CHANSON AND MADRIGAL
1480-1530

ISHAM LIBRARY PAPERS II

CHANSON
& MADRIGAL

1480-1530

STUDIES IN COMPARISON
AND CONTRAST

A Conference at Isham Memorial Library

SEPTEMBER 13–14, 1961

Edited by James Haar

HARVARD UNIVERSITY PRESS

Cambridge, Massachusetts

1964

Publication of this volume has been aided
by a grant from the Ford Foundation

Library of Congress Catalog Card Number 63–19137
Printed in the United States of America

PREFACE

CURT SACHS, speaking as chairman of the first Isham Conference, in 1957, praised what he called the "coherence and vitality" of the papers and discussions in that meeting; he felt nonetheless that these qualities could be intensified in future meetings, through concentration of subject matter and allowance for longer discussions. To that end the organizers of the second conference, Professor A. Tillman Merritt and his colleagues in the Harvard Department of Music, restricted the material to a comparatively narrow temporal and topical span, invited three men to read papers, and provided discussion time equal to that taken by the papers themselves. The speakers and nine panelists, all of them "fresh" from the meetings of the International Musicological Congress held in New York the week before, assembled in the Houghton Library at Harvard on September 13 and 14, 1961, to treat the subject of possible relations between the Parisian chanson and the early Italian madrigal.

This volume represents the proceedings of the second Isham Conference. As in the first volume of this series,* the papers are printed with only slight changes from their spoken form; the discussions have been modified in language and in some instances rearranged in order, but their content is reproduced as faithfully as possible. The editor is responsible for translating those portions of the discussion conducted in French, for the modifications already mentioned, and for the footnotes in the discussion sections. Although some of the verve and scholarly charm displayed by the panelists has been lost in the process of editing, it is hoped that their thought is accurately set down here.

* *Instrumental Music: A Conference at Isham Memorial Library, May 4, 1957,* ed. David G. Hughes, Isham Library Papers I (Cambridge, Mass., 1959).

PREFACE

The editor acknowledges with thanks the expert workmanship of Mrs. Christa Eisenbraun, who prepared the musical examples. These examples, although grouped together at the end of the volume, illustrate three papers of markedly individual character; the slight differences in presentation of the three groups of examples are further reflection of the authors' independence in thought and scholarly method.

My thanks are due also to Miss Blair McElroy for her expert editorial assistance.

James Haar

Cambridge, Massachusetts

CONTENTS

CONTENTS

MUSICAL EXAMPLES

CONTENTS

INTRODUCTORY ADDRESS

A. TILLMAN MERRITT

I N M A Y 1957, a conference on instrumental music was held at the
Isham Memorial Library. This conference, in contrast to the first,
deals with a much more restricted subject. The decision to do this
was made at the time the first meeting was planned, for we wished
to progress from a general field to a more specific problem.

Mrs. Ralph Isham, through her faithful and generous support of
the Isham Library, has made possible its steady growth and success
and has thereby provided the stimulus for the conferences that have
taken place here; without the Isham Library there would have been
little reason for these meetings. We are most grateful to her and
are disappointed that she was unable to be present this time.

Professor Gustave Reese of New York University is no stranger
at Harvard. His exceptional knowledge and talents are universally
known, and we here have repeatedly benefited by his generosity in
teaching and advice. Again we were most fortunate in gaining his
consent to serve us by acting as moderator at this conference. We
are indebted not only to him but also to the three distinguished gentlemen who agreed to read papers: Professor Howard Brown of the
University of Chicago, Professor Walter Rubsamen of the University
of California at Los Angeles, and Professor Daniel Heartz of the
University of California at Berkeley.

Our very special thanks are due the illustrious trio of French
scholars who participated in the discussion of the papers: Madame
Nanie Bridgman, M. François Lesure, and Madame G. Thibault, all
of Paris.

The panel to discuss Professor Brown's paper consisted of Mrs.
Isabel Pope Conant, M. Lesure, and Mme. Thibault. The panel for
discussion of Professor Rubsamen's paper was composed of Mme.

Bridgman, Professor Frank D'Accone of the University of Buffalo, and Professor Nino Pirrotta of Harvard. The panel to discuss Professor Heartz's paper consisted, finally, of the late Professor Erich Hertzmann of Columbia University, Professor Alvin Johnson of the University of Pennsylvania, and Professor Claude Palisca of Yale University, as well as any of the other six panelists who, on account of the comprehensive nature of Professor Heartz's paper, wished to join the discussion.

Much credit is due my colleagues Professors David Hughes, Nino Pirrotta, John Ward, and Dr. James Haar, for planning this conference with me. To the director of the Harvard College Library, Professor Paul Buck, I should like to express gratitude for his friendship and assistance to us not only on this occasion but over a period of many years. We are particularly grateful to Professor William Jackson, who, in addition to being a willing and enthusiastic host to us in Houghton Library, arranged a most interesting exhibit from this library's holdings of medieval and Renaissance music and musical literature. Miss C. E. Jakeman of the Houghton Library was also most kind.

It remains for me to say only that I feel confident that this second Isham Conference will be followed in due time by another, and that the series of Isham Papers will continue in the future.

· · · · ·

His many friends at Harvard and elsewhere were saddened by the death of Erich Hertzmann on March 3, 1963. Professor Hertzmann was an honored guest and active panelist at both the first and second Isham conferences. His wide knowledge, inquiring mind, and joyous spirit will long be missed in the world of musical scholarship.

CHAIRMAN'S PREFACE

GUSTAVE REESE

EVEN though the period with which we are here to be concerned was not strongly given to the writing of crab canons, I should like in making a brief introduction to proceed backwards. Mr. Heartz, whose paper is last, has chosen for his title *"Les Goûts réunis,* or the Worlds of the Madrigal and the Chanson Confronted." On the surface, at any rate, there would seem to be little doubt that the word *réunis* is applicable in this instance; an interpenetration of chanson and madrigalian styles seems fairly likely. However, a re-examination of the facts is certainly in order; if there was mutual influence the question of which side came first is certainly pertinent, as well as the problem of depth and breadth of influence. With regard to precedence there is room for considering several infusions, and priority with regard to each of them, not just the first. There is no reason why differences on such points should not generate enough heat to make our sections lively, and let us hope that this happens.

First, Mr. Brown presents the case for the chanson. Mr. Rubsamen's paper then deals with the matter of madrigalian types, not just the madrigal proper. And finally, Mr. Heartz presents his composition in two-part counterpoint, interweaving French and Italian lines. After each paper the soloist is followed by choral response, which is hearty and full-throated. Although the solos are of predetermined nature, the choruses are not fixed, at least as to form; to some extent they are predetermined as to length, and as for tempo the chairman recommended a *moderato* without too much of an inclination toward *presto.* Now for the *prima pars.*

CHANSON AND MADRIGAL
1480-1530

ABBREVIATIONS

Das Chorwerk *Das Chorwerk,* ed. F. Blume and K. Gudewill (Wolfenbüttel, 1929—).

DTO *Denkmäler der Tonkunst in Oesterreich* (Vienna, 1894–1938).

JAMS *Journal of the American Musicological Society*

MGG *Die Musik in Geschichte und Gegenwart,* ed. F. Blume (Kassel, 1949—).

RISM *Répertoire international des sources musicales, Recueils imprimés, XVIᵉ–XVIIᵉ siècles, Vol. I: Liste chronologique* (Munich, 1960).

Bologna, Bibl. Cons.	Biblioteca del Conservatorio (Liceo Musicale)
Bologna, Bibl. Univ.	Biblioteca universitaria
Florence, Bibl. Cons.	Biblioteca del Conservatorio
Florence, Bibl. Nat.	Biblioteca nazionale centrale
Paris, Bibl. Nat.	Bibliothèque nationale

Ockeghem's "Les desleaulx" (Example 1), from Eugénie Droz, Geneviève Thibault, and Yvonne Rokseth, eds., *Trois chansonniers français du XVᵉ siècle* (Paris, 1927), is published by permission of Librairie Droz, Geneva.

Josquin des Prez's "Mille regretz" and "Plus nulz regrets" (Examples 2 and 3), from *Werken,* ed. Albert Smijers (Amsterdam and Leipzig, 1921—), are published by permission of G. Alsbach & Co. (N. V. Basart), Amsterdam.

Antoine de Févin's "En amours n'a sinon que bien" and "Il fait bon aimer l'oyselet" (Examples 6 and 7), from Howard Mayer Brown, *Theatrical Chansons of the Fifteenth and Early Sixteenth Centuries* (Cambridge, Mass., 1963), are published by permission of Harvard University Press.

I

THE GENESIS OF A STYLE:
THE PARISIAN CHANSON,
1500–1530

HOWARD M. BROWN

IN APRIL 1528 the publisher Pierre Attaingnant put on sale, in his shop in the rue de la Harpe near the church of S. Cosmé in the university quarter of Paris, a two-volume set of *Chansons nouvelles en musique à quatre parties*. This was not the first collection of polyphonic music to be printed in France; Daniel Heartz has recently pointed out that another of Attaingnant's volumes, containing music in a somewhat older style, deserves that distinction.[1] The occasion is nevertheless noteworthy since this anthology of *chansons nouvelles* was the first publication to contain songs of the sort especially identified with the composer Claudin de Sermisy. And it begins a long and distinguished series of similar collections brought out by the same firm. Within two years after the *Chansons nouvelles* Attaingnant had published more than 300 songs. And in the course of the next two decades the grand total swelled to almost 2000.

The Parisian chanson of the 1520's and 30's began as something new on the musical scene. But nothing in the history of human endeavor is so new that it does not owe an enormous debt to its own past. And changes of style do not take place overnight. My primary task here is to describe the musical events leading to the appearance of the Attaingnant chansons in an effort to relate them to their own tradition. Investigating their background and discovering their immediate predecessors will illuminate those aspects of their style which are unique or novel and those which are derived from older models.

[1] Daniel Heartz, "A New Attaingnant Book and the Beginnings of French Music Printing," *JAMS*, XIV (1961), 9–23. The conclusions of this article supplant those in Maurice Cauchie, "Les deux plus anciens recueils de chansons polyphoniques imprimés en France," *Revue de musicologie*, VIII (1924), 72–76, which remains, however, the only study on the contents of the *Chansons nouvelles*.

For constructing a family tree often gives insight into the character and personality of the descendants.

Most of the chansons published by Pierre Attaingnant were written by composers living and working in the capital city of France. The sobriquet "Parisian chanson" seems in this case to be quite accurate. A specific style appears to have been closely associated with a specific place. Or perhaps it would be better to connect the chansons with a specific institution, the royal court, for beginning with the reigns of Charles VIII and Louis XII, but especially under Francis I, the importance of the court in the intellectual and artistic life of the country increased enormously. At the court the advance guard of the nation assembled; the newest philosophy, art, music, and literature were fostered and flourished in the king's household.[2]

Unfortunately, detailed registers of the king's music have not survived from the first third of the sixteenth century. Nevertheless an incomplete picture may be sketched in with the aid of less specific documents: Guillaume Crétin's well-known laments on the deaths of Ockeghem and of Févin and Lourdault; the list of musicians marching in the funeral procession of Louis XII in 1515; the roster of composers contributing to the Medici Codex, recently so brilliantly described by Edward Lowinsky; and finally, the notices of payments to the royal singers during the years 1532 and 1533, published by Michel Brenet.[3] From these documents it becomes clear that the de-

[2] It should be pointed out that the royal court did not stay in Paris permanently, but traveled frequently about the country. See Francis Decrue de Stoutz, *La Cour de France et la société au XVIᵉ siècle* (Paris, 1888), pp. 141–142, and John S. C. Bridge, *A History of France from the Death of Louis XI, Vol. V: France in 1515* (Oxford, 1936), pp. 295–297.

[3] Crétin's lament for Ockeghem, "Déploration dudit Crétin sur le trespas de feu Okergan, Trésorier de Sainct Martin de Tours," is printed in Guillaume Crétin, *Œuvres poétiques,* ed. Kathleen Chesney (Paris, n.d.), pp. 60–73. His lament for Févin and Lourdault, "Plainte sur le trespas de feu maistre Jehan Braconnier, dit Lourdault, chantre," is printed *ibid.,* pp. 210–216. See André Pirro, "Notes sur Jean Braconnier dit Lourdault," *Revue musicale,* IX (1928), 250. The musicians who marched in the funeral procession of Louis XII are listed in Ernest Thoinan, *Les Origines de la chapelle-musique des souverains de France* (Paris, 1864), pp. 91–92. The Medici Codex is described in Edward Lowinsky, "The Medici Codex: A Document of Music, Art, and Politics in the Renaissance," *Annales musicologiques,* V (1957), 61–178. Composers named in the registers of the chapel royal for 1532 and 1533 are listed in Michel Brenet, "Deux comptes de la chapelle-musique des rois de France," *Sammelbände der internationalen Musikgesellschaft,* VI (1904–5), 3–7. A history of musical life in Paris remains to be written. Brenet, pp. 1–2, lists and evaluates the studies written so far.

velopment of the chanson between 1500 and 1530 involves four generations of composers. At the very end of the fifteenth century Johannes Ockeghem and his contemporaries Agricola and Verjust were members of the royal chapel. Ockeghem, the aged and revered master, had faithfully served three kings, Charles VII, Louis XI, and Charles VIII, for more than forty years. By the time of Ockeghem's death there were as well men of Josquin's generation working in the king's service. These were the composers who were born in the middle of the fifteenth century, but who lived through the first decades of the sixteenth. Prioris and Compère are the prominent figures in this group, and possibly Josquin himself, although the precise nature of his connection with the French kings remains unclear. In 1511 Antoine de Févin, a brilliant young composer, died prematurely at the age of 35 or 40. To judge by Crétin's lament on that tragic occasion, as well as by details of the king's funeral a few years later, the chapel at that time still had in it some of Josquin's contemporaries, but to them had been added younger men, notably Jean Mouton, whose fame was almost as great as Josquin's. And finally, as early as 1515 Claudin de Sermisy and his followers began their activities. The young Claudin had moved from the Sainte Chapelle, where he was in 1508, to the chapel of the king. And he, like Ockeghem, was to enjoy a long and glorious career at the French court, serving under Louis XII, Francis I, Henry II, and Francis II. By examining the works of representatives of each of these generations we can survey the music written and performed during this period. Investigating the songs of Ockeghem, Josquin, Févin, Mouton, and Claudin should make clear the developments of the first thirty years of the sixteenth century.

These chansons are to be found in a great variety of books and manuscripts. The volumes of French secular music printed between 1500 and 1530 can be divided into three groups: books printed in Venice by Ottaviano Petrucci, those printed in Rome and Venice by Andrea Antico, and those brought out by the Parisian firm of Pierre Attaingnant. The most varied fare is offered by the earliest of the three printers, Petrucci,[4] who did not publish any music with French text after 1508. His most important and rightly famous three-volume set, the *Odhecaton,* contains pieces primarily from the generation of

[4] His volumes are listed in Claudio Sartori, *Bibliografia delle opere musicali stampate da Ottaviano Petrucci* (Florence, 1948).

Josquin. But there are also chansons in it by older composers, Ocke-ghem and Hayne van Ghizeghem, and chansons in the latest styles, by Jean Mouton and Ninot le Petit. The repertory of Andrea Antico, active about 1520, is more catholic. Paradoxically enough this Italian printer reflects the preferences of the French court at the end of the reign of Louis XII. Here are the works of Mouton, Févin, and the young Adrian Willaert. The appearance of this music in Italian books does not mean that these composers were ignored in Paris, or that Antico's sources were not Parisian. For Antico worked mostly in Rome with the cooperation of the pope, who had given him print-ing privileges, and Leo X was a notorious Francophile, at least in musical matters; the constant interchange between the royal chapel in Paris and the papal choir in Rome ensured that music lovers in the Italian city kept in touch with French musical tastes.[5] Attain-gnant's presses began shortly before 1528, first with a reissue of one of the Antico anthologies, and then with volumes containing music in the newer style.[6] Not surprisingly, the production of these three printers corresponds more or less with the division of the French royal chapel into generations: Petrucci favors Ockeghem and Jos-quin, Antico favors Févin and Mouton, and Attaingnant favors Claudin de Sermisy. And in general composers published by one of these three are not published by the others; the repertories are kept quite separate.

Most of the preserved manuscript sources of secular music were the personal songbooks of rulers, or of the wealthier courtiers and bourgeoisie. Some, the more elaborate and the more elegant, may have been presentation copies, written to commemorate an impor-

---

[5] The volumes printed by Antico are listed in *RISM*. The volumes containing French secular music printed before 1530 are *RISM* 1520[3], *RISM* 1520[6], and *RISM* [1521][7]. The *Catalogue des livres précieux et des manuscrits avec miniatures com-posant la bibliothèque de M. E. M. B[ancel]* (Paris, 1882), p. 177, lists a volume of *Vingt-trois chansons gaillardes et amoureuses* (s.l.n.d.) as being from Antico's presses. On closer inspection, however, the volume turns out to be identical with *Il primo libro de le canzoni franzese* (Venice: O. Scotto, 1535 = *RISM* 1535[8]). Bancel owned the altus part book only; this is undoubtedly the copy now in Paris, in the Bibli-othèque Nationale.

[6] The Attaingnant volumes containing chansons printed before 1530 include *RISM* 1528[3], [c. 1528][4], [c. 1528][5], [c. 1528][7], [c. 1528][8], 1529[2], 1529[3], and 1529[4]. The earliest volumes printed by Attaingnant are all listed chronologically in Daniel Heartz, "La Chronologie des recueils imprimés par Pierre Attaingnant," *Revue de musicologie*, XLIV (1959), 176–192.

tant event. Others were prestige symbols, albums designed for consultation, perhaps, but not for constant, heavy wear. A few may well have been practical workbooks, written by a teacher for his aristocratic pupil, or by a music lover for his own amusement. Not unnaturally the best sources of music by French composers are those manuscripts prepared for members of the royal court. The manuscripts which once belonged to Diane de Poitiers, Françoise de Foix, René de Vaudémont, and Charles de Bourbon, the traitorous *connétable,* are all invaluable for discovering the tastes of Louis XII's courtiers.[7] A few more chansonniers, important sources of the period, are associated with other courts and different cities. Several manuscripts with chansons can be identified as the property of Henry VIII of England. Cambridge, Magdalene College, MS. Pepys 1760, may have been a gift from someone in France to the young Prince of Wales. Its exclusively French repertoire contrasts strikingly with the contents of the so-called King Henry's Manuscript (British Museum, Add. MS. 31922), which presents a much more plausible picture of what the musical king would have preferred.[8] Italians also collected French music. There are manuscripts from the Medici, and especially from the fanatically music-loving Leo; and one of the best sources of chansons in the first quarter of the century is the Rinuccini chansonnier, MS. Basevi 2442 of the Biblioteca del Conservatorio in Florence,

[7] Bologna, Bibl. Cons., MS. Q 19, dated 1518, once belonged to Diane de Poitiers; see Lowinsky, "The Medici Codex," pp. 98–106. London, British Museum, MS. Harley 5242, dated ca. 1515, once belonged to Françoise de Foix, wife of Jean de Laval-Montmorency and mistress of both Charles de Bourbon and Francis I; see Paule Chaillon, "Le Chansonnier de Françoise," *Revue de musicologie,* XXXV (1953), 1–31. René de Vaudémont owned Paris, Bibl. Nat., MS. fonds fr. 1597; see Gaston Paris, *Chansons du XVe siècle* (Paris, 1885), p. xii. Paris, Bibl. Nat., MS. fonds fr. 9346, the Bayeux Manuscript, was prepared for Charles de Bourbon; Théodore Gérold, *Le Manuscrit de Bayeux* (Strasbourg, 1921), is a modern edition of this collection of monophonic melodies.

[8] On the Pepys manuscript see *Bibliotheca Pepysiana. A Descriptive Catalogue of the Library of Samuel Pepys* (London, 1923), Vol. III: "Mediaeval Manuscripts," by M. R. James, pp. 36–38; B. Kahmann, "Über Inhalt und Herkunft der Handschrift Cambridge Pepys 1760," *Bericht über den internationalen musikwissenschaftlichen Kongress Hamburg 1956* (Kassel, 1957), pp. 126–128; and A. T. Merritt, "A Chanson Sequence by Févin," *Essays on Music in Honor of Archibald Thompson Davison* (Cambridge, Mass., 1957), pp. 91–99. On King Henry's manuscript see John Stevens, *Music and Poetry in the Early Tudor Court* (London, 1961), *passim;* the manuscript is indexed there on pp. 388–425. For a modern edition of Add. MS. 31922, see *Music at the Court of Henry VIII,* ed. and transcr. John Stevens, Musica Britannica, 18 (London, 1962).

an almost exclusively ribald collection of songs by Josquin and his younger colleagues.[9] In contrast Marguerite of Austria's albums reflect the melancholy preoccupations of that melancholy ruler.[10] Less exalted, several miscellanies now in the Stiftsbibliothek of St. Gall were apparently written by foreign students in Paris. Among the Swiss humanists studying abroad, two at least, Johannes Heer and Aegidius Tschudi, spent a part of their *Studienjahre* between 1510 and 1520 collecting music in the French capital.[11]

Necessary as it is to explore the histories of printed and manuscript collections, and to inquire into the personnel of various European chapels, my chief end here is neither biographical nor bibliographical. The genesis of a style can be explained only by going to the music itself. The ancestry of the Attaingnant chanson can be uncovered by describing selected aspects of the music and pointing out elements of continuity—traces of a Parisian tradition.

My survey begins with Ockeghem, even though he lived and worked before the turn of the century. His chansons can then be used as a norm against which to test the developments of later generations. He is included here as a Frenchman, in spite of his Netherlandish origins, since he spent all of his creative life in the king's service.[12] Like others of his generation Ockeghem set to music poems by the *rhétoriqueurs*. These poems almost invariably deal with courtly love, often with the lover scorned by his cruel but beautiful

[9] Manuscripts belonging to the Medici include Cortona, Bibl. del Comune, Codd. 95 and 96 (altus and superius part books), and Paris, Bibl. Nat., MS. nouv. acq. fr. 1817 (tenor part book)—discussed and the texts printed in Gustav Gröber, "Zu den Liederbüchern von Cortona," *Zeitschrift für romanische Philologie*, XI (1887), 371–394, and in Rodolfo Renier, "Un mazzetto di poesie musicali francesi," *Miscellanea di filologia e linguistica in memoria di Napoleone Caix e Ugo Angelo Canello* (Florence, 1886), pp. 271–288; Rome, Bibl. Casanatense, MS. 2856, described briefly in Knud Jeppesen, *Der Kopenhagener Chansonnier* (Copenhagen and Leipzig, 1927), p. lxxiii; and Rome, Vatican Library, Cappella Giulia, MS. XIII, 27, described briefly by Jeppesen, p. lxxiii.

[10] On Marguerite of Austria see Martin Picker, "Three Unidentified Chansons by Pierre de la Rue in the *Album de Marguerite d'Autriche*," *Musical Quarterly*, XLVI (1960), 329–343. This is part of a larger, unpublished study of Marguerite's two chansonniers, Brussels, Bibl. Royale, MSS. 228 and 11239.

[11] On these two manuscripts, St. Gall, Stiftsbibliothek, MSS. 462 and 463, see Arnold Geering, *Die Vokalmusik in der Schweiz zur Zeit der Reformation* (Aarau, 1933), pp. 91–93 and 185–187, with indexes of the two manuscripts given on pp. 224–232.

[12] Dragan Plamenac, "Ockeghem," *MGG*, IX, 1825–38, is the best survey of his life and works, with a complete bibliography of studies on the composer.

mistress. And this stereotyped subject matter is treated in one of a very limited number of predetermined formal schemes, rondeaux, virelais, or ballades. Indeed, the great majority of Ockeghem's chansons are rondeaux, either with four-line refrains rhyming *abba,* or with five-line refrains rhyming *aabba.*[13] With their rigid forms and monotonous subject matter these texts are exercises in stylized language; the poets cared less about what they said than about the way in which they said it. The stilted, artificial verses have a certain richness, filled as they are with identical sounds, puns, alliterations, and various other tricks of rhyme and rhythm. Take, for example, the refrain of "L'autre dantan":

> L'autre dantan, lautrier passa
> Et en passant me trespassa
> D'un regard forgé a Millan
> Qui m'a mis en l'arriere ban
> Tant mauvais brassin me brassa.[14]

But few of the poets rise above the level of skillful craftsmen.

Ockeghem's music for these poems displays a stylistic unity characteristic of his age. Since convention plays so large a part in shaping the words, it is not surprising that on the largest formal level all of Ockeghem's chansons in any one category are exactly alike. The individuality of a composition operates within limits strictly prescribed by tradition. With medieval exactness all of his rondeau settings, for example, conform outwardly to one pattern. The composer sets the refrain as a composition divisible in two. The first part ends with a half cadence and the repetition scheme of the two sections of music corresponds with the large formal outline of the poem: *AB aA ab AB.* But the connection between text and music ends with this formal relation. Ockeghem writes one phrase of music for one phrase of text, but each of the musical phrases is different. That is, the refrain settings are through-composed. The only exceptions to this

[13] Of the 22 chansons listed by Plamenac, 16 are rondeaux (15 for three voices and one, "Je n'ay deuil," for four). There are four virelais by Ockeghem: "Ma bouche rit," "Ma maistresse," "Presque transi," and "Tant fuz gentement resjouy"; and one ballade, "Mort tu as navré," the lament on Binchois' death, using a plain chant cantus firmus. For the twenty-second chanson of Ockeghem, see note 17, below. On the poetry, see Henry Guy, *Histoire de la poésie française au XVIe siècle, Vol. I: L'École des rhétoriqueurs* (Paris, 1910).

[14] Modern edition in Eugénie Droz, Geneviève Thibault, and Yvonne Rokseth, eds., *Trois chansonniers français du XVe siècle* (Paris, 1927), no. 17.

practice occur when Ockeghem chooses to use musical rhyme to underscore the rhyme scheme of the poem. In "Les desleaulx ont la saison"[15] (Example 1) the last phrase of the superius (mm. 26 to the end) resembles the first phrase, underlining the fact that the refrain of this rondeau quatrain rhymes *abba*. But this sort of sophistication is quite foreign to Ockeghem's lesser contemporaries; more often than not there is no repetition of formal units within any one refrain setting.

The statement that each phrase of music corresponds to one line of text might well be challenged, so diverse are the transcriptions offered by modern editors. Placing the words beneath the music is often very difficult. The manuscript sources are frequently careless in this respect, and there are usually many more notes than syllables. The solution of Droz, Thibault, and Rokseth to the problem of text underlay in "Les desleaulx" is probably correct in its broad outlines. Each phrase begins more or less syllabically, and a long melisma occurs toward the end of each. This general rule takes into account the fact that repeated notes often appear at the start of a phrase, and common sense dictates that the syllable change at such a place. But the details can be worked out in many different and equally convincing ways. And this multiplicity of solutions would appear to be a fundamental characteristic of the style. An Ockeghem chanson is "abstract," an autonomous musical complex supplied with text. The words are hung on an independent frame. They do not fit the melodic line in one inevitable way. Important words in a phrase are not necessarily emphasized, and the position of the melismas is determined almost entirely by purely musical considerations.

The fifteenth-century musician composed by writing one line completely from beginning to end, and then adding a second line to the first. To this two-part framework the composer would then fit a third voice to fill out the otherwise bare texture and to complete the chords. Toward the turn of the century, when even fuller sounds were preferred, a fourth voice as well would have been added. By the fifteenth century this so-called discant-tenor technique was a procedure already long established, in theory as well as in practice.[16]

[15] Modern edition in Droz, Thibault, and Rokseth, no. 9.

[16] On the technique of successive composition see Edward Lowinsky, 'The Concept of Physical and Musical Space in the Renaissance," *Papers of the American Musicological Society* for 1941 (New York, 1946), pp. 57–84.

The two-part substructure was self-sufficient. The superius and tenor, both constructed with careful regard for their melodic outlines, can be played together, and nothing essential will be missing from the composition. The two voices produce no awkward or forbidden voice leadings, they always cadence correctly, and all of the dissonances are resolved properly. The contratenor, on the other hand, skips around with little regard for an intelligible melodic shape, sounding many large and awkward intervals. The contratenor in "Les desleaulx" is especially fragmentary; while the superius and tenor expose all of the significant melodic material, and form together a solid framework, the third voice, moving in small discrete units, alternately fills in pauses, enriches the sonority, and connects the end of one phrase with the beginning of the next. "Les desleaulx" exemplifies this traditional procedure more closely than most of Ockeghem's chansons, for Ockeghem differs from his contemporaries in trying usually to disguise the hieratic structure. He unifies his compositions by making the contratenor approach more closely the other voices in melodic importance, and by using imitation, sequences, and motives to make a well-integrated texture. Even in "Les desleaulx" there is some evidence of these refinements. All of the phrases save the first begin with imitation between superius and tenor, and sometimes the contratenor joins in as well. A short imitative sequence introduces the last phrase (mm. 21–22), and the material on which it is based seems to be derived from the opening of the piece, and to be expanded at the end. The musical rhyme has already been discussed.

The technique of successive composition, emphasizing so strongly the horizontal aspect of music, invalidates a chord-by-chord analysis of the harmony. In spite of the fact that a chanson like "Les desleaulx" contains a good many chords the roots of which are a fourth or a fifth away from the preceding or following harmonies, harmonic planning within phrases was still not a primary concern of the composer. An awareness of tonality and a feeling for chord progressions developed during the fifteenth and sixteenth centuries, but in Ockeghem's chansons these modern tendencies manifest themselves chiefly in the construction of cadential formulas. There are two aspects to consider: the structure of the cadences, and the "tonal" degrees on which they occur. The tonal plan of "Les desleaulx" is rather typical. Like so many Ockeghem chansons, it is in the Dorian mode, here untransposed. The poem is a rondeau quatrain, so there are four phrases of music, cadencing on D (m. 6), E (m. 13), A (deceptive cadence: V–IV in mm. 17–18), and D. This pattern has a readily discernible logic, based on the circle of fifths. And although not all of the chansons of Ockeghem operate in exactly the same way, the following generalization can be made: the first phrase cadences on a relatively stable degree, either I or V, and in the middle there is a half cadence, either a real one on the dominant, or, as here, a Phrygian one on II of the "home key." This middle cadence is the most important internal one, for there the refrain divides in half, and from there one must be able to return to the beginning. Notice how carefully Ockeghem has disguised these breaks. The contratenor must finish its phrase after the important middle cadence of measure 13, and the third cadence, in measures 17–18, comes three measures too early; by the time the postlude has run its course, the last phrase has already begun.

The structure of the cadences in "Les desleaulx" is also typical. The final one is an example of the most important type of the later fifteenth century. In this so-called Burgundian cadence, the tenor moves from supertonic to tonic, the superius has an 8–7–8 suspension, and the contratenor leaps an octave. The resulting V–I cadence is really a midway point between the more purely contrapuntal VII⁶–I of earlier generations and the full-fledged V–I with suspension of later generations. And there are as well in this chanson the other cadences common to Ockeghem: the deceptive (mm. 17–18), the Phrygian (mm. 12–13), so useful for the half-cadence function, and the Burgundian in which the contratenor fails to skip an octave, leaving the tenor and superius alone to make the resolution (mm. 5–6). The one aspect they all have in common is the disposition of the two-voiced framework; for in all of them the tenor descends from supertonic to tonic, and the superius has an 8–7–8 suspension.

Within reasonable limits the outline of Ockeghem's style just presented describes all of the composer's chansons—with one notable exception. Whereas in most of his songs the structural framework consists of two voices which are both newly invented by the composer, there is one which uses borrowed material. In the four-voiced "S'elle m'amera," reprinted in Gombosi's study of Obrecht,[17] Ocke-

---

[17] The chanson, without text and with the title "Petite camusette," is printed in Otto Gombosi, *Jacob Obrecht* (Leipzig, 1925), appendix, no. 6. The sources which

ghem appropriates a pre-existing popular melody, "Petite camusette," which he presents quite simply in the tenor. Over this, as his
superius, he writes a rondeau setting, "S'elle m'amera." But aside
from this composition Ockeghem's chansons are all quite similar in
style, technique, and form.

Such unity is not to be found in the secular music of Josquin des
Prez. Generalizations about him can apply only to a segment of his
work: to his early settings of poems in *formes fixes,* to his mature
chansons with no borrowed material, or to his arrangements of popular melodies. Even in the most external matters Josquin observes
no rigid set of conventions: he writes, for example, pieces for three,
four, five, or six voices with equal ease. This variety of approach may
well be related to the fact that Josquin traveled widely in the course
of his long and varied career. Thus he would have tried his hand at a
number of local dialects: older-style pieces during his student days
(with Ockeghem in Paris?) and in his early years in Italy, chansons
in the Parisian manner for Louis XII, and somber, melancholy
compositions for Marguerite of Austria. Unfortunately very little is
known as yet about the chronology of his chansons, and it is hazard-
ous to state when or where any one of them was written. Even the
important dates in the composer's life are not clearly established.[18]
He was in Italy until the last decade of the fifteenth century, and he
returned to that country again to be chapel master at the court of
Ferrara for a few years, from 1503 to sometime after 1505. Later he
was connected with the court of Marguerite of Austria, and he spent
his last years at Condé, enjoying a prebend obtained for him by Marguerite. His principal sojourn in Paris, then, must have taken place
between 1494 and 1503, after he left the papal choir, and before he
went to Ferrara. Probably Helmuth Osthoff is correct,[19] however, in
suggesting that Josquin worked for the French king even after 1503,
as a *Kapellmeister von Haus aus,* a nonresident composer who sent
his latest works to the court from time to time. Apparently he was
still supplying the chapel royal with music in 1515, for his five-voiced

give both the "Petite camusette" text and the rondeau text are listed in Dragan
Plamenac, "A Postscript to Volume II of the *Collected Works* of Johannes
Ockeghem," *JAMS,* III (1950), 36–37.

[18] For a survey of Josquin's life and works and a bibliography of studies about
him see Helmuth Osthoff, "Josquin Desprez," *MGG,* VII, 190–214, and Osthoff,
Josquin Desprez, vol. I (Tutzing, 1962).

[19] *MGG,* VII, 195.

motet "De profundis" was evidently written to be sung at the funeral of the king.[20] The only two secular pieces definitely connected with Josquin's stay in Paris are "Vive le roy," the fanfare based on a *soggetto cavato dalle vocali*,[21] and "Guillaume s'en va chauffer," the unpretentious little canon commissioned for performance by the unmusical king himself.[22] To these two may be added a few others which are likely to have been a result of the composer's work in Paris. These are the seven three-part arrangements of popular melodies in a style associated with the court of Louis XII.[23]

Biographical material helps us little in establishing a chronology of Josquin's chansons. Bibliographical studies are no more revealing. The number of Josquin's chansons his contemporaries knew, and how those were transmitted, are among the most pressing problems of research on Josquin. Between 1501 and 1503 Petrucci in Venice printed more than fifteen,[24] but the main corpus was not published until 1545, some twenty years after the composer's death. These appeared in the commemorative edition brought out as volume VII of the series of chanson anthologies published by Tielman Susato in Antwerp; and they were reissued in 1549 as volume XXXVI in Attaingnant's series.[25] But between 1503 and 1545, only a handful of

[20] Osthoff, *MGG* VII, 194.

[21] Modern edition in Arnold Schering, *Geschichte der Musik in Beispielen* (Leipzig, 1931), no. 62a. Osthoff (*MGG*, VII, 194) is not convincing when he argues that Josquin's "Adieu mes amours" was written for Louis XII because it contains the lines "vivrai-je du vent, si l'argent du roi ne vient pas souvent?" since this is an arrangement of a pre-existing popular melody; see note 40, below.

[22] This chanson is listed in Osthoff's catalogue of Josquin's works (*MGG*, VII, 204) as "Lutuichi regis Franciae jocosa cantio" after Glarean, *Dodecachordon* (Basel, 1547). But the text "Guillaume s'en va chauffer" is given in the copy of this composition in the Johannes Heer Liederbuch, St. Gall, Stiftsbibliothek, MS. 462, p. 101, along with the date 1510.

[23] The seven are "En l'ombre d'un buissonnet," "La belle se siet," "Quant je vous voy," "Qui belles amours," "Si ja voye Marion," and "Si j'ay perdu mon amy," all listed in *MGG*, VII, 203-204, and the three-voiced "Entre je suis," listed in Martin Picker, "Polyphonic Settings c. 1500 of the Flemish Tune 'In minen sin,'" *JAMS*, XII (1959), 94.

[24] Chansons of Josquin published by Petrucci include "Adieu mes amours," "Bergerette savoysienne," "Cela sans plus," "De tous biens playne," "La plus des plus," and "Madame helas," all in Helen Hewitt and Isabel Pope, eds., *Harmonice Musices Odhecaton A* (Cambridge, Mass., 1942); the chansons from *Canti B* and *Canti C* are listed in Sartori, *Bibliografia Petrucci*, nos. 2 and 12.

[25] Susato's volume is listed as *RISM* 1545[15]. The title of Attaingnant's reissue is *Trente sixiesme livre contenant xxx. chansons Tres Musicales, A Quatre Cinq & Six parties . . . Le tout de la composition de Jeu Josquin des prez* (Paris: Pierre Attaingnant, March 14, 1549 [= 1550 N.S.]).

Josquin's songs were printed: a few of the three-part popular arrangements by Antico and Abbate in 1536, and a few five- and six-part chansons by Melchior Kriesstein of Augsburg in an anthology edited by Sigmund Salblinger in 1540.[26] The following discussion of Josquin as a link between Ockeghem and later styles must take into account the possibility that Mouton and Claudin were not acquainted with the compositions from Josquin's last years and, indeed, that these late works were written after the establishment of Claudin's style.

Josquin set almost no poems in formes fixes. The very few that he does set, "La plus des plus" in the *Odhecaton,* for example, resemble Ockeghem's in many ways.[27] They differ from works by the earlier composer mostly in being more "classical." That is, their formal outlines are clearer, cadences are not disguised, the rhythmic structure of the melodic lines is more readily apparent, and Josquin uses sequence and imitation more consistently. On occasion Josquin arranged some of the older chansons, but these usually involve some technical tour de force. For example, he added a close two-part canon beneath two voices of Hayne van Ghizeghem's "De tous biens playne," in the arrangement printed in the *Odhecaton.* And his six-voiced arrangement of Ockeghem's "Ma bouche rit" anticipates the application of parody technique to secular music.[28] Josquin uses Ockeghem's superius as his superius, but he quotes all three voices of the model in their original relations at the very beginning.

[26] *RISM* 1536¹ and 1540⁷.

[27] "La plus des plus" is printed in Hewitt and Pope, no. 64. "Madame helas," *ibid.,* no. 66, may also be a rondeau setting, although the text is lost; the music is divided in half as for a rondeau. There are no other settings of poems in a forme fixe among Josquin's works, except for those which use a cantus firmus. The following discussion of Josquin's chansons does not take into account those using a plain chant cantus firmus, such as "Cueurs desolez / Plorans ploravit," "Fortune d'estrange / Pauper sum ego," and "Nymphes des bois / Requiem aeternam," all listed in *MGG,* VII, 203–204.

[28] Josquin's "De tous bien playne" is printed in Hewitt and Pope, no. 95; "Ma bouche rit" is in Josquin des Prez, *Werken,* ed. Albert Smijers (Amsterdam and Leipzig, 1921—), chanson no. 19. The Hayne model of "De tous bien playne" is in Hewitt and Pope, no. 20, among other places, and the Ockeghem model of "Ma bouche rit" *ibid.,* no. 54. Josquin borrows material from Dufay in his cantus firmus chanson "L'amye a tous / Je ne viz oncques," in Josquin, *Werken,* chanson no. 25. Parody technique, basing a new work on all of the voices of a model, figures again in Josquin's work in connection with his setting *a 4* of "Le villain jaloux" in Augsburg, Staats- und Stadtbibliothek, Cod. 142a, fol. 44ᵛ. It begins like Jean Mouton's "Le vilain jaloux" in Bologna, Bibl. Cons., Cod. Q 19, fol. 200ᵛ, but the two versions continue in a different but related way. One is a parody of the other.

Throughout the rest of the piece Josquin accompanies the borrowed superius with an ostinato built on the opening motive of the model.

The absence of poems in the formes fixes from those Josquin chose to set may be the most obvious difference between his chansons and Ockeghem's, but this change is not as radical as it might appear, and it would be a mistake to assume that there is no continuity at all from the one composer to the other. In fact, Josquin also set poems by the rhétoriqueurs, but not those in the traditionally acceptable forms. Jean Molinet, Guillaume Crétin, Jean Lemaire de Belges, Claude Bouton, and possibly even Marguerite of Austra herself all furnished verses for the composer, and these poets make up the last generation of the grands rhétoriqueurs.[29] Unfortunately most of the poems that Josquin chose are anonymous, but presumably they too came from the same literary circles. Not surprisingly the language of these poems resembles the language of Ockeghem's chansons—the diction is still that of the fifteenth century. Take, for example, the first stanza of Marguerite's poem:

> Plaine de dueil et de melancolye
> Voyant mon mal qui tousjours multiplye,
> Et qu'en la fin plus ne le puis porter,
> Contraincte suis pour moy reconforter,
> Me rendr'à toy le surplus de ma vie.[30]

And the poets still write about the same things, although a subject other than unrequited, courtly love is occasionally introduced. But the forms of the poems are unlike those used by Ockeghem; Josquin's texts are organized in a great variety of ways. Many of them are strophic, with a rhyme scheme and meter repeated for a number of stanzas. Some are simple quatrains or cinquains. The only scheme which recurs often enough to constitute a separate category and deserve special comment is the decasyllabic five-line stanza, rhyming *aabba*, as in "Plaine de dueil." [31] This pattern is exactly the same as the refrain of a rondeau cinquain, but that we are not dealing here with one of the formes fixes is proved by the existence of the subse-

---

[29] Josquin's poets are discussed by Osthoff in *MGG*, VII, 211–212.

[30] Josquin, *Werken*, chanson no. 4.

[31] Other chansons of Josquin with the rhyme scheme *aabba* include "Cueur langoureulx," "Douleur me bat," "Incessament livre suis," "Nesse pas ung grant desplaisir," "Parfons regretz," "Plusieurs regretz," and "Vous larez s'il vous plaist," all listed by Osthoff in *MGG*, VII, 203–204.

quent stanzas, or by the music itself, which is not divisible into two parts to allow for the conventional repetition scheme of the rondeau.

Another important difference between Ockeghem's music and Josquin's mature chansons without borrowed material involves the way each musician composed. Whereas Ockeghem wrote one line at a time, Josquin conceives all of the voices of his polyphonic fabric simultaneously. He works with all of the voices at once, and each has a more nearly equal share in the effect of the whole. Edward Lowinsky has discussed this change from successive to simultaneous composition in some detail, most recently in his article on early scores, and examination of "Mille regretz" (Example 2) will confirm his conclusions.[32] Imagine the superius and tenor of this chanson played together without the other two voices, and contrast them with Ockeghem's "Les desleaulx." The two voices by Josquin are fragmentary and discontinuous; they cadence at the end on the wrong degree, and they make occasional awkward voice leadings, as in measure 31. If only these two voices are played alone, much that is essential to the composition is omitted. The discant-tenor technique has been supplanted. And since these two voices no longer constitute a self-sufficient structural framework, the composer has a much freer series of possibilities open to him to construct and to unify his compositions.

In the first place the texture can be lightened and made more varied by the use of imitative duets and choral dialogue, if the latter term can be used to characterize the technique of opposing one section of an ensemble against the others in ever-changing combinations. In "Mille regretz," for example, one voice is sometimes opposed to the other three (mm. 17-19), or two voices can answer the other two (either in an imitative duet, mm. 19-21 and 21-23, or with a continuation of the same phrase, mm. 27-29 and 29-31), or else three or all four voices can join together in homorhythmic passages (mm. 15-16 and 34 to the end). Short phrases can be repeated with few but subtle changes, as in measures 7-9 and 10-12, and one of the more remarkable aspects of this chanson is the way the central motive, a simple descending tetrachord, can, with great imagination, be harmonized, reharmonized, and placed in a variety of contexts (such

[32] See note 16, above, and Edward Lowinsky, "Early Scores in Manuscript," *JAMS,* XIII (1960), 126-173. "Mille regretz" is printed in Josquin, *Werken,* chanson no. 24, and in *Das Chorwerk,* III, no. 1.

as mm. 7–9, 13–14, 15–16). The master stroke, however, is the condensed summary at the end of much that has gone before (compare mm. 5–6 with 32–33, and 13–17 with 34 to the end). I cite "Mille regretz" notwithstanding the fact that it is one of the very last of Josquin's chansons, possibly written for Charles V in 1520,[33] and consequently after Claudin's style was already established. For this is one of the most subtle and perfect of all of Josquin's chansons.

Canon is a second method of construction to replace the outmoded discant-tenor technique, and this is Josquin's favorite means of building a musical structure, especially in his five- and six-voiced chansons. A large percentage of his songs are built around a two-part canon. "Incessament livre suis a martire," "Douleur me bat," and "Plaine de dueil" are but three such pieces.[34] Above and below the two anchoring voices the other lines are fitted, each taking an equal share in the imitative counterpoint.

Along with greater freedom in choice of texts and a wider range of possibilities in manipulating textures, Josquin also invents more varied forms for his chansons. Those which use imitative duets and choral dialogue extensively are usually through-composed. In such pieces one point of imitation is taken up per phrase; a new line of text will call forth a new point of imitation. This generalization describes more accurately "Plus nulz regretz" than it does "Mille regretz."[35] Formal analysis must adapt to the individual demands of each composition in this category.

But in the large number of chansons which are constructed around a canon, the formal structure of the poem is usually mirrored in the music. Individual solutions differ, but in general Josquin bases his schemes on the premise that the repetition of a rhyme demands the repetition of the musical phrase which sets the line of text. In other words phrase repetition becomes the central formal principle, and balance and symmetry of identical sections are much more impor-

[33] Osthoff, *MGG* VII, 197.

[34] Other chansons of Josquin using canon include "A l'heure que je vous," "Cueur langoureulx," "Du mien amant," "Nesse pas ung grant desplaisir," "Parfons regretz," "Plusieurs regretz," "Pour souhaitter," "Regretz sans fin," "Se congie prens," "Vous l'arez s'il vous plaist," and "Vous ne l'aurez pas," all listed by Osthoff in *MGG*, VII, 203–204. See also note 41, below.

[35] "Plus nulz regretz" is printed in Josquin, *Werken,* chanson no. 29. Other through-composed Josquin chansons include "En non saichant," "J'ay bien cause de lamenter," "Je ne me puis tenir d'aimer," "Mi lares vous," and "Plus n'estes ma maistresse," all listed by Osthoff in *MGG*, VII, 203–204.

tant in Josquin's chansons than they are in Ockeghem's. This correspondence between verse form and musical form can be quite
straight-forward, as for example in "Incessament livre suis," one of
the canonic settings of a cinquain rhyming *aabba*.[36] The music repeats
according to the pattern *AABBC*. "Douleur me bat," another canonic
cinquain, is only slightly more complex.[37] The joints between sections are smoothed over with connective tissue, and the final phrase
of music is repeated, sung twice to the same line of text, with a coda
appended. The result may be diagrammed *AA'BB'CC coda*. Still a
third canonic cinquain, "Plaine de dueil," [38] offers a slightly different
solution, but one which is again but a variation of the basic principle. In this chanson the second line of text (mm. 12ff) is set to
music similar to the first line, but transposed up a fifth. The fourth
line of text (mm. 31ff) uses music similar to the third line but transposed down a fifth. Moreover, the last line of text sung by the canonic voices rhymes musically as well as textually with the first line
(compare the superius, mm. 5-8, with the same voice in mm. 45-47).
In all three of these examples, two constructive principles are at work
simultaneously: canon, holding together the texture, and the formal
repetition scheme, mirroring the rhymes of the poem.

Like Ockeghem, Josquin writes one phrase of music for one line
of text, but here the similarity between the two composers' methods
ends. Instead of Ockegehm's freely asymmetrical melodies which
seem to be abstractly conceived, Josquin writes simpler, "squarer"
melodies, invented with a keen ear for the declamation of the verses.
In Josquin's chansons there is seldom serious doubt about how the
words fit the music. For one thing, the number of melismas is
sharply reduced. In the two pieces just discussed there are almost
none. Certainly the short melisma in the first line of "Mille regretz"
is unambiguous, and the words for the canonic voices of "Plaine de
dueil" *must* be sung as indicated in Smijers' transcription, for the
setting is syllabic throughout. Instead of long, freely unfolding melodies Josquin writes a series of succinct motives. He usually takes into
account the poetic caesura in the middle of each line, so that one
phrase is divisible into two parts. This simplicity is particularly striking in the canonic voices, but the accompanying lines are only

[36] "Incessament" is printed in Josquin, *Werken*, chanson no. 6.
[37] "Douleur me bat" may be found in Josquin, *Werken*, chanson no. 18.
[38] Josquin, *Werken*, chanson no. 4, and in *Das Chorwerk*, III, no. 3.

slightly more complex. Instead of being an abstract musical complex, a Josquin chanson supports and elucidates the text, not only on a larger formal level, but also within any one phrase. The music grows out of the text, and the miracle of the composer is that he, like Mozart, can reflect the poetry without sacrificing musical logic.

The clarity of Josquin's formal structures has perhaps less to do with the fact that the forward motion is stopped at the end of each phrase by means of prominent cadences than with the fact that the melodic material is clear and simple, so that the beginning of a new section is immediately apparent. Certainly the cadence structures of "Mille regretz" and "Plaine de dueil" are complex and irregular enough to give the lie to the statement that Josquin's important cadences are always authentic, with a few plagal and deceptive ones added for contrast. On the other hand, that statement is more accurate than these two chansons would indicate. To balance the picture Example 3 lists the eight cadences of "Plus nulz regretz," [39] one of Josquin's through-composed chansons on a poem by Jean Lemaire de Belges, the first stanza of which consists of eight lines, rhyming *abab bcbc*. As the arrangement on the page suggests, the music divides into four sections. Each couplet of the poem cadences on the tonic, the first couplet ending with an old-fashioned VII^6–I cadence, the others with the more modern V–I. The first lines of each couplet end in a less stable manner, with deceptive cadences, or plagal ones, or none at all. In other words a hierarchy of cadences is established, the most important and most stable ones being reserved for the important points of articulation in the form. And some traces of the older discant-tenor technique can still be found, for whenever there is an authentic V–I cadence, the tenor almost invariably has the characteristic 2–1 voice leading, and the superius an 8–7–8 suspension.

Edward Lowinsky in his recent monograph on tonality and atonality in the sixteenth century [40] has pointed out that a result of the establishment of the technique of simultaneous composition was an increased awareness of the vertical aspect of the music, and a new sensitivity to chord progressions. This novel attitude toward harmonic planning is evident, for example, in the first phrase of "Plaine

[39] See note 35, above.
[40] *Tonality and Atonality in Sixteenth Century Music* (Berkeley and Los Angeles, 1961).

de dueil." The sense of tonal direction instilled by the progress of the first eight measures around the circle of fifths is quite different from Mozart's or Haydn's but the logic is nonetheless clear. The same traces of vertical organization can be found in "Mille regretz." And Josquin's other innovations—the substitution of two-part canon and imitative counterpoint for the older discant-tenor technique, and the closer union of text and music at all levels—are equally important in distinguishing his music from Ockeghem's.

Investigating those chansons without borrowed material tells only half the story, for Josquin wrote almost as many arrangements of monophonic popular melodies as he did settings of poems in the courtly tradition of the rhétoriqueurs. At least once he uses the same technique as Ockeghem, putting a popular tune, in this case "Adieu mes amours," in his tenor as a cantus firmus, and writing over it a rondeau setting, beginning also with "Adieu mes amours." Quite often Josquin arranged the borrowed melody in two-part canon, in the manner of the chansons already discussed, and some of his best-known compositions, "Allegez moy," "Faulte d'argent," and "Petite camusette," were the results.[41] Some of his four-voiced chansons, those written probably around the turn of the century, paraphrase a popular tune, with no one voice stating the melody complete. "Bergerette savoysienne" in the *Odhecaton* is one of these;[42] as in the other chansons of this group, the superius and tenor of "Bergerette" have most of the responsibility for stating the significant melodic material, and the discant-tenor technique lurks just around the corner. And finally there are the three-voiced popular arrangements already mentioned and presently to be discussed.[43] In considering Josquin's secular works these polyphonic arrangements of popular melodies must not be ignored, and they must be clearly distinguished from those of his chansons which utilize only newly invented material.

[41] For a modern edition of "Adieu mes amours" see Hewitt and Pope, *Odhecaton*, no. 14. Other chansons of Josquin using popular melodies in canon include "Baisez moy," "Belle pour l'amour de vous" (a free canon), "Comment peut avoir joye," "En l'ombre d'un buissonnet" (a double canon), "Entre je suis," and "Une musque de Buscaye," all listed by Osthoff in *MGG*, VII, 203–204.

[42] Other chansons of Josquin which paraphrase popular material include "Si jey bien dire" and "Si j'ay perdu mon amy" (*a 4*), listed by Osthoff in *MGG*, VII, 203–204.

[43] See note 23, above.

Elsewhere, in connection with music in the secular theater, I have justified calling these monophonic melodies popular.[44] Suffice it to say here that, as with most things popular, much used, and very old, the sources of the words as well as of the music are unknown, and their histories obscure. Aside from the numerous printed anthologies of the sixteenth century which reproduce the texts without the music, the largest repertoire of these chansons survives in two well-known manuscripts, the Bayeux Manuscript and Paris, Bibliothèque Nationale, MS. fonds fr. 12744, both available in modern editions.[45] Although these or similar melodies were performed throughout the fifteenth century, they were not frequently used as the basis for polyphonic arrangements until the following century. The texts differ radically from the poems of the courtly tradition. In the first place they deal with a wide variety of things, and not just courtly love. They treat of love from many points of view; shepherds and shepherdesses, unfaithful wives and senile husbands, erotic monks and nuns all play their part. The poems are mostly of the middle class or lower, some are obscene, and many are commonplace. The formes fixes, with the exception of the virelai, never made any inroads into the popular domain. Most of these poems are strophic; many have refrains of one sort or another, but there are neither metric peculiarities nor predetermined forms and rhyme schemes. The language is that of the popular song: less elegant than the rondeaux and ballades, sometimes quite direct and colloquial, often quite charming, and often filled with clichés.

The tunes which accompany the texts are, like most popular music, a collection of elements—melodic, rhythmic and harmonic—assembled by a composer, rather than brilliantly inspired melodies. They are a series of conventional patterns strung together. The melodies are simple and straightforward; the ranges are narrow, the phrase structure regular, and the rhythm uncomplicated. Usually each phrase of a melody begins with a short, concise rhythmic motive and closes with one of several cadential formulas. Example 4, setting out the beginnings of four tunes from the Bayeux Manuscript, will suffice to demonstrate the kinds of similarities to be found in these

[44] Howard Mayer Brown, *Music in the French Secular Theater: 1400–1550* (Cambridge, Mass., 1963); "The *Chanson rustique*: Popular Elements in the 15th- and 16th-Century Chanson," *JAMS*, XII (1959), 16–26.

[45] Gaston Paris, *Chansons du XVe siècle,* and Gérold, *Le Manuscrit de Bayeux.*

tunes. A good many more of their clichés could easily be listed: their formulas for opening gambits, rhythmic patterns, melodic configurations, and closing phrases. The tunes reflect the rhyme scheme and metrical structure of the poems much more clearly than they do the meaning of the words. After all, the same music had to serve all of the stanzas of the poem, and often the tunes were reused with different words altogether. But the repetition of the musical phrases, as in Josquin, almost always corresponds to the rhyme scheme of the poem.

These popular songs enjoyed a great vogue at the court of Louis XII.[46] The Bayeux Manuscript, one of the two great monophonic chansonniers, was prepared for one of the king's *grands seigneurs,* Charles de Bourbon. And all of the Parisian composers of the time have left us large numbers of polyphonic arrangements of these melodies. Conventions for working with popular material soon grew up, and composers were fond of using the tunes in one of two ways. These two new chanson styles of the reign of Louis XII may be characterized as the three-part popular arrangement and the four-part popular arrangement, but only if the terms are understood to refer to a specific style, and not merely to the number of voices present.

The three-part popular arrangement is the easier of the two styles to formulate. The composer lays out the cantus prius factus, unadorned, in the tenor. The outer voices, usually fairly equal in range to the tenor, imitate the borrowed material, and all three of them cadence together at the end of every phrase. This characteristic disposition of the voices is plain to see in Example 5, a setting by Antoine de Févin of "J'ay veu la beauté," a melody found in both of the largest monophonic chansonniers.[47] In this chanson, as in most others in this style, the outer voices almost invariably begin the imitation, so that the tenor each time enters last—the first phrase here is an exception. Since the texture is so imitative, the composer's main problem is to write a series of continuations for his simple, given melody. To say the same thing in another way, the tenor has the plainest ver-

[46] See Paule Chaillon, "Les Musiciens du nord à la cour de Louis XII," *La Renaissance dans les provinces du nord* (Paris, 1956), pp. 63–69.

[47] "J'ay veu la beauté" of Févin is in Cambridge, Magdalene College, MS. Pepys 1760, fol. 65ᵛ. The tune on which it is based is in Gaston Paris, no. 64, and Gérold, no. 20.

sion of the cantus prius factus just because it enters last; the composer, wanting the voices to cadence together, does not have an opportunity to write a continuation for that voice. With superius, tenor, and bass all sharing the principal melodic material, songs in this style sometimes resemble paraphrase chansons, in which no one voice has the melody complete. And, indeed, some of the three-part popular arrangements do use this technique. But this is merely a slightly more complex solution to the problem of exposing the pre-existing material; it may involve nothing more than writing continuations for all three voices, including the tenor, although there are chansons in which the popular tune is parceled out almost equally. Josquin's "La belle se siet" is a paraphrase chanson, and both Févin and Mouton used this technique too.[48]

A description of the three-part popular arrangement makes it appear that the composer has used the old-fashioned method of writing one line at a time. Since the tenor existed previously, it might well have been written down first, and the other voices added individually. But in fact there are important differences between chansons in this style and the older ones. The relation of the voices to each other is not the same in a three-part popular arrangement as in a fifteenth-century Burgundian chanson. In the first place the superius and tenor in the newer style do not make a self-sufficient two-part framework. These two voices create an awkward 6/4 chord, for example, in measures 54 and 64 of "J'ay veu la beauté." And the cadence between superius and tenor in measures 13–14 of "En amours n'a sinon que bien"[49] (Example 6) is impossible without the addition of the bass. The lowest voice, when it does not share the important melodic material, functions as a real harmonic bass, confirming the roots of the chords. There can be no doubt that the composers of these chansons worked with all of the voices at once. For none can be omitted without sacrificing an essential part of the composition.

My description of these chansons also suggests that they epitomize a truly contrapuntal style. They use a variant of the cantus firmus technique, and their texture is consistently imitative. But in fact, these chansons are not necessarily contrapuntal at all. In the opening

[48] "La belle se siet" is in *RISM* 1536[1], fol. 20. For Févin's and Mouton's use of paraphrase see notes 56 and 59, below.

[49] Modern edition in Howard Mayer Brown, *Theatrical Chansons of the Fifteenth and Early Sixteenth Centuries* (Cambridge, Mass., 1963), no. 17.

phrase of "Il fait bon aimer l'oyselet" [50] (Example 7), the superius runs along in parallel sixths with the cantus prius factus, while the lowest voice clarifies the harmony. And even in the first phrase of "En amours," the imitation is so harmonically oriented that it can scarcely be called pure counterpoint. Long sections of these chansons are based either on parallelisms or on polyphonically elaborated triads; the counterpoint is usually quite unobtrusive, with few dissonances, and those few introduced and resolved smoothly.

The three-part popular arrangements exhibit the same increased awareness of chords and chord progressions as does Josquin's music. At the beginning of "Il fait bon," an entire phrase can be analyzed profitably in modern terms. I–IV–I–VII–I (VI)–V–I is certainly an intelligible series of harmonies. And frequently there are harmonic progressions which are not tonal, but which do have a modal logic of their own, as in the first phrase of "J'ay veu la beauté." The cadence formulas are much more regular than in Josquin. Almost all of them are authentic or half-cadences (see the two in Example 6). The authentic ones are invariably arranged with the conventional disposition of voices: the tenor moving from the second degree to the tonic, and the superius with an 8–7–8 suspension.

In these three-part popular arrangements there is often a distinct break in style at the point where the composer drops his simple given material and begins his fancier continuation. The popular and the courtly collide head on. But, like the borrowed melodies, the continuations themselves are apt to be made up of clichés. Over and over again, Févin writes close canons which turn out be be based on a single chord (see, for example, mm. 32–33, and also mm. 47–50 of "J'ay veu la beauté,") or else the outer voices move in parallel tenths (see, in the same song, mm. 35–36). Vacillating between two notes (mm. 35–36), and writing scale fragments in near sequence (mm. 39–41 of the superius), or in isolation (m. 54) are but a few of the regular tricks of Févin's trade. Indeed, this is really a style of clichés: the melodic and rhythmic clichés of the pre-existing popular tunes plus the melodic and rhythmic clichés of the composer's continuations, and, at the end of every phrase, the traditional cadential formulas.

The three-part popular arrangement is best represented in the works of Antoine de Févin, but a number of other composers as well

---

[50] Modern edition in Brown, *Theatrical Chansons*, no. 27.

write in this style. Josquin, Mouton, Willaert, Richafort, Moulu, Gascongne, and Jacotin all composed similar pieces, published in anthologies by Andrea Antico, and preserved in the manuscript songbooks of Louis XII and of his contemporaries.[51] The other new style formulated during that king's reign, the four-part popular arrangement, is best represented in the works of Jean Mouton, but a number of minor masters, Bruhier and Ninot le Petit for example, and even Compère, the slightly older contemporary of Mouton, also produced some of them.[52]

The borrowed material in these four-part popular arrangements undergoes a greater transformation than in the three-part chansons. All of the voices in Mouton's "La, la, la, l'oysillon du bois s'en va" [53] allude to the monophonic cantus prius factus, but the tenor and superius state it most completely; as in Josquin's "Bergerette savoysienne" mentioned earlier, the old-fashioned discant-tenor technique is hiding just below the surface. Normally, however, Mouton paraphrases the popular tune—all of the voices share it equally—so that he can give free rein to his imagination in disposing of sections of the melody as he will. In "Resjouissez vous bourgeoises" [54] (Example 8) the pre-existing melody alternates between altus and superius throughout the first half, and is parceled out equally among the voices in the second half.

If the aesthetic point of the three-part popular arrangement was to write a series of continuations upon a given beginning, the point of the four-part chansons is to juxtapose fragments of the popular tune in interesting and amusing relationships. Often the composer will break off a bit of the given melody and toss it about among the voices, adding comparatively little new material, as in the section of Example 8 beginning at measure 26. This creates a mosaic-like counterpoint, a series of rapid and amusing stretti, which are brought to a close by a tutti homophonic passage (as at the end of Example 8,

[51] For example, *RISM* 1520[6], *RISM* 1536[1]; London; British Museum, MS. Harley 5242; Cambridge, Magdalene College, MS. Pepys 1760; and Florence, Bibl. Naz., MS. Magl. XIX, 117.

[52] For example, Bruhier's "Latura tu," Compère's "Alons ferons barbe" and "Nous sommes de l'ordre de saint Babouyn," and Ninot le Petit's "Nostre cambrière si malade estois," all printed in Hewitt and Pope, *Odhecaton,* nos. 94, 26, 37, and 32.

[53] Modern edition in Brown, *Theatrical Chansons,* no. 46.

[54] In Florence, Bibl. Naz., MS. Magl. XIX, 117, fol. 45[v], and Cambrai, Bibl. de la Ville, MS. 124, fol. 12[v].

and see also mm. 9–10 and 22–25). Indeed, homorhythmic passages often interrupt the busy contrapuntal sections, for contrast and variety, and sometimes, as in Mouton's "James james james" in the *Odhecaton,* or at the end of "Ils sont bien pelez" in *Canti C,*[55] these tutti phrases will change abruptly from duple to triple meter, with the important melodic material rewritten accordingly. And these triple-meter interruptions can also bounce along contrapuntally, before changing back, with equal abruptness, to the original meter. In other words, the four-part popular arrangements are not so different in style and technique from those chansons of Josquin which exploit imitative duets and choral dialogue extensively. The important difference between the two styles is that Mouton and his colleagues base their works on a pre-existent melody, and they simplify Josquin's techniques in the interests of entertainment.

These two new styles, the three- and the four-part popular arrangement, were the most significant developments in the field of secular music during the first fifteen years of the sixteenth century. That is, they mark the beginning of a specifically Parisian tradition. At least this hypothesis appears reasonable at the present stage of our knowledge, for the two styles were adopted and cultivated especially by the composers closest to the French royal chapel. But if I have talked about the history of the chanson from Ockeghem and Josquin to the newer styles as though it were one continuous development, I have not meant to imply a regular chronological progression. In truth, these many different styles were all being written at the same time. Ockeghem died around 1495, but some of his contemporaries continued to write music similar to his into the sixteenth century. Josquin lived and worked during the last part of Ockeghem's career, but he and his contemporaries were composing until the 1520's. Févin died in 1511; the three-part popular arrangement must have flourished during the first decade of the sixteenth century. This is precisely the time when the four-part popular arrangements also flourished, for they first appear in the *Odhecaton* and its supplementary volumes. That is, these two new styles came into being before many of the late Josquin chansons.

Antoine de Févin's position in the history of the chanson may be understood most easily by comparing his attitude toward pre-existing

[55] "James james james" is printed in Hewitt and Pope, no. 36, and "Ils sont bien pelez" in Brown, *Theatrical Chansons,* no. 29.

popular melodies with the attitudes of Josquin and Ockeghem. The oldest of the three composers set texts in the courtly tradition of the fifteenth-century rhétoriqueurs almost exclusively. He made but one excursion into the domain of popular music. Josquin wrote approximately equal numbers of settings of courtly texts and arrangements of popular melodies. Almost all of Févin's chansons are based on popular monophonic tunes; he had but little to do with the rhétoriqueurs. In fact, most of Févin's songs are three-part popular arrangements. More often than not, these are the simplest sort, with the tenor stating the cantus prius factus completely. Févin does, however, occasionally use the paraphrase technique, as in "Petite camusette" and "Très doulce dame." And he sometimes writes a four-part popular arrangement.[56]

One Févin chanson, "Adieu soulas" (Example 9), deserves special mention. Its superius is a variant of the top voice of a less skillfully made three-voiced chanson in the Johannes Heer Liederbuch.[57] Presumably, then, this top voice is a pre-existing melody, although the tenor might just as well be, for when it is not imitating the superius it is moving in parallel sixths with it. The bottom line is rhythmically subservient to the tenor; it discreetly supplies the chord roots. The remarkable aspect of this composition is its close resemblance to Claudin's chansons. Although its over-all tonal design [58] is not at all typical of the later composer, many of Claudin's songs begin with chords on I, VI, and V in exactly the same rhythm; and innumerable songs continue with three quarter-note anacruses on the same pitch. The shape of the melodic line is the same; the lightly imitative texture is the same; and the formal proportions are the same. This is a

[56] On Févin's life and works, see B. Kahmann, "Antoine de Févin—A Bio-bibliographical Contribution," *Musica Disciplina,* IV (1950), 153–162, and V (1951), 143–155. The list of works in Kahmann, "Févin," *MGG,* IV, 142–144, is more complete than that in *Musica Disciplina.* Of the 17 surviving chansons of Févin, 13 are three-part popular arrangements (two of which use paraphrase technique). Two, "Naimez jamais" and "Pardonnez moy," are four-part popular arrangements, one is related to a fifteenth-century chanson (Ockeghem's "Fors seulement"), and one, "Fuyez regretz," has no borrowed material.

[57] Févin's chanson is in Cambridge, Magdalene College, MS. Pepys 1760, fol. 63ᵛ; Florence, Bibl. Naz., MS. Magl. XIX, 117, fol. 45ᵛ; and in London, British Museum, Add. MS. 35087, fol. 53ᵛ. The anonymous version is in St. Gall, Stiftsbibliothek, MS. 462, p. 98. The second stanza of text in the London manuscript reads: "Je meneray lassus au vert bochage / Ou je feray fonder ung ermitage / Pour les regretz que j'ay de mon amy, / Ellas, ellas, il ma fally."

[58] The composition is in the Lydian mode. The phrases cadence on g, g, and F.

surprising piece, considering that it was written before 1511, the year of Févin's death.

Like Févin, Jean Mouton wrote arrangements of popular melodies almost exclusively. He, too, composed three-part popular arrangements, but all of his paraphrase their monophonic cantus prius factus.[59] And he is the best composer of the four-part popular arrangements.[60] There is still a third sort of chanson represented in Mouton's works, the five- and six-voiced song with a borrowed melody in the superius, or else using paraphrase technique, but a discussion of these would lead us too far afield; the mere mention of their existence must suffice.[61] Just as there was one of Févin's chansons which seemed to adumbrate Claudin's style, so there is one Mouton chanson, "De tous regretz," [62] which shares many features with the works of the later composer. Like so many of the chansons published by Attaingnant, this is a setting of a decasyllabic quatrain rhyming *abba*. And like so many of the later compositions, this has the form *ABCA* with the last section repeated to the same text. Like Claudin, Mouton begins homophonically, and continues with imitative counter-

---

[59] On Mouton's life and works, see Paul Kast, "Mouton," *MGG, IX*, 679–686, and Kast, "Remarques sur la musique et les musiciens de la chapelle de François 1er au camp du drap d'or," *Fêtes et cérémonies au temps de Charles Quint* (Paris, 1960), pp. 135–146. Mouton's three-part popular arrangements include "Dieu gard de mal" (Cambridge, Magdalene College, MS. Pepys 1760, fol. 68v), "Jamais naymerai masson" (*RISM* 1520⁶, no. 12, and London, British Museum, Add. MS. 35087, fol. 55v; see also Nanie Bridgman, "Christian Egenolff, imprimeur de musique," *Annales musicologiques*, III (1955), 122–123); "Le grant desir" (*RISM* 1536¹, fol. 5); and "Prens ton con" (*RISM* 1536¹, fol. 3).

[60] Mouton's four-part popular arrangements include "James james james," printed in Hewitt and Pope, *Odhecaton*, no. 36, "La, la, la, l'oysillon du bois," printed in Brown, *Theatrical Chansons*, no. 46, "Le vilain jaloux" (see note 28, above), "Resjouissez vous" (see Example 8 of this study), and "Velecy velela," Florence, Bibl. Cons., MS. B 2442, fol. 92.

[61] Mouton's five- and six-part chansons include "Ce que mon cueur pense," "Du bon du cueur," "La rousée du mois de may," "Le berger et la bergère," "Vray Dieu d'amours maudite soit la journée," and "Vray Dieu qu'amoureux ont de peine," all in the 1572 *Mellanges* published by Le Roy and Ballard in Paris; see François Lesure and Geneviève Thibault, *Bibliographie des éditions d'Adrian le Roy et Robert Ballard* (Paris, 1955), no. 165. Mouton also wrote several canonic chansons: "En venant de Lyon," printed in Heartz, "A New Attaingnant Book," ex. 2, and "Qui ne regrettoit," printed in Dragan Plamenac, "Deux pièces de la Renaissance tirées de fonds florentins," *Revue belge de musicologie*, VI (1952), 19–20, both of which are double canons, and 'Je le lesray puisqu'il m'y bat," printed in Brown, *Theatrical Chansons*, no. 36.

[62] Modern edition in *Das Chorwerk*, LXI, no. 9.

point. Nevertheless no one could mistake this for a work by Claudin. It is still too profuse with its musical material; it is too contrapuntal; its rhythms are not patterned enough, and its harmonies not as tonal. But it is in chansons such as this that the process of refinement and simplification took place which led from Josquin to Claudin.

The discussion of the poetry which fifteenth- and sixteenth-century musicians chose to set to music has centered thus far around two opposing traditions: the courtly and the popular. In the 1520's these two opposites were reconciled by Clément Marot, a figure as important in the history of music as he is in the history of literature.[63] Marot, the favorite poet of Claudin and of his followers and imitators, gave new life to the worn-out tradition of lyrical poetry in sixteenth-century France by infusing into its precious veins a healthy dose of good, red blood. He, more than any other individual, brought the old ways to an end and ushered in the new. To be sure, most of his best poems still deal with love, although he can on occasion cry, "Changeons propos, c'est trop chanté d'amours . . . chantons de la serpette." [64] But a new personal note has crept in. A stanza like

> Jouyssance vous donneray,
> Mon amy, et si meneray
> A bonne fin vostre esperance;
> Vivante ne vous laisseray,
> Encores, quand morte seray,
> L'esprit en aura souvenance [65]

is altogether refreshing in its directness. Sometimes his debt to popular poetry is openly acknowledged. "En entrant en un jardin/Je trouvay Guillot Martin/Avecques s'amye Heleine" has literally dozens of genuinely popular antecedents.[66] Some of his verses not primarily intended for music, but set nevertheless, are not merely popular in tone: they are frankly obscene, like "Martin menoit son

[63] On Marot's chansons see Jean Rollin, *Les Chansons de Clément Marot* (Paris, 1951), esp. pp. 78ff. This work should be used with care—Rollin presents some ideas with incomplete or misleading documentation—but his discussion of the poetic forms in Marot's work is very good. See also Henry Guy, *Histoire de la poésie française au XVIe siècle, Vol. II: Clément Marot et son école* (Paris, 1926).

[64] *RISM* [c. 1528]⁸, no. 2.

[65] Modern edition in Gustave Reese, *Music in the Renaissance* (New York, 1954), p. 292.

[66] Text and bibliography printed in Rollin, p. 177. For similar popular songs, see Gaston Paris, *Chansons du XVe siècle*, nos. 8, 9, 76, 82, 104, etc.

pourceau au marché" and "Frère Thibaut." [67] Whether lyrical, erotic, or bibulous, the vigor of unaffected language has transformed the old artifices.

An analogy can be made with the musical situation in the 1520's. The chansons published by Pierre Attaingnant also reconciled the courtly and the popular. It is no accident that Marot's poems were the ones most often set by the new composers. Precisely when this reconciliation took place remains one of the mysteries in the history of the chanson. Certainly Claudin's style was already well established by 1528, the year of the first volume published by the new generation, the *Chansons nouvelles*. Perhaps the birth of the chanson associated with Claudin can be pushed back as far as 1515, the year Francis I ascended the throne, and the first year that Claudin's position in the royal chapel can be documented. In view of Févin's "Adieu soulas" and Mouton's "De tout regretz," it would seem unwise to place the beginnings of the new style much later.

As is the case with the works of the first two decades of the century, the music of Claudin's chansons follows the form of the text closely. Many of the Marot poems are strophic, but it would be difficult to find two in which the arrangement of stanzas is exactly the same. At any rate the formes fixes are dead and buried. In the music which sets these texts repetition of a phrase usually coincides with the rhyme scheme of the poem. If the rhyme is the same, the musical phrase will be the same. But within this very general practice a great variety of individual solutions is possible.

To illustrate this procedure the *Chansons nouvelles* of 1528 may usefully serve as samples of the new style in its first stages. In that volume there is one large group of chansons which does conform to a single pattern, suggesting that for the composers if not for the poets, new conventions were springing up. About a third of the chansons in the 1528 anthology, nine out of thirty-one, are settings of decasyllabic quatrains, presumably the first stanzas of strophic poems. [68] All of

---

[67] There are a number of settings of these poems by Marot. "Martin menoit" was set by Claudin (*RISM* 1535[6], no. 14), Janequin (*RISM* 1535[6], no. 13), and Alaire (*RISM* 1534[14], fol. 10[v]). "Frère Thibault" was set by Certon (*RISM* 1540[11], no. 1) and Janequin (*RISM* 1540[12], no. 6). See also François Lesure, "Autour de Clément Marot et de ses musiciens," *Revue de musicologie*, XXXIII (1951), 109-119.

[68] The *Chansons nouvelles* survive in an incomplete state (see *RISM* 1528[3]). But all of the chansons in the volume can be reconstructed from reprints in later Attaingnant volumes (see Cauchie, "Les deux plus anciens recueils"; *RISM*

these quatrains rhyme *abba,* while the music repeats according to the scheme *ABCA,* or rather *ABCAA,* for more often than not the last phrase is repeated along with the last line of text. This formal diagram, one of the most common in Claudin's chansons, corresponds almost exactly with the form of the verses.

To judge by the examples in the *Chansons nouvelles,* the tonal schemes in this group of compositions also follow one basic design. Needless to say one phrase of music sets one line of text, making four cadences in a chanson with the form *ABCA.* Compositions in the Dorian mode invariably cadence on d, F, a, and d. Often this mode is transposed a fourth higher to G, with a key signature of one flat, as in "Si j'ay pour vous" [69] (Example 10), one of the songs complying with this convention. Chansons in the Lydian mode, like "J'attens secours" [70] (Example 11), always cadence on F, F, C, and F. The second cadence on F is invariably a less stable VII^6–I progression, so that the over-all tonal plan is not as static as it would first seem. These two tonal plans, one for the Dorian and one for the Lydian mode, were regularly applied to quatrain settings. They may be regarded as norms against which to consider the other pieces in this repertory, for Attaingnant chansons are almost all in one of those two modes. In the 1528 anthology, for example, the Mixolydian mode is represented by two compositions, the Aeolian by one, and all of the rest are about equally divided between Dorian and Lydian. [71]

But in spite of the fact that many of these chansons have a stereotyped formal outline, and a conventional tonal scheme as well, not all of Claudin's chansons are built in exactly the same way. Often the song will be constructed of four phrases, regardless of the number of lines in the text strophe, but almost always there is some correspondence between the phrase repetitions and the shape of the poem. Example 12, summarizing for a number of examples from *Chansons nouvelles* the musical repetition schemes, the rhyme schemes of the

[c. 1528][8] contains a good many of them). The nine quatrain settings are "Si j'ay pour vous" (Example 10 of the present study), "Le triste cueur," "Veu le grief mal," "J'attens secours" (Example 11 of the present study), "Languir me fais," "C'est a grand tort," "Aupres de vous," "Le cueur est bon," and "Las, je m'y plains." "Le departir" and "De resjouyr" are both quatrains, but they are not decasyllabic.

[69] *RISM* [c. 1528][8], no. 13.

[70] *RISM* [c. 1528][8], no. 28.

[71] "C'est a grand tort" and "Le cueur est bon" are in the Mixolydian mode; "Aupres de vous" is in the Aeolian mode.

poems, and the degrees on which the phrases cadence, will make this point better than a prose analysis. Even if the music cannot be diagrammed *ABCAA,* sections are apt to recur: either the first phrase or two will be repeated immediately with new words, or the opening of the piece will return at the end, and, in any case, the final section is usually supplied with repeat marks. In other words, Claudin, like Josquin, considered phrase repetition the most important formal principle, but smaller proportions, a less complex texture, and the greater simplicity of the schemes themselves distinguish the works of the younger composer from those of the older.

Many of the chansons in the 1528 anthology are made up of decasyllabic lines. Very often in setting these words Claudin divides the ten syllables, marking a caesura after the fourth. The result is a characteristic rhythmic pattern which reappears often in his works. A clear-cut, fairly slow, rhythmic motive begins each phrase, and this is followed by quicker motion, often introduced by three anacruses on the same pitch, and concluded with a cadential formula:

Time and time again this or a similar pattern forms the basis of the rhythmic life of a piece. Several superius parts which conform to this convention are reproduced as Example 13. Even if a complete statement of the whole pattern never recurs, elements from it are apt to be broken off and used throughout a chanson as a device to unify a composition. But sometimes the repetitions are so frequent and so literal, as in the samples reproduced in Example 14, that the melodies are almost isorhythmic. Moreover this recurring rhythmic scheme is not very different from the procedure adopted by Févin in his threepart popular arrangements. Instead of a popular beginning and a fancy continuation, Claudin writes a clear-cut opening motive followed by a faster drive to the cadence.

Along with the increasing stylization of form, over-all tonal planning, and rhythmic structure goes a heightened awareness of the organizing possibilities of harmonic progressions. By this time, of course, cadential formulas are quite standardized; important points of articulation progress from V to I with an 8–7–8 suspension in the superius and a 2–1 descent in the tenor, and less stable resting places use less final series of chords: VII⁶–I, IV–I, V–VI, or I–V. But a sense of tonality involves more than writing cadential formulas. It is clear from the music that the mysterious relationship between dominant and tonic, the keystone of tonality, was becoming more and more clearly understood. Most chansons begin, for example, with a drive towards the dominant. The opening motive is often harmonized I–VI–V, I–IV–VI–V, I–VI–II–V, or with some similar set of chords designed to bring the music to a momentary stop on the dominant, tonally the most significant chord. Both Examples 10 and 11 behave in this way. Moreover, entire chansons can now be analyzed intelligently by using the familiar system of Roman numerals. To be sure this apparatus of analysis, devised for functional harmony of the sort found in music written after 1700, must be used with discretion when applied to a sixteenth-century chanson. And the harmonic system of the 1520's is admittedly different from the harmonic system of the 1750's. Chansons in the Dorian mode on G, for example, emphasize the mediant, Bb, and the subdominant, C, almost as much as the dominant; and Lydian compositions can use the supertonic, G, as an important secondary area. Nevertheless, it is clear that controlling chordal progressions and planning phrases harmonically were conscious preoccupations of the composers. Indeed, I suspect that those critics who emphasize the term "homophonic" in speaking of Claudin [72] really mean "harmonic," for the quality they refer to has less to do with texture than with regulation of the harmonic rhythm.

The texture of the chansons published by Attaingnant varies greatly, which is hardly surprising in view of the fact that there are some 2000 of them. The first phrase of Claudin's "Changeons propos" [73] (Example 15) is as imitative as any of Josquin's chansons, although there are many in the new style which are more genuinely homophonic. A division truer than that between imitative and non-imitative chansons may be made between settings of lyrical as opposed to narrative texts. The narrative settings—"Ung jour Robin" in *Chansons nouvelles* is one of them [74]—usually tell some light erotic anecdote. They are apt to be in a simplified Josquin-like imitative style with prominent homorhythmic sections. In other words they resemble in many ways the four-part popular arrangements by Mouton. Just so, the Févin three-part popular arrangements, and I

[72] See, for example, Reese, *Music in the Renaissance,* pp. 291ff., and the authorities quoted there.
[73] *RISM* [c. 1528]⁸, no. 2.
[74] Complete in *RISM* [c. 1528]⁸, no. 31.

am thinking especially of the rather unusual "Adieu soulas," may be equated with the Claudin lyrical settings. In them a chordal texture is enlivened by lightly imitative counterpoint.

The superius of Claudin's chanson is the most important voice melodically. This can be demonstrated, if proof is needed, by pointing out that when Claudin's chansons are used as *timbres* in noels, and political and religious songs, it is normally the superius which is borrowed.[75] But the tenor has still not entirely lost its importance. Often the superius and tenor move in parallel motion (see, for example, the first phrase of "J'attens secours," Example 11), and the next-to-lowest voice frequently states more than an equal share of the significant melodic material. The lowest voice is almost entirely a harmonic bass, verifying the root progressions while being subservient melodically and rhythmically to the superius. The altus is a filler voice, completing harmonies or doubling chord components for a richer sonority. Omitting the altus will not remove anything essential to the composer's conception. Indeed, in Attaingnant's volume of three-voiced chansons, the *Quarante et deux chansons musicales à troys parties* of 1529, some of the compositions are identical with four-voiced songs published elsewhere by the same printer, except that the altus part is missing.[76] Whether the altus part was left out, or whether it was written later, it clearly is not an essential voice.

There is some justification for supposing that Claudin's earliest chansons were written for only three voices. Four of Attaingnant's *Quarante et deux chansons,* "Amy souffrez," "J'ay trop aymé," "C'est grand plaisir," and "C'est grand erreur," were also published in different but related settings for four voices, and in every case the four-voiced version is the more complex.[77] In "Amy souffrez," for ex-

[75] See, for example, the *souterliedekens* based on "Languir me fais" and "Dont vient cela" in Elizabeth Mincoff-Marriage, *Souterliedekens* ('s-Gravenhage, 1922), nos. 158 and 160, and the examples of Buus's *chansons spirituelles* cited in Howard Brown, "The *Chanson Spirituelle,* Jacques Buus, and Parody Technique," *JAMS,* XV (1962), 145–173.

[76] Three chansons from *Quarante et deux chansons* are the same in the versions *a 3* and *a 4.* They are: "En regardant son gratieux maintien," (*a 4* version in *RISM* [c. 1528]⁹), "Ces fascheux sotz" (*a 4* version in Cambrai, Bibl. de la Ville, MSS. 125–128, fol. 139), and "Je ne scay point" (*a 4* version in Munich, Bayerische Staatsbibliothek, Mus. MS. 1516, no. 33).

[77] The version *a 4* of "Amy souffrez" is in *RISM* [c. 1528]⁴, fol. 10ᵛ; the version *a 4* of "J'ay trop aymé" in *RISM* [c. 1528]⁴, fol. 13ᵛ; the version *a 4* of "C'est grand plaisir" in *RISM* [c. 1528]⁶, fol. 8ᵛ; and the version *a 4* of "C'est grand erreur" is

ample, a setting of a quatrain rhyming *abba,* the form of the three-voiced version is *ABCA.* The four-voiced version uses a variant of the other's superius as its superius, but when the first phrase returns at the end it is rewritten, so that the four-voiced chanson must be diagrammed *ABCA'.* Clearly it is the later version, a more elaborate arrangement of the simpler, original three voices. The four-voiced "C'est grand erreur" is a parody of the fewer-voiced version. And the other two examples from this volume also confirm the priority of the three-voiced chanson. Moreover, the description just made of a texture typical of Claudin, with superius and tenor in parallel sixths and the bass, subservient rhythmically, supplying the roots of the chords, fits as well some of the Févin three-part arrangements, not only "Adieu soulas" (Example 9) but also the more typical "Il fait bon" (Example 7). In other words, a comparison of the music by the two composers supports the view that Claudin evolved his style from that of the earlier man. The most important difference between the two is that Févin bases his compositions on pre-existing popular melodies whereas all of Claudin's are newly invented.

The absence of popular material marks off Claudin and his contemporaries from the previous generation. This is not to say that Attaingnant never published a polyphonic setting of a popular, monophonic melody. There are a few, but they are not very frequent.[78] Some are by composers of the older generation, and possibly some are by particularly conservative musicians. But this technique had clearly passed out of fashion. Claudin was, however, influenced by popular styles, or at least by those composers most interested in such things. And paradoxically, Claudin's own compositions became the popular songs of his and the following generations. They soon began to appear in the cheap anthologies of song texts, and the melodies were adapted for use as noels, political songs, and both Catholic and

printed in Albert Seay, ed., *Thirty Chansons for Three and Four Voices from Attaingnant's Collections* (New Haven, 1960), no. 11 (the version *a 3* is printed there as no. 1).

[78] For example, Févin's "On a mal dit," printed in Seay, no. 3, after *Quarante et deux chansons* (*RISM* 1529[4]). *RISM* 1529[4] contains other settings of monophonic melodies as well: "J'ay mis mon cueur," "Mais que ce fust," and "He dieu qui me confortera." Other chansons of Attaingnant with popular melodies include "En l'ombre d'un buissonet," in *RISM* [c. 1528][9], "Gentil galans," in *RISM* [c. 1528][4], "Le bon espoir," in *RISM* [c. 1528][5], and "Voicy le may," in *RISM* 1530.[5]

Protestant *chansons spirituelles*.[79] By the 1530's the distinction be-tween courtly and popular, once so clear, can no longer be success-fully made.

The transformation of the courtly tradition by an infusion of popu-lar elements has been one of the recurrent themes of this study. The sudden interest in strophic poems using simple and direct language and associated with a traditional monophonic music was one of the greatest innovations in secular music in France in the first quarter of the sixteenth century. Composers stopped writing long, rhythmically free, asymmetric melodies, onto which they hung a text, and began using melodies which closely reflected the shape of the words. Me-lodic repetitions mirrored rhyme schemes; and syllabic text settings took into account the necessity for good declamation. In music by Févin and Mouton, the closer union of text and music was caused by the fact that the significant melodic material existed already. And possibly even Josquin's late chansons were influenced in this respect by what he knew of popular styles. In any case, Claudin learned how to write a melody and how to fit it with words, either from Févin, Mouton, and their contemporaries, or else directly from those com-posers' own sources of inspiration. And in many other ways as well Claudin reveals the debt he owed his immediate predecessors in the royal chapel. His music is a simplification and stylization—in form, harmony, tonal planning, melodic construction, and rhythmic organ-ization—of generations past. Even the texture is not so different from Févin's and Mouton's, for although the superius now dominates, the tenor has not relinquished all of its importance. Like Clément Marot's lyric poetry, Claudin's chansons reconcile the two traditional poles: the courtly and the popular.

I have tried to show the continuity of a specifically Parisian tradi-tion without ever going outside France. If Italian musicians influ-enced Claudin, their effects were not of primary importance. There is no doubt that he and his contemporaries knew Italian music. Claudin, Janequin, and Prioris, among others, all set to music Italian

[79] See, for example, *S'ensuyvent plusieurs belles chansons nouvelles avec plu-sieurs aultres retirées des anciennes impressions* (Paris, 1535); *S'ensuyvent plusieurs belles chansons nouvelles et fort joyeuses avec plusieurs autres retirées des anciennes impressions* (Paris, 1537); Clément Marot, ed., *Les Chansons nouvellement assem-blées oultre les anciennes impressions* (s.l., 1538), and the many other similar col-lections listed in the bibliography of Brown, *Music in the French Secular Theater*.

poems.[80] Members of the French royal chapel accompanied their employers on their campaigns of conquest in the south. Both Louis XII and Francis I brought back with them to Paris Italian musicians, mostly, as far as we know, cornettists and other minstrels rather than "serious" composers.[81] And, as we have seen, there was a strong and direct connection between the royal chapel and the papal choir in Rome.[82]

But if there was an Italian influence, what was it? Or to ask the question in another way, what was new in Claudin's chansons? How does one differ from a chanson by Ockeghem? I have suggested two major innovations. Claudin's attitude towards his text is quite unlike Ockeghem's. In the works of the later composer there is a much closer connection between words and music. But this change came about through the penetration of French popular music, transmitted as monophonic melodies, into courtly circles. Secondly, Claudin's chansons are written in a new harmonic style, but this is a crystallization of tendencies already present in the music of Josquin and his contemporaries. The roots of Claudin's new sensitivity to chords and chord progressions go back at least to the beginning of the century within France itself. It would be intriguing to argue that Josquin's quickened awareness of tonality was at least partly a result of his experiences in Italy with the frottola and related forms, but such a conclusion can be made only after more detailed investigation and further proofs. Originally Italian or not, this new harmonic style was inherited by Claudin from native French composers. For Claudin was the true son of his father, the rightful heir of his Parisian forbears.

DISCUSSION

PANELISTS: MME. THIBAULT, MRS. CONANT, MR. LESURE

MME. THIBAULT: I quite agree with Mr. Brown's description of Ockeghem's chansons as dialogues for superius and tenor, with an

[80] See, for example, Claudin's "Altro non el mio amor" (*RISM* 1534[12], fol. 2[v]), Janequin's "Si come il chiaro," printed in François Lesure, ed., *Anthologie de la chanson parisienne au XVIe siècle* (Monaco, 1953), no. 9, and Prioris' "Consumo la vita mia," in Cambridge, Magdalene College, MS. Pepys 1760, fol. 86[v], among other places.

[81] See Henry Prunières, "La Musique de la chambre et de l'écurie sous le règne de François Ier, 1516-1547," *L' Année musicale,* I (1912), 219-236.

[82] See André Pirro, "Leo X and Music," *Musical Quarterly,* XXI (1935), 1-16.

added third voice. But I don't know that whether this voice was composed at the same time or later is very important; I think it is the final result that counts. Sure as I am that the contratenor was an added voice in compositions prior to Ockeghem, I should not be surprised if in his time the three voices were conceived at once, even though superius and tenor remained more important than contratenor.

MR. BROWN: I meant to stress result rather than method with regard to Ockeghem's chansons; however, I chose "Les desleaulx" (Example 1) because it shows perhaps the least well integrated of all of Ockeghem's contratenors, behaving like an added voice whether or not it was one.

MME. THIBAULT: You chose very well!

MR. HERTZMANN: But even in this piece there is imitation, showing an intention on the part of the composer to integrate the three voices.

MME. THIBAULT: And not only imitation, but rhythmic spacing and other details show a careful contrapuntal relation, too well constructed for the third voice to have been added later.

MR. BROWN: That is true. I really meant, in using "Les desleaulx," to show two different things: the traditional "Burgundian" technique and also Ockeghem's modifications of that technique.

MR. REESE: It seems likely, or at least very possible, that Ockeghem's contratenors were written simultaneously with the other parts. On the other hand we see Pietro Aron [83] pleading for simultaneous composition, at a time which is already rather late for Ockeghem. Would he have made such a plea if this sort of thing were common practice?

MME. THIBAULT: Theorists' comments often come after composers have done their work. Ockeghem proves himself a thorough polyphonist in his religious music; why should he have adopted a quite different way of writing for his chansons? It does not seem in character for a composer who thinks polyphonically in three or four parts to change over to writing duos and then adding a third voice.

[83] In his *De institutione harmonica* . . . (Bologna, 1516), bk. III, chap. x, Aron describes simultaneous composition as his own practice and that of the best composers of his day. This passage and a similar one from the *Thoscanello de la musica* of 1523 are quoted in Lowinsky, "Physical and Musical Space in the Renaissance," p. 67. Aron's own method of teaching was the traditional one of beginning with two-part composition, however.

MR. JOHNSON: I quite agree that in Ockeghem's chansons the contratenor is certainly no mere filler. But the priority of the two upper parts seems still to be indicated by their self-sufficiency.

MME. THIBAULT: They are self-sufficient, but this does not mean that one could remove the contra and perform the chansons as duets. Many of Dufay's and Binchois' pieces can be performed as duos; but in Ockeghem one would miss the third voice were it removed. Another proof of this point is that in Ockeghem's period we begin to see different names given to the contratenor; it is called different things when it begins to belong more to the inner fabric of the chanson.

MRS. CONANT: Ockeghem occasionally arranged chansons by other composers; I am thinking of the example by Cornago,[84] a three-voice piece which Ockeghem set for four parts, changing the contratenor radically in order to do it. Could that be an additional argument for his thinking of the whole contrapuntal fabric at once?

MR. REESE: Yes, although it may be simply part of the old tradition of borrowing a melody and reworking it.

MR. PALISCA: As for Pietro Aron, I think he may have stressed the distinction between simultaneous and successive composition because his contemporaries were still teaching counterpoint in the successive method. Even Zarlino begins by teaching two-part counterpoint, saying that when the rules are learned one can add more parts;[85] he gives consonance tables just as the early sixteenth-century theorists did. I think that Aron was perhaps more in contact with what composers did, and realized that they did not write in a successive way unless they were composing over a cantus firmus. Even in the fifteenth century no one could have written a canon in anything but a simultaneous way.

[84] The three-voice "Qu'es mi vida preguntays," attributed to Cornago in Monte-cassino, Archivio, MS. 871 N, p. 380, is found in a four-voiced arrangement in the same manuscript (pp. 257–258), attributed to Cornago and "Oquegan." The four-voice version is also in Seville, Bibl. Colombina, MS. 7–1–28, fol. 24ᵛ–25, here anonymous. See H. Anglès, ed., *La música en la corte de los reyes catolicos: Poli-fonia religiosa I.* Monumentos de la música española, 1. (Madrid, 1941), p. 104; H. Anglès, "Cornago," *MGG,* II, 1681; Plamenac, "Ockeghem," *MGG,* IX, 1836. A discussion of the piece may be found in I. Pope, "La Musique espagnole à la cour de Naples dans la seconde moitié du XVᵉ siècle," in *Musique et poésie au XVIᵉ siècle* (Paris, 1954), pp. 49–50.

[85] Gioseffo Zarlino, *Le istituzioni armoniche,* bk. III, chap. xl. The passage is given in translation in O. Strunk, *Source Readings in Music History* (New York, 1950), p. 245.

MR. PIRROTTA: Of course Ockeghem was able to write three or more parts at once. But one may think of his writing pieces in which the two upper parts are self-sufficient and the third an "added" part (not necessarily in a temporal sense) as yet another skill. I am inclined to think that although in other types of music Ockeghem conceived all the parts at once, in the chanson' he intended to preserve the identity of the self-sufficient two upper voices.

MR. REESE: He may, in other words, have been carrying on part of the chanson tradition.

MR. BROWN: As Mme. Thibault suggests, one is never going to find out exactly when this old tradition came to an end; my point is simply that there is a real difference in style between Ockeghem and Josquin, and that Ockeghem represents the older tradition, in however modified a way.

MME. THIBAULT: Mr. Brown's mention of "popular" arrangements suggested some interesting examples: there is a group of four-part chansons in the latter part of the Dijon manuscript,[86] where two "popular" voices, derived from popular refrains, are somehow "framed" by two newly composed voices, a superius and bassus. These pieces, from the period around 1470, are prior to the *chansons rustiques* we have been considering here. The style of these chansons, which may have exerted some influence on late-fifteenth-century chansons, would be interesting to look into. But that form of composing voices two-by-two is quite another thing from the three-part chansons of the period, the ones we have been discussing.

You spoke, Mr. Brown, of a style of composition in which little bits of melody are put together, separated by stops, and called it a characteristic of the Févin school; Example 5 demonstrates this style. In the *Odhecaton* there is a chanson called the "Dit le burguygnon"[87]—proof that Italians considered it to be in Burgundian style—which is full of short phrases, using characteristically French rhythmic formulas, and separated by pauses. The piece is a medley of French songs; some of the authors may be Burgundian, but I do not like to make this distinction since I believe that the chanson is simply the French chanson, even in the fifteenth century. At any

[86] Presumably the chansons on fols. 171ᵛ–186 of Dijon, Bibl. de la Ville, MS. 517. See the catalogue of this manuscript in S. Morelot, "Notice sur un manuscrit de musique ancienne de la Bibliothèque de Dijon," *Mémoires de la Commission des Antiquités du Département de la Côte-d'Or,* IV (1856), 133–160.

[87] No. 18, fols. 20ᵛ–21; printed in Hewitt and Pope, *Odhecaton,* no. 18.

rate the piece is an early example of the style you spoke of in con-- nection with Févin.

MR. REESE: This piques my curiosity. How does one know that it was the Italians rather than the French who gave the name "Dit le burguygnon" to this piece?

MME. THIBAULT: Simply because it was published in Venice by Petrucci; it may have been given to the publisher by French mu- sicians who were there. This is only a hypothesis; the name may be French-given, except that usually one doesn't call oneself something. It is other people who bestow descriptive names. I have no absolute proof, except that one does find fragments of well-known French songs in the piece.

A peculiarity of the Févin chansons is that he does not use voices in the traditional manner, but instead very often has three upper voices or three lower voices—either three feminine voices, or those of young boys, or three male voices. This is quite new, and it is something Claudin does not follow. Could these chansons have been written for performance in school plays, to be sung by young boys or girls? There must be some reason for this peculiarity of style.

I might speak here of another detail in your paper, this with re- gard to the texting of Ockeghem's chansons. You spoke of "L'autre dantan." [88] It is a sixain, is it not?

MR. BROWN: No, I think it is a cinquain.

MME. THIBAULT: But I believe it is really a sixain, with part of the text missing, after "Tant mauvais brassin me brassa."

MR. BROWN: I was of course only reading it from your *Trois chansonniers* . . .

MME. THIBAULT: The texting there was done by Eugénie Droz and myself many years ago, and I no longer agree with it! I have an- other version of the text which falls in much better with the music, the extra verse explaining a good deal. The long melisma at the end should have some text supplied to give an accent. At any rate the older texting can no longer be regarded as completely correct. This is of course just a detail; in general I quite agree with your proposed lines of division. I think of Claudin de Sermisy as almost a separate figure in his own time, because he has a very fluent per- sonal style, in rhythm and in melody, which is not at all that of many of his contemporaries. He has in addition a way of writing the

[88] See text at note 14.

inner parts very fluidly, again peculiar to him; this may be a reason why the lutenists adopted his chansons in preference to those of others. So I think that while Claudin's style was a good one to select, it is a personal one, and in a way even an exceptional one within the field of the Parisian chanson. Perhaps he is exceptional because he is a first-rate composer.

MR. BROWN: Precisely.

MME. THIBAULT: But when one is trying to find rules, it is usually with the less important composers that one deals. The good men hide their little tricks; the poorer ones let us analyze them more easily.

MR. BROWN: I agree. But since I tried to restrict myself for the most part to the *Chansons nouvelles* [89] in giving examples, it seemed appropriate to concentrate on Claudin. And I feel that other chanson composers of the period are not so much different from Claudin as they are less good.

MME. THIBAULT: As for the literary form of Claudin's chansons, I think that, as you said, it is the combined result of different traditions, that of the chanson rustique being one. If one studies the inner shape of a stanza in strophic chansons, one sees that the repetition of the last line practically makes these poems into five-line stanzas, just as in the cinquain. The musical schemes support this; and if one tries to set all the stanzas, not just the first, to the music, a pattern that is really very traditional emerges.

One further point about your linking of Claudin with Févin: besides Claudin's being a real melodist, which I think puts him in a different category from Févin, his counterpoint is very euphonious, while a characteristic of Févin's style is all those seconds that rub up against one another. It is a different, more rugged style, without the softness of melody one associates with Claudin. Your Févin examples, again very carefully chosen for your purposes, are perhaps not entirely typical of the whole of his work—if one may be permitted to speak of the whole of any composer's work in this way.

MR. LESURE: I trust that I may be forgiven for using the language of the chanson to comment on Mr. Brown's paper. One of the original features of his view of the chanson is, I think, his setting back a bit the date of inception of the "Parisian" style, a style which has hitherto been defined in a quite narrow way as a certain type of chanson beginning with Attaingnant and ending about the middle

[89] See note 68, above.

of the century. Mr. Brown has in fact taken the Parisian chanson back to the end of the fifteenth century, into the reign of Louis XII, the time of Févin, Mouton, and their contemporaries. The Mouton example "De tous regretz," which you have spoken of [90] has in fact many of the characteristics of the Attaingnant-published chansons (and Attaingnant even printed a few of Mouton's works); but is it true that all the work of this man and of his contemporaries is in this style? There may be resemblances between individual chansons of Claudin and Févin, but nonetheless a fundamental difference of style does exist between the two generations. I wonder, then, if your selection of examples has not been perhaps rather "precise," in its intention of proving your point. Although I do not know the chansons of Mouton and Févin in close detail, I question the appropriateness of using terminology ordinarily applied to Claudin's generation for them.

MR. BROWN: I think I said that "De tous regretz," like Févin's "Adieu soulas" (Example 9), is an exceptional work for its composer. "Resjouissez vous" (Example 8) is much more characteristic of Mouton's style, and it seems to me that what I have called the Parisian chanson under Louis XII is the kind of piece represented by "Resjouissez vous" and by "J'ay veu la beauté" (Example 5), which are much more typical Mouton-Févin pieces. I use the term "Parisian chanson" in connection with this style simply because the composers who wrote these pieces were all men who were working in the royal chapel.

MME. THIBAULT: Mr. Lesure has just said that the term "Parisian chanson" when used for the chanson of the period from 1530 to 1550 can be quite precisely defined; however, if one brings together chansons of Josquin and Mouton, and those of the generation of Bruhier and Ninot le Petit, one finds that they do not fit this definition. If they are occasionally written on the same general plan, this has only the effect of complicating the chronological question.

MR. BROWN: I was careful never to call Josquin's chansons Parisian chansons.

MME. THIBAULT: But those of Mouton and others, you did. If one speaks of "genesis" that is one thing; to move the Parisian chanson back to the generation of 1500 to 1530 is quite another.

MR. BROWN: I agree, but it does seem to me that Févin's style in

[90] See text at note 62.

particular is really a local dialect, written specifically in Paris or, at any rate, for the court.

MME. THIBAULT: Certainly; the grands seigneurs of the period of Louis XII and Francis I favored the chanson rustique as Marie Antoinette favored pastoral themes—it was à la mode. But although a fashion may modify the existing style of writing, it may be a passing thing, without real lasting effect.

MR. BROWN: Févin's style is, I admit, a special thing.

MME. THIBAULT: It is, then, very useful in supporting your thesis as to the "genesis" of the Parisian chanson; that does not make it identical with the later style.

MR. LESURE: I should like to add something about the courtly-popular distinction, after all not a thing particularly restricted to the fifteenth century. Every languorous piece is not courtly, nor is every gay one popular; so one cannot always tell simply by the character of the text. Then, as for Mr. Brown's identification of the Parisian chanson with the work of Claudin, I suggest that one must deal as well with his contemporaries, whose work appeared also in the first publications of Attaingnant. These composers do not all write quite like Claudin—a happy thing, for every man should have something of his own style. Nevertheless there are strong similarities among composers of the period from 1520 to 1540: extreme simplicity of rhythmic style, of musical and even of literary form. And as Mr. Brown has said, there are evident analogues to this in some of the work of Févin and Mouton. It is possible that the Claudin-Janequin style existed some time before Attaingnant's first publications, since they were quite well-established composers when Attaingnant began to print. The two men were in fact first published in Italy: Claudin in, I believe, a religious publication of 1526,[91] and Janequin in an Antico print [92] including an early version of his "L'Alouette." Thus one could move the Parisian chanson back from 1528 to, say, 1520; nevertheless, it would seem well to reserve the term "Parisian" for the work of this generation.

MR. REESE: The term "Parisian chanson" has been criticized a good

[91] *RISM* [c. 1526][5], *Fior de motetti e canzoni novi* . . . (Rome, G. Giunta). The motet "Aspice Domine de sede sancta tua," ascribed to "Claude," appears in this publication.

[92] *RISM* 1520[6], *Chansons à troys* (Venice; Antico, 1520). See François Lesure, "Clément Janequin: Recherches sur sa vie et son œuvre," *Musica Disciplina,* V (1951), 158.

deal. If it does not seem applicable to the generation of Févin because a quite unified French style was to follow that generation, could it be used as a general term to illustrate the contrast between it and another style of the period of Claudin and Janequin, the more polyphonic chanson cultivated in the Low Countries by men like Gombert and Willaert?

MR. BROWN: Exactly. I couldn't even talk about such a figure as Pierre de la Rue, because he is totally outside the Parisian tradition.

MR. REESE: He does of course have a few pieces which seem to be related to Parisian style; a chanson such as "Au feu d'amour" [93] is a little like those of Claudin's generation.

MR. LESURE: Of course composers may from time to time have felt the need or wish to write in Parisian style. In publications of the first generation of Phalèse and Susato there are occasional examples of pieces in the Claudin-Janequin style.

MME. THIBAULT: Perhaps the term *chanson de cour* would be clearer for us to work with. A concept of the chanson at the court of Louis XII or the young Francis I, with its emphasis on Paris as the focal point of the court, might give a truer idea of what we have been talking about.

MR. RUBSAMEN: I find that there are certain advantages in choosing, as you did, Mr. Brown, a few important composers as the basis of your paper; but on the other hand I feel that there are some missing links, and that avoidance of men such as Bruhier, Ninot, Pierre de la Rue, and Brumel results in a rather indistinct picture of the period. For instance, the homorhythmic texture so prevalent in Claudin's chansons is quite different from the more transparent texture of Févin, Mouton, and especially Josquin. It is much more likely that the point of departure for adoption of this homorhythmic texture can be found in the chansons of Bruhier and Ninot and Brumel. In these men one can also find chansons with the clear formal structure you spoke of as characteristic of Claudin.

MR. BROWN: One can find them even in Josquin, for that matter. As for Bruhier and Ninot, it seems to me that their four-part chansons are very like the "popular arrangement" chansons of Févin and Mouton. Then, I do not see why Brumel and Pierre de la Rue

[93] Printed in R. Eitner, ed., *60 Chansons zu vier Stimmen aus der ersten Hälfte des 16. Jahrhunderts,* Publikation älterer praktischer und theoretischer Musikwerke, 18 (Leipzig, 1899), no. 33; also in H. Riemann, ed., *Musikgeschichte im Beispielen,* 3d ed. (Leipzig, 1925), no. 24.

should be brought in, since they did not work for the French court and so do not qualify for my definition of the Parisian chanson.

MR. RUBSAMEN: I mention Brumel because a chanson such as "Dieu te gart" [94] is very much in the style you have called the four-part "popular" chanson.

MR. BROWN: In the same tradition are the narrative chansons of Claudin, such as "Un jour Robin," [95] pieces which combine homorhythmic sections with mosaiclike counterpoint.

MR. RUBSAMEN: I got the impression that in your chronological survey you suggested that the four-part chanson emerged from Josquin's style. I would ask a rhetorical question: where in Josquin are the shifts from duple to triple meter that are so common in the four-part chanson?

MR. BROWN: I don't think I quite said that, but rather that Josquin's late chansons, Févin's three-part popular arrangements, and Mouton's four-part popular arrangements all existed at once. I don't think there is time here to go into the origins of the four-part popular arrangement.

MR. RUBSAMEN: Perhaps we shall consider this in the next session. One minor point: you mentioned Josquin's having had some connection with the court of Marguerite of Austria. Did you mean that he was attached to the court in some way? I have never seen his name in any list of her musicians.

MR. BROWN: No, I merely said that there was some relation, clear from the fact that she wrote to Condé to ask how he was. [96] Mr. Rubsamen's questions are, if I interpret them rightly, leading up to the matter of Italian influence, which I think we all agree can be left for the next session. My chief point in any event was that if there was any Italian influence on Claudin it came by way of Mouton and his French contemporaries.

MR. REESE: How do we know there was Italian influence on Mouton?

MR. BROWN: We don't. The question might well be asked; however, I did not do so here. By way of a general answer to Mr. Rubsamen's remarks, I admit that I had to skip a good many details, but

---

[94] In Florence, Bibl. Cons., MS. B 2442, p. 132.

[95] *RISM* [c. 1528]⁸, fol. 4.

[96] For Josquin's relations with the court of Marguerite of Austria see Osthoff, "Josquin Desprez," *MGG*, VII, 197.

I feel that this was necessary in order to represent, in however generalized a way, the work of several generations of composers.

MR. HERTZMANN: Several questions occurred to me as I listened to Mr. Brown's paper. The first has to do with how "popular" the material of the chanson was. I do not know; but I am reminded that at a symposium here at Harvard [97] we discussed the same question as to the fifteenth-century dance. We did not really find the answer to that either; but I shall repeat what I said then: I no longer believe what I wrote on the subject some thirty-five years ago.

As to the matter of pushing back the date of the "Parisian" chanson, although, as you say, Claudin may have started writing at the time of his first appointment at the royal court, Clément Marot, who is certainly an important moving force in this whole movement, did not start that early; to my knowledge he began only in the 1520's. I therefore don't think that we can push the whole thing back so far.

I rather agree with Mr. Lesure that your emphasis on Claudin does not quite do justice to the period; I don't mean that you should have spoken of lesser composers, but of Janequin as a counterpart to Claudin. The 1528 chansons of Attaingnant, which appeared anonymously, contain pieces by Janequin as well as chansons of Claudin. Surely Janequin deserves a place in the discussion. I myself leaned heavily toward Claudin in my youth because I thought he was the more musical man; he had more melodic invention, was more pleasing, more "harmonic"—in short, was more appealing. Janequin, on the other hand, seems to have commanded a quite different contrapuntal technique, possibly more skillful than that of Claudin. There are a few rather intricate chansons by Claudin, displaying a sort of flamboyant Gothic style, if one may use this expression. But most of them are very simple. One thing that is characteristic of Claudin as an individual composer, though not of the Parisian chanson as a whole, is a kind of interchange between the discant, always important melodically, and the tenor, which often seems of primary structural importance. Most composers after Claudin concentrate on the melody of the top line, not on a tenor and/or discant structure.

[97] The first Isham Library Conference. See *Instrumental Music: A Conference at Isham Memorial Library, May 4, 1957,* ed. David G. Hughes, Isham Library Papers I (Cambridge, Mass., 1959). Mr. Hertzmann's remarks on the fifteenth-century dance, reversing his earlier views, may be found on pp. 27-28, in the discussion following the paper of Otto Kinkeldey, "Dance Tunes of the Fifteenth Century."

Finally there is a matter of relations between text and music in Claudin. Poetry and music are close if one thinks of prosody, and to a slight degree, of text interpretation; but one must remember that these chansons are stanzaic. Then, even with the music the singers would not have had all the stanzas, which were not all printed by Attaingnant; they were printed separately, in the case of the Marot chansons after the music had come out. The matter of text interpretation should then be taken with some caution.

MR. BROWN: I was really concerned only with prosodic relations; I never claimed that there was any attempt to express the meaning of the text.

MR. HERTZMANN: There may be limited attempts, such as invocations and the like. But this sort of expression really goes back to the fifteenth century.

MR. BROWN: One of the principal aims of my paper was to show that there was little Italian influence on the "Parisian" chanson; as a consequence I felt no need to show any kind of madrigalian tenddency to express the meaning of the text in the music. If I had had room for Janequin I could perhaps even have strengthened my point, since as you say, Janequin is in many ways a more French composer, more in the tradition, than Claudin. Another reason for my omitting Janequin is that the early part of his career was not spent in Paris. I tried to limit myself to people who were connected with the court.

MR. HERTZMANN: Janequin did have an indirect connection with the court.

MR. BROWN: Yes, but the men I discussed were the principal composers of the royal chapel. Neither Févin nor Mouton, as far as I know, worked anywhere but at the court. This is true of Ockeghem, then of Claudin. The exception is Josquin, whose relation is a more tenuous one.

MR. HERTZMANN: I do, however, agree with Mme. Thibault and Mr. Lesure that we should not mix up the issues and call everything from 1500 on "Parisian." Our concept of the Parisian chanson as the body of works published by Attaingnant is a well-established one.

MR. BROWN: The nomenclature is not too important, do you think? As for your question about "popular" chansons, my book *Music in the French Secular Theater* takes up this matter in some detail, and I refer you to that. I admit that the question is a difficult one to decide with any certainty.

MRS. CONANT: The chansons of Ockeghem were meant, presumably, to be sung by one voice with instrumental accompaniment. It seems to me that a major structural change in the chanson comes about when the parts are all texted and are all vocal in character. This apparently takes place in the early sixteenth century, but there are fifteenth-century examples, and at least some of these seem to have been popular in nature. Could there be a connection between fully vocal style and popular elements?

MR. BROWN: I had not thought of the two together. The change to fully texted voices, like the change from successive to simultaneous composition, occurs somewhere around 1500, give or take fifteen years. On the other hand, the "popular" style of Févin is effective— if I may use such a bland word—if a singer performs the cantus prius factus and instruments play the other two voices. Nevertheless it is true that the important change of style takes place in 1500 rather than in 1530; and one sees this change between a piece by, say, Ockeghem and a piece like the "Mille regretz"[98] of Josquin, the latter not so much a popular piece as a kind of choral dialogue.

MRS. CONANT: If I may revert to Spanish material, which I know better, one is struck by the fact that in the *Cancionero de Palacio* in the Palace Library in Madrid the songs on really popular texts are sung by all voices; this is true even of quite early songs, and is in contrast to later but more courtly songs, where it seems apparent that one voice, texted, is sung while the others are played on instruments.

MR. BROWN: The songs in French farces and moralities are, it seems to me, more often than not sung *a cappella;* and these all use popular material.

MR. REESE: Could the change to fully texted style not have been made for purely musical reasons, a stylistic change characteristic of the Josquin generation?

MME. THIBAULT: The change can be seen in the difference between *Canti C* and *Canti A* and *B*.

MR. BROWN: But don't you think that *Canti C* contains at least some instrumental pieces?

MME. THIBAULT: That is a question in itself. One must decide whether there is an instrumental style per se or whether songs of several stanzas have not simply been embroidered by singers so that one can't tell if the pieces are instrumental or not.

[98] See Example 2, printed after Josquin, *Werken,* chanson no. 24.

MR. REESE: Did you say, Mr. Brown, that there was no fundamental change in texture between Josquin's generation and that of Claudin?

MR. BROWN: Not quite. There is of course a change, but one rather like that between Dufay and Ockeghem with relation to the contratenor; in Ockeghem one can still see the old superius-tenor framework, and in Claudin one can see a good many elements from Josquin, even though the result is quite different.

MR. REESE: Isn't there more difference between Josquin and Claudin in texture—as we ordinarily think of that term—than between Josquin and the Susato-published school of Netherlandish composers?

MR. BROWN: It seems to me that Josquin stands in the middle, with the Netherlanders complicating him, the Parisians simplifying him. Mouton might be very important here; his five- and six-part chansons seem very much like those of the Netherlanders.

MME. THIBAULT: I should like to return to a point made by Mr. Hertzmann: the tenor is often important in the chanson of this period. Of course when a chanson was used as timbre in a noel it was the superius, but in fricassées it could be the tenor as well as the superius that was borrowed.

MR. BROWN: Yes, but more often than not it was the superius. Then, think of the "Jouyssance" as a basse danse.[99]

MME. THIBAULT: And often the simplest version of a tune is in the tenor, the superius having a more elaborate form.

MR. HERTZMANN: Of course the superius has to be a bit more elaborate in order to accommodate the discant cadence, whereas the tenor can move down simply from second to first degree; this is a technical, not a substantial difference.

MME. THIBAULT: But if the same theme is exposed in the superius and in the tenor, separately, the question is, in which part is it the more ornate?

MR. PALISCA: I should like to ask Mr. Brown if in Claudin he does not find some mixing of styles such as one finds in the madrigal, according to the meaning of a particular phrase; that is, one phrase

---

[99] Claudin's "Jouyssance vous donneray," which first appeared in Attaingnant's *Chansons nouvelles,* was used as a basse danse in Thoinot Arbeau's *Orchésographie* of 1589, the dance being a free version of the chanson tenor. The chanson and dance tenors are printed together in J. Tiersot, *Histoire de la chanson populaire en France* (Paris, 1889), pp. 113–114. For a discussion of the chanson and the basse danse, and a bibliography of the sources of each, see Brown, *Music in the French Secular Theater.*

will be treated contrapuntally, another in declamatory style. If this is actually determined by the text you find the kind of *Figurenlehre* that occurs later in motets. "Si j'ay pour vous" (Example 10) seems to bear this out. At one point you have "secourez-moi" (mm. 9-10), a sort of call for help, in homophonic style; then, a bit later, there is "prenez pitié" (mm. 15-17), with a descending semitone in the superius, imitated more or less exactly by all the voices, as you might find it in later madrigals. This seems almost a rhetorical approach to setting the text.

MR. BROWN: Yes, but often the chansons are stereotyped; the second phrase is declamatory whether or not the text says "secourez-moi."

MR. REESE: As a brief concluding remark, I might say a word in defense of Mr. Brown's selection of examples. It may not be at all a bad thing to pick one's examples with care; if they are not completely characteristic of the period, they may be just the sort of thing that starts a new trend. After all, a new development has to be set in motion by something not characteristic of an older style.

II

FROM FROTTOLA TO MADRIGAL:
THE CHANGING PATTERN OF
SECULAR ITALIAN VOCAL MUSIC

WALTER H. RUBSAMEN

DURING the half century between 1430 and approximately 1480 three textures or styles are discernible in vocal music set to secular Italian texts. One represents the lingering tradition of the Italian Ars Nova, in which the uppermost voice noticeably exceeds the others in activity and floridity, the verses being for the most part amorous lyrics ascribed to Leonardo Giustiniani. Among the chief repositories of this type are Bologna, University Library, MS. 2216; Escorial, Monastery Library, MS. IV.a.24; Florence, Biblioteca Nazionale, MS. Magl. XIX, 176; and Petrucci's sixth book of frottole.

These and several other sources of the period, notably the Chansonnier Cordiforme of the Bibliothèque Nationale in Paris, contain examples of a second style, that of the simplified, essentially homophonic and isometric Justiniana. In the compositions beginning "Ayme sospiri," [1] "Merce te chiamo" [2] (Example 16), and "Perla mia cara" [3] (Example 17), for instance, the solo voice begins passages with repeated notes in declamatory fashion, while simultaneous holds or pauses in all three voices clearly demarcate the ends of phrases. Apparently this became the prototype of the later frottola, although

[1] Escorial, Monastery Library, MS. IV.a.24, fols. 85ᵛ–86; published in modern transcription by Walter Rubsamen in "The Justiniane or Viniziane of the 15th Century," *Acta Musicologica,* XXIX (1957), 180–182.

[2] The original setting for two voices is in Bologna, Bibl. Univ., MS. 2216, fols. 27ᵛ–28; the same, with the addition of a third voice, in Montecassino, Archivio, MS. 871 N, pp. 348–349, and Escorial, Monastery Library, MS. IV.a.24, fols. 82ᵛ–83 (incomplete).

[3] Paris, Bibl. Nat., Chansonnier Cordiforme, fols. 11ᵛ–12. A different, incomplete setting of the text is contained in Paris, Bibl. Nat., MS. nouv. acq. fr. 4379, fol. 66ᵛ.

it has been shown that the singer embellished the discant of the basic structure with improvisatory melismas during actual performance, the *fermate* or rests probably serving the accompanying instrumentalists as an indication of phrase endings.[4] A chief reason for the homophonic nature of the Justiniana lay in the manner of performance by the poet-improvisators of the fifteenth century, such as Giustiniani himself, who either accompanied themselves on the lute, lira da braccio, or viol, or relied upon minstrels for this purpose as they sang love songs for the delectation of the courtiers and their ladies. As they were musical amateurs, their accompaniments must have been relatively simple, and so devised as not to interfere with the understandability of the text.

The Flemish-Burgundian and English musicians who lived in Italy, or whose works were performed there during the period in question, contributed songs in a third style, that with independent, polyphonic, but usually nonimitative parts. For solo voice or duet with instrumental accompaniment, these settings of Italian texts play only a minor role in the secular manuscripts of the time, as compared with the dominant chanson. Some are equivalent stylistically to the chanson, others show by their melismatic upper voice that the influence of the Italian Ars Nova was still strong, and some are actual chansons in which the French has been replaced by Italian. Among the compositions in question are Dufay's "Dona i ardenti rai,"[5] "Donna gentile, bella come l'oro,"[6] and "Vergine bella,"[7] the latter one of the few settings of Petrarch in the Quattrocento; "Tanto è l'afano," a textual alteration of Caron's chanson "Le despourveu infortuné;"[8] Johannes Bedingham's "Fortune helas," recast in Italy as "Gentil madonna, de non m'abandonare;"[9] and Busnois' "Chon

---

[4] Rubsamen, "Justiniane," pp. 175ff.

[5] Oxford, Bodleian Library, Canonici Misc. MS. 213, fol. 73.

[6] New Haven, Yale University Library, Mellon Chansonnier, pp. 84-85; Paris, Bibl. Nat., Chansonnier Cordiforme, fols 2ᵛ-3; Pavia, Bibl. Univ., MS. Aldini 362, fols. 52ᵛ-53 (anon.).

[7] Published in *Das Chorwerk*, XIX, 7ff.

[8] Rome, Vatican Library, Cappella Giulia, MS. XIII, 27, fols. 38ᵛ-39; Rome, Bibl. Casanatense, MS. 2856, fols. 67ᵛ-69; Bologna, Bibl. Cons., Cod. Q 18, fols. 25ᵛ-26; Seville, Bibl. Colombina, MS. 5-I-43, fols. 52ᵛ-53; and many other sources. Published by H. Ringmann, *Das Glogauer Liederbuch*. Das Erbe deutscher Musik, series I, vol. 4 (Kassel, 1936), p. 52. See Dragan Plamenac, "A Reconstruction of the French Chansonnier in the Biblioteca Colombina, Seville," *Musical Quarterly*, XXXVIII (1952), 250-251.

[9] For the sources see Plamenac, pp. 112-113, 246.

tutta gentileça"[10] (Example 18), which may also be based on a French model. Judging from the phraseology of the various voice parts, only the discant of Busnois' composition appears to have been intended for vocal performance.

Often all three techniques—the melismatic upper voice, homorhythmic writing, and polyphonic equivalence of the parts—alternate in the same composition. By 1480, however, the melismatic style had died out, to all intents and purposes, except as it continued to be improvised in the Justiniana and the *strambotto*. Examples of such written-out improvisations may be found in Petrucci's *Frottole Libro VI*, where they apparently served as examples of an archaic form. The earlier frottola manuscripts [11] contain strambotti marked by a series of holds perhaps marking melismas sung by the poet-improvisator. Among the examples are "Mille prove ho gia facto," "Alta regina a ti piangendo," Serafino Aquilano's "Risguardo il viso mio," and "La nocte è curta" (Example 19), all in the Paris manuscript analyzed by Mme. Bridgman.[12]

It appears probable that improvisators of the late fifteenth century made the rhapsodic ornamentation of a simple melodic line an integral part of their performance. Among the most famous of these poet-musicians were those at the Ferrarese court, Giovanni Cieco di Parma and Francesco Cieco di Ferrara; a Spaniard who entertained at the Neapolitan court, Benedetto Gareth (Il Chariteo); Francesco Cei; Bernardo Accolti, called "l'unico Aretino," and the most celebrated of them all, Serafino Aquilano. The master examples of sonnets or *capitoli* printed by Petrucci as models for poets and other performers bear witness to the fact that the improvisatory singing of poetry was still very much in vogue during the first decade of the sixteenth century. Thus, in *Strambotti, Ode, Frottole, Sonetti. Et*

[10] Florence, Bibl. Naz., MS. Magl. XIX, 59, fols. 52ᵛ–53 (anon.); Paris, Bibl. Nat., MS. fonds fr. 15123, fols. 13ᵛ–14.

[11] Florence, Bibl. Naz., MS. Magl. XIX, 141, and MS. Panc. 27; Florence, Bibl. Cons., MS. B 2441; London, British Museum, MS Egerton 3051; Milan, Bibl. Trivulziana, MS. 55; Modena, Bibl. Estense, MS. a.F.9.9; Paris, Bibl. Nat., Dépt. Mus, Rés. Vm.⁷ 676.

[12] Respectively nos. 16, 19, 27, and 105 of Paris, Bibl. Nat., Dépt. Mus., Rés. Vm.⁷ 676. For the concordances see Nanie Bridgman, "Un Manuscrit italien du début du XVIᵉ siècle à la Bibliothèque Nationale (Département de la Musique, Rés. Vm.⁷ 676)," in *Annales musicologiques*, I (1953), 177ff. A transcription of "Alta regina" appears there on pp. 260–262.

modo de cantar versi latini e capituli. Libro quarto (1505) one finds a composition entitled "Aer de capituli," and another, "Modo de cantar sonetti." As late as 1514–1518, Castiglione in *The Courtier* [13] states that his favorite manner of performance is "il cantare alla viola per recitare," but urges the potential poet-improvisators among his readers to consider their age, as it is displeasing to see an old, white-haired, toothless man singing and playing the viola to a group of women—"perche il più delle volte cantando si dicon parole amorose, e ne' vecchi l'amor è cosa ridicula."

The isometric, homophonic texture of the frottola, whose roots apparently lay in the writing down of a basic structure that was to be embellished with improvisatory ornaments in the discant, became predominant in Italian secular music during the last decades of the fifteenth century, while the Netherlanders continued to write polyphonic works with Italian texts. Manuscript collections entirely devoted to frottole began to appear in the 1490's. The title *Frottole* used by Petrucci in his eleven books of frottole, published between 1504 and 1514, is a collective term embracing many different Italian verse forms and compositional types, including the *barzelletta* or frottola proper, which was related to the ballata in structure, the strambotto, *oda,* capitolo, sonnet, canzone, Justiniana, *canto carnascialesco,* rudimentary *villotta,* and even a few settings of Latin poems. Probably derived from the medieval Latin *frocta,* the term originally signified an assortment of enjoyable verses. During the Trecento and early Quattrocento a frottola was a poem of irregular length of line containing many proverbs and witty sayings. Groups of short, septisyllabic rhyming lines alternate with those of eleven or twelve syllables, but the short, rhyming verses gives to the poem a folklike tone that also characterized the later frottola—hence the revival of the term by Petrucci. For example, a Trecento frottola attributed to Petrarch begins:

> Di rider ho gran voglia,
> Se non fosse una doglia.
> Che m'è nata nel fianco
> Di sotto al lato manco.

The most frequently used poetical forms in the frottola collections —the barzelletta, oda, and strambotto—evince the common characteristics of popular verses, extreme regularity in length of lines and

[13] Bk. 2, chap. xiii.

rhyming schemes. Given the close connection between text and music in at least the uppermost voice, the consistent repetition of trochaic, octosysyllabic lines in the barzelletta-frottola resulted in symmetrical patterns of accents, equal periods, and repeated notes at ends of phrases to match the inevitable feminine endings of the verses. The alternation of *ripresa* and strophes in the barzelletta usually determined the musical form, *ABA or ABABABA* depending on the number of strophes.

The music itself consists of a few well-defined phrases, repeated here and there because of rhyming lines, or merely because the composer decided that too many new phrases would be wasteful. General traits of musical style in the frottola are simplicity, clarity of form through the repetition of phrases and sections, avoidance of complex polyphonic devices, and full-voiced writing throughout, thus contrasting strongly with the imitative polyphony and more transparent writing of the contemporary Flemish-Burgundian composers. In the basic frottola all voices are homorhythmic, the bass serving as a harmonic fundament, and the middle parts filling in the chordal structures. As a result, only the discant is vocally smooth, the others often having awkward, unvocal skips. Phrases begin and end simultaneously, and imitations, if they exist at all, occur between the middle voices as incidental embellishments of the homophony. Generally the composer provides only the discant with a complete text, making it syllabic and unmistakably vocal in character. Its declamatory nature betrays its derivation from the musical recitation of the poet-improvisators. Subsidiary voices that flow without pause and do not correspond to the phraseology of the text are clearly intended for instruments; even if homorhythmic with the discant, they generally betray their harmonic conception by jumping about in a quite unvocal manner.

Frottole cannot be classified as folk songs, for they were sung by and for the aristocracy and the cultivated middle class. The prevailing meter is duple, except that in rare instances closing sections, especially those with villotistic undertones, may be in triple time. The early frottola utilizes the standard three-voiced complex that prevailed during the Quattrocento until about 1490, but the classical variety has four voice parts. In comparison with the contemporary chanson and the later madrigal, the musical setting of a barzelletta, oda, or strambotto is quite short, whereas that of the instrumentally accompanied canzone shows the trend toward greater length that was to culminate in the extended, through-composed works of the madrigal era. No particular effort is made in the frottola to express the inner meaning of the text, but tone painting on individual words sometimes occurs. In comparison with the madrigal, however, such usage is rare.

A more elaborate type of frottola, characterized by an activated homophony in which the middle voices contain extensive runs and figuration, may be found in Petrucci's publications and those of the transitional period. The inner parts of barzellette and ode by Tromboncino and Cara, for example, often demonstrate a semipolyphonic independence, but the basic structure remains homophonic, and the voice parts often end phrases simultaneously. Quite distinct from these are the instrumentally accompanied canzoni, capitoli, sonnets, and ottave rime by Tromboncino, Cara, Capriolus, and others that begin to appear in Petrucci's prints from 1507 (*Libro VII*) on, and in the other frottola publications of the second and third decades. Here the lower voices play almost continuous accompaniment to a declamatory discant intended for the voice, filling in the gaps between the discant's phrases and activating the cadences.

The choice of texts in these compositions also shows the trend toward a more artistic form of secular vocal music in Italy. From the mass of barzellette and ode in Petrucci's collections emerge an occasional sonnet, beginning with Niccolò da Correggio's "Quest'è quel locho, amore" in *Frottole Libro II* (1504), and Antonio Tebaldeo's "Va posa l'archo" in *Frottole Libro IV,* and other examples of elegant poems in the classical tradition, the canzone, capitolo, and sestina. Particularly important in this respect is Petrucci's *Frottole Libro VII,* which contains three of Petrarch's canzoni in musical setting by Tromboncino, and one by Capriolus of a canzone from Bembo's *Gli Asolani.*[14] The new bent can be recognized with the publication in 1510 of Antico's *Canzoni nove,* in which appeared no fewer than seven of Petrarch's lyrics, and in Petrucci's *Libro XI* (1514), where examples of classical types of poetry make up approximately a third of the collection. Much credit for this change of taste is due to Isabella d'Este, marchioness of Mantua, who had the musi-

[14] All four have been published in the supplement to Walter Rubsamen's *Literary Sources of Secular Music in Italy (ca. 1500)*, University of California Publications in Music, vol. I, no. 1 (Berkeley and Los Angeles, 1943), pp. 53–65.

cians in her employ, Tromboncino and Cara, set to music many verses by Petrarch and the Petrarchistic poets in her circle of friends and acquaintances. One of these men, Pietro Bembo, had already greatly stimulated the cult of Petrarch with his edition of the *Canzoniere* in 1501.

The growing popularity of the canzone in musical setting during the transitional period between frottola and madrigal was particularly significant because its form differed so greatly from that of the barzelletta or oda. Free alternation between septi- and endecasyllabic lines and an irregular rhyming scheme in the canzone result in musical phrases of unequal length, and avoidance of the barzelletta's symmetry and sometimes monotonous regularity of accentuation. Significantly, a similar irregularity of phrasing was to become one of the chief traits of the madrigal. The strambotto must also have contributed to this artistic asymmetry because its phrases in musical setting, separated by holds or pauses, are much less uniform in length than those of the barzelletta. Since the strambotto lacks a refrain, major repetitions do not take place in the music, except for the recurrence of the entire composition within the framework of its over-all strophic form. An example from the Paris frottola manuscript, "Iti, suspiri, la dove amore" [15] (Example 20), will illustrate the freedom of phraseology to be found in the strambotto.

But musically the canzoni, sonnets, and other elegant verse schemes set by Tromboncino and Cara were still frottole, that is, strophic songs for solo voice with instrumental accompaniment, showing the usual frugality in the use of musical material. In his setting of Petrarch's canzone "Si è debile il filo," [16] for example, Tromboncino employs only nine different musical phrases for sixteen lines of the strophe, repeating some once or even twice, either at random or for rhyming reasons. The frottolists intended only the discant of the canzone to be sung, in a declamatory fashion that clearly anticipates operatic recitative. In Venice, Biblioteca Marciana, MS. Cl. It. IV, 1795-98, for example, even though the texts are written out in all voice parts of the "literary" compositions by Tromboncino and Cara, it is obvious from the lack of rests in the lower voices that these were intended for instruments. Although their choice of texts was madrigalesque, the Mantuan frottolists exerted little or no influence upon

[15] Paris, Bibl. Nat., Dépt. Mus., Rés. Vm.[7] 676, fols. 74[v]–75.
[16] Modern edition in Rubsamen, *Literary Sources*, p. 53.

the musical texture of either the madrigal-to-come or the French Renaissance chanson.

Characteristic of the true madrigal, on the other hand, are both a text of high literary quality and a basically through-composed form, each stanza being set to new music. Repetition of phrases may occur, but then for structural reasons, not for economy. The expressive, melodic voices of the madrigal, each created in the image of its text and conceived vocally, build equal parts of a homorhythmic or polyphonic whole, except that the bass as the harmonic fundament cannot be as smoothly flowing as its companions.

Of vital importance to the emergence of the madrigal in the Cinquecento, therefore, was the gradual development of a secular Italian style in which all voices were melodic and textually conceived, and in which the musical accentuation and phraseology matched that of the poetry throughout the parts. During the last decades of the fifteenth century the texture of Italian compositions written by the Franco-Netherlanders changed to polyphony that was more consistently imitative, especially at the openings of pieces. Johannes Martini, who was attached to Duke Ercole's court in Ferrara from 1475 to 1492, and Johannes Ghiselin, alias Verbonnet, who served the same duke in 1491 and probably had done so since 1487,[17] and who subsequently joined the chapel of the cathedral in Florence,[18] transferred the equivalence of voices characteristic of the chanson around 1490 to secular Italian song, or simply replaced the texts of compositions that were originally French. Although the scribes usually wrote out only the textual incipits in the manuscripts, equivalence of voice parts and presence of points of imitation probably indicate the composer's intention to have been an all-vocal performance. Among the examples of this style are Martini's "Se mai il cielo" and "Odi prudenze forte,"[19] Ghiselin's "De che te pasci, Amore"[20] (Example 21), and the anonymous "Nel cuor si destruge."[21]

Most of the Italian frottolists ignored this development, partly because it did not match their needs or tastes, and partly because they

[17] Clytus Gottwald, "Johannes Ghiselin-Janne Verbonnet: Some Traces of His Life," *Musica Disciplina,* XV (1961), 107–108.

[18] Frank A. D'Accone, "The Singers of San Giovanni in Florence during the 15th Century," *JAMS,* XIV (1961), 345.

[19] Both in Florence, Bibl. Naz., MS. Magl. XIX. 59, nos. 5 and 7; "Se mai" is also in MS. Magl. XIX, 178, fol. 65ᵛ.

[20] Rome, Bibl. Casanatense, MS. 2856, fols. 138ᵛ–139.

[21] Rome, Vatican Library, Cappella Giulia, MS. XIII, 27, fols. 58ᵛ–59.

may have lacked the capacity to write contrapuntally. Evidently the great majority of frottole were intended to be performed by a solo vocalist with instrumental accompaniment, but it can be documented that all voice parts of the homorhythmic frottola were sung when the occasion demanded. If the subsidiary parts easily fit the text and flow quietly within a legitimate vocal range, one may assume that they could be sung, even though the full text appears only under the discant in the printed or manuscript sources. Compositions that submit to this definition certainly must have been one of the points of departure for the homorhythmic and chordal quality of the early madrigal.

One Italianized Netherlander, Heinrich Isaac, contributed measurably to the "vocalization" of Italian secular music by composing both frottole and polyphonic songs in this manner. He and a pleiad of musicians in the patronage of Lorenzo de' Medici and his successors, including Alexander Agricola, Alexander Coppinus, Bartholomaeus Florentinus Organista, Francesco de Layolle, and the young Bernardo Pisano, set to music the ballate of Lorenzo and his circle, as well as the *canzoni a ballo* and canti carnascialeschi associated with the Tuscan carnival season.

Pisano' early works are three-voiced *ballate grandi* of high literary quality, in which the partly polyphonic, partly homorhythmic texture of the opening ripresa is intended to be sung in all parts, each of which is vocally conceived and provided with a text in the unique source, MS. B 2440 of the Conservatory in Florence. But in the second and third sections of these compositions, *piedi* and *volta,* respectively, a text appears under the discant only, which probably was intended for unison singing with instrumental accompaniment. In "Amor sia ringraziato," for example, the text added to the lower voices of the piedi and volta by Gandolfi [22] does not fit the music well, and in "Questo mostrarsi lieta a tutte l'hore" the volta text suits only the discant.[23] All voices of "Una donna l'altrier fixo mirai" [24] (Example

[22] R. Gandolfi, "Intorno al codice membranaceo di ballate e di canzoncine di autori diversi . . . nella biblioteca del R. Istituto Musicale di Firenze, N. 2440," *Rivista musicale italiana,* XVIII (1911), supplement, p. 4, from Florence, Bibl. Cons., MS. B 2440, pp. 48–51.

[23] Published by Alfred Einstein in *The Italian Madrigal* (Princeton, 1949), III, 3, from Florence, Bibl. Cons., MS. B 2440, pp. 40–43.

[24] Florence, Bibl. Cons., MS. B 2440, pp. 100–103; Florence, Bibl. Mediceo-Laurenziana, MS. Ashb. 606, fol. 134 (text only).

22) seem singable, however, not only in the ripresa, which has the text throughout the parts, but in the single-texted remainder also.

Similar works by Isaac, Layolle, and Bartholomaeus may also be found in the manuscript B 2440. It should be pointed out that the ballate by Poliziano and others set to music by these composers are of a higher level qualitatively, and are less regular in their musical phraseology than the barzelletta-frottola because of the alternation between septi- and endecasyllabic lines. Were it not for the frottolistic repetition of the music for the piedi, and the abandonment of the all-vocal texture in the later sections, the Florentine ballata could readily be called an anticipation of the early madrigal. In his setting of "Questo mostrarsi lieta a tutte l'hore" [25] Layolle not only created all voices in the image of their text but also conceived them melodically, without the awkward skips of the usual frottola. Only one early work by this potentially important participant in the development of the madrigal seems to have been preserved. He apparently left Italy for Lyons around 1520 and then devoted himself primarily to the composition of church music.[26] Yet a collection of madrigals entitled *Cinquanta canzoni à 4 voci* was published in Lyons around 1542, shortly after his death.[27] Perhaps some had been written early enough to have played a role in the crystallization of madrigalian texture.

Bartholomaeus' setting for four voices of "Questo mostrarsi lieta a tutte l'hore" (Example 23) has been published by Hans Engel [28] in incomplete form, without the piedi and volta sections. Judging from this and his setting of Poliziano's ballata "Questo mostrarsi adirata de fore," [29] the Florentine organist's music alternates between points of

[25] Published by Gandolfi in "Codice membranaceo," supplement, pp. 2–3; in Florence, Bibl. Cons., MS. B 2440, pp. 32–35, and Florence, Bibl. Naz., MS. Magl. XIX, 117, fols. 16ᵛ–17. I am grateful to Mr. Frank D'Accone for the information that the text is by Lorenzo Strozzi.

[26] François Lesure, "Layolle," *MGG*, VIII, 398.

[27] E. Vogel, *Bibliothek der gedruckten weltlichen Vokalmusik Italiens aus den Jahren 1500–1700* (Berlin, 1892), I, 363. A collection of *Venticinque Canzoni a 5 voci* by Layolle was published in Lyons in 1540 (Vogel, I, 362).

[28] Hans Engel, *Das mehrstimmige Lied des 16. Jahrhunderts in Italien, Frankreich und England,* Das Musikwerk, 4 (Cologne, n.d.), p. 13. The sources are Florence, Bibl. Cons., MS. B 2440, pp. 26–29; Florence, Bibl. Naz., MS. Magl. XIX, 141, no. 11; MS. Palat. 1178 (B.R. 337), no. 8; and Florence, Bibl. Mediceo-Laurenziana, MS. Ashb. 606, fol. 119 (text only).

[29] Published by Gandolfi in "Codice membranaceo," supplement, pp. 1–2, from Florence, Bibl. Cons., MS. B 2440, pp. 22–25.

imitation and isometric homophony, with excellent prosody in all voices of the ripresa, whereas only the discant of the remainder is intended to be sung.

Lorenzo de' Medici himself wrote the poetry of several canzoni a ballo, usually in the form of barzellette, which were sung and danced to by the crowds who caroused in the streets during the Calendimaggio, or carnival season, between May 1 and St. John's Day, June 24. Closely related to the canzone a ballo in function were the canti carnascialeschi, which may be subdivided into *carri,* sung by people dressed as craftsmen who appeared on floats; *trionfi,* which presented popular fables or classical myths embodying some reference to love; and *mascherate,* sung by masked men who wandered about Florence serenading the ladies. According to legend Lorenzo insisted that special music should be written for each purpose. Unfortunately, Isaac's music for what was reportedly the first of this genre to be sung at a carnival (about 1490), Lorenzo's *Canto dei bericuocolai* (song of the sellers of gingerbread and spice cakes), has not been preserved, but his canzone a ballo "Hora è di Maggio" [30] possesses the traits of many other polyphonic carnival songs of the period: alternation between frottolistic homophony and imitative polyphony, and between duple and triple meter. Isaac's piece stresses the points of imitation somewhat more than do similar compositions by Italians; it starts with successive entrances of voices that are independent, textually conceived melodic lines, then shifts to a danceable homorhythmic texture in triple meter.

Many of the carnival chants by Coppinus, Bartholomaeus, and others in the Florentine circle [31] similarly consist of alternations between the homorhythmic style of the frottola and imitative polyphony, and shift from duple to triple meter, especially at the close; all are vocally conceived throughout the parts. The anonymous composition "per scriptores," beginning "Orsù, orsù," [32] for example, an-

---

[30] *DTO,* vol. XVI, pt. 1, p. 206, from Florence, Bibl. Naz., MS. Palat. 1178 (B.R. 337), no. 40, and MS. Magl. XIX, 164–167, no. 34 (anon.).

[31] Preserved in several manuscripts of the Biblioteca Nazionale in Florence: MS. Magl. XIX, 141; MS. Panc. 27, MS. Magl. XIX, 121; also in MS. B 2440 of the Conservatory in Florence, and in Petrucci's books of frottole. See the compositions published from the first-named manuscript by Paul Masson, ed., in *Chants de carnaval florentins* (Paris, 1913), and by Federico Ghisi in *Feste musicali della Firenze medicea (1480–1589)* (Florence, 1939).

[32] Published by Johannes Wolf from Perugia, Bibl. Comunale, MS. G 20, in *Music of Earlier Times* (New York, 1946), pp. 49–51.

swers this description, an imitative passage on "venga ad nui" contrasting with the basically isometric texture of the whole. Coppinus, who worked in Florence from the last years of the rule of Lorenzo (d. 1492) until he went to Rome as a papal singer in 1513, wrote carnival chants intended entirely for vocal performance, like the *Canto dei naviganti*,[33] beginning "Contrari i venti," in which sections in triple time twice contrast with the prevalent duple meter; and the *Trionfo de' diavoli*,[34] beginning "Dall' infelice grotte," which contains successive imitative duets in madrigalesque style, the first of which takes the word "fuggiti" as its point of departure, and ends with a danceable phrase in triple time. In their approximation of the early madrigal these compositions lack only a refined text in a classical verse form.

Some of the earlier frottole in manuscripts, such as "Vivo sol di mirar" and "Poi che la lingua mia" in MS. Egerton 3051 of the British Museum, are in triple rhythm throughout, while others close with a gagliarde-like section. In Petrucci's frottole, on the other hand, short end sections in ternary meter may occur, but entire compositions of this nature are very rare. Among the many carnival chants printed by Petrucci in his books of frottole are a vendor's song, "Pan de miglio caldo donne," [35] in which women are invited to buy the best hot bread, and a mascherata of foreign singers, "Forestieri a la ventura" [36] (Example 24), in praise of music and its therapeutic qualities. "Forestieri," although short and simple compared with the canti carnascialeschi of Coppinus, Bartholomaeus, and Isaac, displays a similarly accurate setting of the text throughout the voices (Petrucci prints a full text in the discant only) and contrasts duple with gagliarde rhythm.

Evidently there was some close connection between the Florentine carnival chants and the "new" chansons of Bruhier, Brumel, Compère, Mouton, and Ninot le Petit that began to emerge towards the very end of the Quattrocento. Here also the music is textually bound and singable throughout the parts; sections of isometric (frottolistic?) homophony alternate with those in imitative polyphony, and portions in ternary meter enliven the basically duple rhythmic

[33] Ghisi, p. 14.
[34] Engel, *Das mehrstimmige Lied*, p. 16, and Masson, p. 74.
[35] *Frottole Libro VI*, fol. 27.
[36] *Frottole Libro VI*, fol. 44.

pattern. Themes are light and folklike, often in repeated notes of equal value. Among the early examples of this style, several of which were published by Petrucci between 1501 and 1504, are Ninot's "En l'ombre dung aubepin" [37] and "Et levez vous hau, Guillemette" [38] (Example 25), Bruhier's "Frapez petit coup" and "Jacquet, Jacquet;" [39] Mouton's "James james james;" [40] Compère's "Alons fere nos barbes;" [41] Brumel's "Dieu te gart," [42] and his largely homorhythmic "Tous les regretz" [43] (Example 26). It is surely significant that most sources of these compositions are Italian, either manuscripts of Florentine origin or Petrucci's publications of chansons. Furthermore, the beginnings of "Et levez vous" and "Tous les regretz" in particular show a remarkable resemblance to the characteristic opening pattern of Claudin de Sermisy's chansons, leaving little doubt as to the origins of the so-called Parisian style of the late 1520's.

Apparently the Franco-Netherlanders were the first to elaborate Italian popular melodies polyphonically, and to use them in an entirely vocal context, thus laying the groundwork both for the future villotta and the equivalence of textually conceived voice parts in the madrigal. Isaac's quodlibet "Donna di dentro" [44] cites both texts and melodies of several folk songs; Compère's "Che fa la ramacina" [45]

[37] Florence, Bibl. Cons., MS. B 2442, discant p. 27; Florence, Bibl. Naz., MS. Magl. XIX, 164–167, no. 54 (anon.).

[38] Florence, Bibl. Cons., MS. B 2442, discant p. 23; Petrucci, *Canti C* (1504), fols. 81ᵛ–83 (anon.); Cortona, Bibl. del Comune, Codd. 95–96; and Paris, Bibl. Nat., MS. nouv. acq. fr. 1817, fol. 7 (anon.).

[39] Florence, Bibl. Cons., MS. B 2442, discant pp. 61 and 78; Florence, Bibl. Naz., MS. Magl. XIX, 164–167, nos. 56 and 57 (anon.).

[40] Petrucci, *Odhecaton* (1501), no. 36; Florence, Bibl. Cons., MS. B 2442, pp. 179–182; published by Helen Hewitt and Isabel Pope, eds., *Harmonice Musices Odhecaton A* (Cambridge, Mass., 1942), no. 36.

[41] Petrucci, *Odhecaton,* no. 26; see Hewitt and Pope, no. 26, and p. 142 for the concordances.

[42] Florence, Bibl. Cons., MS. B 2442, discant p. 132.

[43] Florence, Bibl. Cons., MS. B 2442, discant pp. 130–131; Brussels, Bibl. Royale, MS. 11239, fols. 8ᵛ–9.

[44] Florence, Bibl. Naz., MS. Magl. XIX, 59, fol. 154ᵛ; Cortona, Bibl. del Comune, Codd. 95–96; and Paris, Bibl. Nat., MS. nouv. acq. fr. 1817, fol. 18ᵛ. Published in A. W. Ambros and O. Kade, *Geschichte der Musik,* 3d ed. (Leipzig, 1911), V, 351; *Das Chorwerk,* XLIII, 4; *DTO,* vol. XIV, pt. 1, p. 35; and A. Smijers, ed., *Van Ockeghem tot Sweelinck* (Amsterdam, 1951), no. 57, p. 191.

[45] Petrucci, *Frottole Libro IV,* no. 80; Bologna, Bibl. Cons., MS. Q 17, fols. 62ᵛ–63; Cortona, Bibl. del Comune, Codd. 95–96; and Paris, Bibl. Nat., MS. nouv. acq. fr. 1817, no. 28 (anon.); Florence, Bibl. Naz., MS. Magl. XIX, 164–167, no. 35 (anon.), with text in all voices. Published in *Das Chorwerk,* LXIII, 9; R. Schwartz, ed., *Otta-*

contains independent voices, now declamatory in nature, now in stepwise movement, as well as the entire apparatus of the chanson, including staggered, partly imitative entrances at the start, and alternating voice pairs; in "Scaramella fa la galla" [46] the same composer at first quotes the familiar tune in the tenor as a sort of cantus firmus, allowing the other parts to imitate motives from it in diminution, then repeats the folk song in the same voice, but this time in ternary meter, accompanied by the other parts in smooth, homorhythmic fashion. Obrecht, in "La Tortorella," [47] probably written in 1487–88 during his stay in Ferrara, starts with an alternating trio and duet, all parts being intended for voices; Josquin in "Scaramella va alla guerra" [48] and Japart in "Questa se chiama" ("Famene un poco di quella mazacrocha") [49] base imitative counterpoint on the folk melody. Once again, the musical techniques are those of the Franco-Flemish chanson and the madrigal to come, but the texts and folk-like nature of the melodic sources remove these compositions from the sphere of the madrigal proper.

One of the first Italian composers of the Cinquecento to write similar works in textually conceived, imitative polyphony was Don Michele Pesenti. Although the poetry of his "Dal lecto me levava" and "O Dio che la brunetta mia," both published by Petrucci in 1504, [50] is

viano Petrucci: Frottole, Buch I und IV, Publikationen älterer Musik, 8 (Leipzig, 1935), p. 92. An entirely different setting of the text, 4 voices and anon., is in Seville, Bibl. Colombina, MS. 5-I-43, fols. 134ᵛ–135.

[46] Petrucci, *Frottole Libro IV,* no. 81; Florence, Bibl. Cons., MS. B 2439, fols. 16ᵛ–17. Published in Schwartz, p. 92; F. Torrefranca, *Il segreto del quattrocento* (Milan, 1939), p. 522; and H. Riemann, *Handbuch der Musikgeschichte,* vol. II, pt. 1 (Leipzig, 1907), p. 349.

[47] Rome, Vatican Library, Cappella Giulia, MS. XIII, 27, fols. 67ᵛ–68; Petrucci, *Canti C,* fols. 90ᵛ–91; Florence, Bibl. Naz., MS. Magl. XIX, 59, fols. 182ᵛ–183, MS. Magl. XIX, 164–167, no. 37 (anon.). Published in Ambrose and Kade, p. 36, and in Jakob Obrecht, *Werken,* ed. Johannes Wolf (Amsterdam, 1908–1921), vols. XV–XVI (*Wereldlijke Werken*), no. 13.

[48] Florence, Bibl. Naz., MS. Magl. XIX, 59, fol. 180ᵛ; MS. Palat. 1178 (B.R. 337), fol. 40ᵛ; MS. Magl. XIX, 164–167, no. 38 (anon.). Published in Ambrose and Kade, p. 134.

[49] Seville, Bibl. Colombina, MS. 5-I-43, no. 156; Petrucci, *Canti C,* fol. 1015ᵛ [115ᵛ].

[50] Petrucci, *Frottole Libro I* (1504), nos. 30 and 40; both are published in Schwartz, *Petrucci,* pp. 20 and 29; G. Cesari and R. Monterosso, eds., *Le frottole nell' edizione principe di Ottaviano Petrucci* (Cremona, 1954), I, 22 and 31; Torrefranca, *Il segreto,* pp. 434 and 573; "Dal lecto" is also in Riemann, *Handbuch,* vol. II, pt. 1, p. 360, and *Das Chorwerk,* XLIII, 7. "O Dio" appears also in Florence,

villotistic and therefore not of a madrigalesque literary standard, their musical style clearly anticipates that of the madrigal. Proof of Don Michele's influence upon the early madrigalists is Verdelot's treatment for six voices of the discant from Pesenti's "Hoime che la brunetta mia."[51] It can be shown, incidentally, that the *Doppelmeister* Michele Pesenti and Don Michele Vicentino identified by various scholars were one and the same.[52] Similar to the aforementioned works in its popular, villotistic tone is Don Michele's "So ben che le non sa,"[53] which contains several points of imitation upon simple, declamatory themes, and rapid alternation of voice pairs in excellent prosody that can only be called madrigalesque. Since Mar-

---

Bibl. Naz., MS. Magl. XIX, 141, fols. 30ᵛ–31; MS. Palat. 1178 (B. R. 337), fol. 70 (as "Ome che la signora mia"); MS. Magl. XIX, 164–167, no. 33 (anon.); Florence, Bibl. Cons., MS. B 2440, pp. 122–123 (as "O me che la brunetta mia"); published from this source by Gandolfi, "Codice membranaceo," supplement, p. 9, and A. della Corte and G. Pannain, *Storia della musica,* 3d ed. (Turin, 1952), I, 278.

[51] *Verdelot . . . a sei voci* (Venice: A. Gardane, 1541 and 1546) (*RISM* 1541¹⁸).

[52] Two polyphonic, villotistic compositions in particular are assigned to Vicentino. "So ben che le non sa" and "Che farala che dirala," both of which were printed in A. Antico's *Canzoni, sonetti, strambotti et frottole Libro III* (*RISM* 1513¹), and in the reprint of 1518, edited by Alfred Einstein as *Andrea Antico: Canzoni, Sonetti, Strambotti et Frottole,* Smith College Music Archives, volume 4 (Northampton, Mass., 1941), appear with the composer's name given as "D. Michael V.," which is practically identical to the abbreviation of Pesenti's name, "Michel V.," in Petrucci's publication in 1511 of Franciscus Bossinensis' *Libro II,* fol. 16. "Che farala" had already been printed by Petrucci in *Frottole Libro XI* (1514) under the initials "D. M." previously used to identify Michele Pesenti as the author of a barzelletta in *Frottole Libro IX* (1508), "Io voria esser cholu." It seems improbable that the publisher would have employed identical initials for two different composers. "So ben" (see text at note 53) may be found in contemporary manuscripts under two frequently used versions of Pesenti's name, "P. Michael" in Florence, Bibl. Cons., MS. B 2440, p. 124) and "Michael" (Florence, Bibl. Naz., MS. Palat. 1178 [B.R. 337], fol. 67ᵛ). The assignment of these pieces to "Vicentino" is based on the fact that the undated reprint of Antico's publication in the Biblioteca Marucelliana, Florence, spells out the name as "D. Michael vicentino"; but in view of the foregoing, this must either be a mistake, or indicate that Pesenti had moved to Vicenza. From a stylistic viewpoint also, the motet "Tulerunt dominum meum," assigned to "Pre michael de ver.[ona]" in *RISM* 1519², as well as Pesenti's villotistic works in *Frottole Libro I,* are every bit as polyphonic and vocally conceived throughout the parts as are the two compositions in question. The motet, anonymous in Petrucci's *Motetti de passione* (1503), fol. 31ᵛ, is mistakenly ascribed to Josquin in two manuscripts of Germanic provenance, according to B. Antonowytch in the International Musicological Society's *Report of the 8th Congress, New York, 1961* (Kassel, 1961), I (papers), 63.

[53] See note 52; anonymous in Florence, Bibl. Naz., MS. Magl. XIX, 164–167, no. 31; modern edition also in Gandolfi, "Codice membranaceo," supplement, p. 10.

guerite d'Angoulème, queen of Navarre, translated the text of Pesenti's proto-villotta "Che farala che dirala" in *nouvelle* 19 of the
Heptaméron (1558),[54] one may assume that his works were well
known in France also, and that they constitute another link between
Italian and French secular music of the period.

Comparable to Pesenti's compositions in its villotistic tone, but dif-
fering from these in its ternary meter and almost exact homorhythm
is Ioannes B. Zesso's "D'un bel matin d'amore," [55] published in 1507
(Example 27). Its bass, which consists almost entirely of the first,
fifth, fourth, and second steps of the scale, anticipates not only the
standard bass formulas of the sixteenth century, but also the harmonic pattern of much Baroque dance music, such as the dance-
songs in the initiation ceremony of Lully's *Le bourgeois gentil-
homme*. Another proto-villotta by an Italian composer, "E d'un bel
matin d'amore," by Antonius Capriolus, was printed by Petrucci
with the text under all of its smoothly polyphonic voices.[56]

From the early elaborations of Italian songs by the Franco-Netherlanders, Pesenti, Zesso, and Capriolus, runs a clear line to the villotte
and villotistic *dialoghi* of the 1520's, which Torrefranca has mistakenly dated some 40 years earlier and has called the "ramo tardivo"
of the Ars Nova *caccia*. Torrefranca has published most of these
works in his controversial but extremely valuable book on the subject,[57] drawing primarily from the Venetian manuscript in the Biblioteca Marciana, MS. Cl. It. IV, 1795-98, for the purpose. Some examples of the full-fledged villotta, which embodies one or more folk
songs in a vocally conceived texture, are settings of dialogues that alternate between imitative polyphony and homophony, as in Fra
Rufino's "Hayme amor, hayme fortuna" [58] and the anonymous
"Amor che fai;" [59] others are more purely homorhythmic compositions in which the tenor sings the folk tune alone at the outset, as in
"De la da l'acqua," by F(rancesco) P(atavino) [60] and "L'ultimo dì de

[54] André Pirro, "Pour l'histoire de la musique," *Acta Musicologica*, III (1931), 52.
[55] Petrucci, *Frottole Libro VII*, fol. 27[v].
[56] Petrucci, *Frottole Libro XI*, fol. 35[v].
[57] Torrefranca, *Il segreto del quattrocento*.
[58] *Motetti e canzone libro I* (*RISM* [1521][6]), no. 17; Venice, Bibl. Marciana,
MS. Cl. It. IV, 1795-98, no. 5; published in Torrefranca, pp. 464-466.
[59] Venice, Bibl. Marciana, MS. Cl. It. IV, 1795-98; Torrefranca, pp. 427-431.
[60] *Canzoni frottole et capitoli . . . Libro I. De la Croce* (*RISM* 1526[6]), fols.
11[v]-12; Venice, Bibl. Marciana, MS. Cl. It. IV, 1795-98, no. 95 (anon.); Torrefranca, pp. 443-444.

Magio," by Sebastian Festa; [61] still others contain the familiar dance-like passages in triple meter, such as Patavino's "Donne, venete al ballo." [62] Fra Rufino in particular demonstrates his mastery of textually conceived, imitative polyphony, and thereby merits more attention than he hitherto has received.

Don Michele Peseñti participated also in the serious, literary trend leading to the madrigal proper by setting to music two odes of Horace, a capitolo, "Ben mille volte," and a canzone, "Alma gentil." "Ben mille volte" (Example 28), subtitled "Modus dicendi capitula" in Petrucci's *Frottole Libro I* (1504), was intended as a model for other verses of the same pattern. All voices of this purely homorhythmic composition could readily be sung, even though Petrucci provided only the discant with a full text. "Alma gentil" (Example 29), contained in the Morgan Library print of 1521(?), *Motetti e canzone libro I,* is smoothly vocal in all the parts but recalls the frottola because the inner prosody is not exact, and several short phrases are repeated for rhyming reasons (mm. 9–11 = 12–14; 17–20 = 26–29; 33–36 = 37–39) or at random (mm. 14–17 = 21–24). Equal note values and repeated motives in all voices at measures 5–8 express the meaning of "fusse equalmente" in madrigalesque fashion. The print in question, as well as Bernardo Pisano's *Musica sopra le Canzone del petrarcha* [63] and manuscripts such as Florence, Biblioteca Nazionale, MS. Magl. XIX, 164–167; Bologna, Biblioteca del Conservatorio, Cod. Q 21; Venice, Biblioteca Marciana, MS. Cl. It. IV, 1795-98, and so on, are now in part books, illustrating the new equivalence of textually conceived voice parts that became the norm in secular Italian vocal music between 1520 and 1530.

Pisano conceived his settings of Petrarch and other poets vocally throughout the parts, and made all the melodic lines except the harmonic fundament relatively smooth, but retained certain elements of the frottola, such as inexact prosody in the subsidiary voices, repe-

---

[61] *Canzoni, frottole et capitoli . . . Libro I. De la Croce* (*RISM* 1526[6]), fols. 30v–31; Venice, Bibl. Marciana, MS. Cl. It. IV, 1795-98, no. 97; Florence, Bibl. Cons., MS. B 2440, pp. 176–177; Florence, Bibl. Naz., MS. Magl. XIX, 164–167, no. 44; Torrefranca, pp. 486–487.

[62] *Canzoni, frottole . . . Libro II de la Croce* (*RISM* 1531[4]), fols. 24v–26; Venice, Bibl. Marciana, MS. Cl. It. IV, 1795-98, no. 93; Florence, Bibl. Cons., MS. B 2440, pp. 170–171; Florence, Bibl. Naz., MS. Magl. XIX, 164–167, no. 42. Published by Gandolfi, "Codice membranaceo," supplement, pp. 13–14; Torrefranca, pp. 445–447; Wolf, *Music of Earlier Times,* no. 45.

[63] Forosemproni: O. Petrucci, 1520.

tition of phrases for reasons of economy in "Amor, se vuoi ch'i torni al giogho antico" [64] (Example 30), and the strophic form in "Che debbio far" [65] and "Nella stagion." [66] In "Amor, se vuoi," the middle voices have lost the jumpiness of the frottola, but contain long, pauseless passages that are adjusted only approximately to the text. Two points of imitation enliven what is basically a homorhythmic structure containing many repetitions (mm. 1-4 = 5-8, 12-14 = 22-24, 57-60 = 61-64, 8-11 = 33-37, and so on). Undoubtedly the Pisano print comprises works composed over a longer period of time, as the haphazard repetition of phrases has practically disappeared from a piece that apparently represents a later phase of the composer's work, "Donna benche di rado," published from Bologna Conservatory Cod. Q 21 by Claudio Gallico.[67] Except for the occasional lack of correspondence between text and music in the middle voices, this could well be called an early madrigal.

Jacopo Fogliano, whose simple barzellette had appeared in several of Petrucci's collections, participated also in the transition to the madrigal with his setting of "Occhi suavi et chiari," published in Siena by Samboneto in 1515 [68] (Example 31). The equivalent and melodically smooth voices are segregated from one another by nonsimultaneous pauses, and a lengthy imitation occurs between discant and tenor, but the text (an oda) lacks the classical elegance required of the madrigal. Fogliano intends his short composition to serve not only the underlaid text, but seven other strophes also, thus betraying his frottolistic background.

Antonio Stringari of Padua anticipated madrigalesque writing, but not its textual quality, in his frottola-dialogo "Don don al foco al foco," [69] which contains a genuine choral dialogue in alternating voice pairs. On the other hand, the well-known composer of liturgi-

[64] Pisano, no. 5; Florence, Bibl. Naz., MS. Magl. XIX, 164-167, no. 9 (anon.).

[65] Pisano, no. 16; Florence, Bibl. Naz., MS. Magl. XIX, 164-167, no. 12 (anon.); Florence, Bibl. Cons., MS. B 2440, pp. 148-153 (anon.); published in incomplete form, without the section intended for the *ritornello,* by Knud Jeppesen in *Zeitschrift für Musikwissenschaft,* XII (1929-30), 86.

[66] Pisano, no. 8; Florence, Bibl. Naz., MS. Magl. XIX, 164-167, no. 6 (anon.).

[67] Claudio Gallico, *Un canzoniere musicale italiano del cinquecento: Bologna, Conservatorio di musica G. B. Martini, MS. Q 21* (Florence, 1961), pp. 128-132; Pisano, no. 6; Florence, Bibl. Naz., MS. Magl. XIX, 164-167, no. 7 (anon.).

[68] *Canzone sonetti strambotti et frottole libro I* (Siena: P. Sambonetti, 1515; *RISM* 1515[2]), fols. 6[v]-7; Bologna, Bibl. Cons., Cod. Q 21, no. 66.

[69] Petrucci, *Frottole Libro XI,* fol. 40[v]; see Alfred Einstein, "Das elfte Buch der Frottole," *Zeitschrift für Musikwissenschaft,* X (1927-28), 618-619.

cal music, Elzéar Genet (Carpentras), set Petrarchan texts [70] for the solo voice with instrumental accompaniment in Tromboncino's manner, hence cannot be recognized as a significant personality in the development of the madrigal.

Although Sebastian Festa, who in 1520 was in the service of the "Rev. Monsignore" of Mondovì in Piedmont,[71] also does not quite achieve the synthesis of stylistic elements recognizable in the true madrigal, he was the only Italian composer of the transitional decade of 1520 to 1530 to have had his secular works republished in both Italy and France during the epoch that followed, and he must therefore have influenced both the early madrigalists and the Parisian school of chanson composers. Obviously intending the Petrarchan sonnet "O passi sparsi" [72] (Example 32) to be sung throughout the parts, he repeats the entire first section in the manner of the frottola, and in the subsidiary voices does not always match music and text, sometimes accentuates the wrong syllables, and neglects to leave enough "air" for vocal performance; but in one respect, that of expressiveness, he comes closer to the madrigal than any of his Italian contemporaries. By returning again and again to a sustained chord for the outcry "Deh!"—especially that into which the discant leaps by an ascending tenth—he effectively gives living meaning to the

[70] A ballata, madrigal, and canzone in Antico's *Canzoni sonetti strambotti* . . . *libro III* (*RISM* 1513[1]), and a canzone in *Fioretti di frottole* (Naples, G. A. de Caneto; *RISM* 1519[4]).

[71] Edward Lowinsky, in "The Medici Codex," *Annales musicologiques,* V (1957), pp. 105 and 117, reprints a letter signed by Giulia Gonzaga in which Festa is identified as a "servitore del Reverendissimo Monsignore de Mondovì mio Zio honorandissimo." From this Lowinsky concludes that Sebastian's patron was a member of the Gonzaga family, specifically, Ercole Gonzaga, whose subsequent patronage of music as Cardinal of Mantua is well documented. But Lowinsky disregards the possibility that Julia's uncle may have been her *mother's* brother, and therefore not a Gonzaga. Francesca Fieschi, Julia's mother, had several brothers, one of whom, Ottobono, was bishop of Mondovì in 1520, the date of Julia's letter. As an apostolic pronotary and nonresident bishop who was made assistant to the pope in 1521, Ottobono and his musical servitor must have lived in Rome during the period in question. See my article, "Sebastian Festa and the Early Madrigal," to be published in the *Kongressbericht* of the International Congress of the Gesellschaft für Musikforschung, held at Kassel in October 1962.

[72] Sebastian Festa in *Canzoni, frottole et capitoli . . . Libro I. De la Croce* (*RISM* 1526[6]), fols. 6[v]–8, and in the enlarged reprint of 1531; anonymous in Bologna, Bibl. Cons., Cod. Q 21, no. 24; Florence, Bibl. Naz., MS. Magl. XIX, 164–167, no. 25, and MS. Magl. XIX, 111, no. 10; Modena, Bibl. Estense, MS. y. L. II. 8, fols. 2[v]–3.

words. Perhaps this heightened sensibility, so unusual in a work of the transitional period (it was first printed in 1526), caused its re-publication between 1544 and 1566 in nine different editions of a madrigal collection devoted primarily to Verdelot.[73]

That Sebastian Festa may have been a key figure in the musical relations between Italy and France during the 1520's is borne out by Attaingnant's publication of both "O passi sparsi" and "Perche'l viso d'amor" [74] in the missing collection once known to have been lo-cated in the German town of Wernigerode, *Chansons musicales à 4 parties* (1533).[75] The editor subsequently included the former work, now erroneously ascribed to Costanzo Festa, in a publication of 1549,[76] from which it was reprinted three times between 1561 and 1573 by Le Roy and Ballard.[77] "L'ultimo dì de Magio" proves that Sebastian Festa was familiar with the purely vocal elaborations of Italian popular melodies, and serves as a document of the relation-ship between the early madrigal and the villotta.

Far surpassing these Italians in output and influence, the man called "il divino Verdelotto" apparently composed his earliest madri-gals toward the beginning of the transitional decade, 1520 to 1530, and thereby set the tone and style of the form in its infancy. Anne-Marie Bragard has shown that Verdelot was *maestro di cappella* at San Giovanni in Florence from July 1, 1523 (if not earlier), until 1525.[78] His "Con suave parlar," published by Gallico from the Bo-logna Conservatory Cod. Q 21, which Gallico dates about 1526,[79] en-tirely lacks points of imitation. As isometric and homophonic as the basic frottola, its phrases begin and end simultaneously in all voices; unlike the frottola, however, these voices are equivalent and exactly mirror the text, which is underlaid throughout the parts, and all ex-cept the harmonic fundament are smoothly melodic or declamatory

[73] *Verdelot a quatro voci* (Venice: A. Gardane, 1544–1566; *RISM* 1544[18] to 1566[22]).

[74] *Motetti e canzone Libro 1* (*RISM* [1521][6]), no. 19; Florence, Bibl. Naz., MS. Magl. XIX, 164–167, no. 24 (anon.); Bologna, Bibl. Cons., Cod. Q 21, no. 10 (anon.); published by Rubsamen in *Literary Sources*, pp. 66–68.

[75] R. Eitner, *Bibliographie der Musiksammelwerke des XVI. und XVII. Jahrhun-derts* (Berlin, 1877), 1533a, fols. 1, 2.

[76] Attaingnant, *Second livre contenant XXIX. chansons* . . . (*RISM* 1549[18]).

[77] *Premier recueil des recueilz de chansons, à quatre parties* . . . (*RISM* 1561[7], 1567[12], 1573[14]).

[78] Bragard, "Verdelot en Italie," *Revue belge de musicologie*, XI (1957), 113ff.

[79] *Un canzoniere musicale*, p. 8; the composition appears there on pp. 178–182.

in nature. Sudden shifts to passages in consistently short note values express the meaning of phrases like "presto s'accorse" and "veloce m'ordinavo" in a text that aptly reflects the Petrarchism of the Cinquecento.

The Venetian MS. Cl. It. IV, 1795–98 contains one of the most unusual and advanced compositions in madrigal style of the transitional decade, "Tanto mi trovo" (Example 33). Its anonymous composer has set to music the ripresa and strophe of a ballata grande that is similar in form to Petrarch's "Di tempo in tempo" (*Canzoniere,* no. 149). Diatonic melodies in a consistently contrapuntal texture, exact prosody in the lower voices as well as in the discant, less jaggedness even than Verdelot in the harmonic fundament—these are traits of the later madrigal that stand in marked contrast to other contemporary works. Except for three repetitions of short phrases, one of which (mm. 30–32 = 33–35) matches the rhyming of brief lines, the ballata is through-composed. Only three of the voices participate in the chief points of imitation (mm. 1–7; 29–36; 63–65), but all are involved in a homorhythmic pair-imitation (mm. 45–49) and in a madrigalesque stretto upon the words "Et fugg' et bramo" (mm. 57–60). Like the classical madrigal, "Tanto mi trovo" is relatively long, comprising 83 measures in comparison with the average frottola of 20 measures, Tromboncino's canzone "Si è debile il filo" of 54 measures, and Pisano's madrigalesque canzone "Amor se vuoi" of 77 measures. Whoever the composer, he deserves a prominent place in the early history of the madrigal.

Most of the forces at play in shaping both the madrigal in its first period and the Parisian chanson of the 1530's are represented directly or indirectly in the Florentine manuscript Biblioteca Nazionale, MS. Magl. XIX, 164–167. Here we find the proto-villotte of Josquin, Obrecht, and Compère that led to Pesenti's popular works in the same vein; the polyphonic carnival song of Isaac, symbolizing the vocally conceived part songs of the Florentine circle around Lorenzo de' Medici; the "new" chansons of Ninot le Petit, Brumel, Bruhier, and Compère that on the one hand so closely resemble the Tuscan canzoni a ballo and canti carnascialeschi, and on the other serve as a point of departure for the thematic patterns and texture of Claudin de Sermisy's chansons; the early madrigals of Pisano, illustrating the end point of a literary trend in the Florentine school that started with Lorenzo himself; and the proto-madrigals of Sebastian Festa, fusing the homorhythmic, homophonic style of the frottola with equivalence of parts created in the image of their poetry, and Petrarchism in the choice of texts. The most necessary element, the parity of textually conceived voices, certainly came from the chansons and Italian compositions of the Franco-Netherlanders, Florentines, and Michele Pesenti.

DISCUSSION

PANELISTS: MME. BRIDGMAN, MR. D'ACCONE, MR. PIRROTTA

MME. BRIDGMAN: Mr. Rubsamen's interesting paper has raised one or two questions in my mind, centering on problems of text and texting. I think it is not quite true to say that the frottola is a solo piece with instrumental accompaniment. In the Paris MS. Rés. Vm.[7] 676 there is a frottola [80] with performing directions for each voice: "pro puero," "pro tenore," "pro alto," "pro basso," showing that it was meant to be sung in all parts. If one saw this same piece without such indications, one would take the three lower parts to be instrumental.

MR. RUBSAMEN: There is certainly no hard and fast rule about performance in the frottola. While the text is written out for the uppermost voice only, the other voices are not necessarily for instruments. Flexibility in this regard may be particularly characteristic of earlier sources such as the Parisian manuscript. But even here I do maintain that most of the pieces seem written for solo performance. Do you agree?

MME. BRIDGMAN: Yes. To go on to another point: I think that perhaps you exaggerated slightly when you spoke of canti carnascialeschi and canzoni a ballo as being almost madrigals, lacking only a serious text of high literary quality. It seems to me that the question of text is here a secondary one; these pieces have really nothing of the madrigal in them.

MR. RUBSAMEN: I was speaking primarily of the vocal quality of the compositions. I realize that all of these early forms—the canto carnascialesco, the early villotta—lack the expressive quality of the madrigal. What I have been looking for is music in which all the

---

[80] "Qual simplice ucellino," no. 93, fols. 103v-104. See Bridgman, "Un manuscrit italien," p. 178.

voices are vocally conceived, and I think that the canti carnasciale-schi are of that nature.

MME. BRIDGMAN: But one should remember that in the fifteenth century voices were treated as instruments; the voice was the most nearly perfect instrument, and voices then sang in an instrumental manner. It is, I think, a modern notion that music is "conceived for the voice."

MR. REESE: There are, nevertheless, individual parts that are more vocal than others. Could one not say that there are some parts written primarily for the voice, whereas others are more neutral in character?

MME. BRIDGMAN: Yes, but this was not a question of great importance for composers of the time. I should like now to turn to another question concerning texts. I am not convinced of the importance of Isabella d'Este's role in the return to Petrarch and to "good" poetry. She herself was a bad poetess; she sponsored, among others, Serafino Aquilano and Chariteo, who wrote verse that was fashionable *poesia per musica* but rather bad poetry as such. I think she was more active in the rise and diffusion of the frottola than of the madrigal.

MR. RUBSAMEN: It is true that Isabella was a patroness of Serafino and of Galeotto del Carretto in the late 1490's, but beginning in the early sixteenth century some of the best poets of the time were in her circle of acquaintances—Sannazzaro and Ariosto, for instance.[81] Perhaps Correggio is not a good poet, but he was at any rate a Petrarchist; his intentions were of the best.

MR. PIRROTTA: It is difficult to distinguish between "bad" and "good" poets; many men who were not very good poets worked nonetheless with the intention of setting literary standards. A distinction should be made between poets writing frivolously or for pastime, and those who worked with the aim of raising the literary standards of poetry. Even Aquilano intended to be a literary poet.

MR. RUBSAMEN: As regards the frottola Isabella's importance is undeniable. She had frottolists in her employ, and when she received poetry from her friends she immediately had it set to music. Where else can one find tangible evidence of this kind? Perhaps, to some degree, in Florence.

[81] Mr. Rubsamen's views of Isabella d'Este as a patroness of poets may be seen in more detail in chapters 2 and 5 of his *Literary Sources*.

MR. D'ACCONE: Certainly the relation between Florentine poets and the three or four Florentine composers whose works have thus far been made known to us is a very close one; so much so that the musicians owed the poets money. I agree that Isabella d'Este deserves the credit given her, that her court was a great center for "refinement" of Italian poetry; but I do think that one must not leave Florence out of the picture. When one considers the literary renaissance that was going on in Florence under Lorenzo de' Medici—himself a pacesetter—and the number of lesser poets whose works were frequently set, one must go back to Florence to see some beginnings of this refinement. I should like to bring up another matter related to texting of the frottola. When you spoke, Mr. Rubsamen, of the pieces in Florence, Conservatory, MS. B 2440,[82] you said that full texts are given for all voices in the first section of pieces by men like Bernardo, Bartholomaeus, and Layolle, but that for the second part, or piedi, only incipits are given. This you said is evidence that the second part may not have been sung by all the voices.

MR. RUBSAMEN: I tried without much success to fit the text to the lower voices in the second section.

MR. D'ACCONE: Codex 2440 is a very sloppily written manuscript in many places. One sees that the scribe got tired of writing in the text for all voices; several works of Pisano, for instance, have text throughout, while others have only incipits. It is hard to believe that this has anything to do with performance practice. It seems rather like laziness on the part of the scribe.

MR. RUBSAMEN: On the contrary, I have noticed that in the ripresa the text is fully written out in almost all cases, but given only for the discant in the piedi and the volta; and while the text fits all the parts excellently in the first sections, that is true neither of the piedi nor the volta in many compositions. The examples—those published by Einstein and those of Gandolfi[83]—I thought illustrated this.

MR. PIRROTTA: This seems logical. It makes sense to me that the

[82] For this manuscript see Gandolfi, "Codice membranaceo," pp. 537–548. But on this article cf. Einstein, *Italian Madrigal*, I, 129.

[83] Two ballate from Florence MS. B 2440 are published in Einstein, *Italian Madrigal*, III, no. 2 (Isaac, "Questo mostrarsi adirata di fore"), and no. 3 (Bernardo Pisano, "Questo mostrarsi lieta a tutte l'hore"). In the Pisano piece the ripresa is fully texted, the stanza texted for cantus only. The Isaac piece is presented as an accompanied solo throughout. As a supplement to his article on the manuscript Gandolfi (see note 22 above) printed eleven pieces selected from it; all of these are fully texted throughout.

ripresa, which for the old ballata was the traditionally choral part, should be sung in all parts while the stanza—piedi and volta—was sung, not in unison even, but by a single person. When one studies the transition from one form to another—including the transition to the madrigal—it is important to consider the philological origins of forms.

MR. REESE: Then the texting of MS. B 2440 would indicate a traditional method of performance.

MR. PIRROTTA: Or a deliberate return to the old ballata form, at least on occasions when the alternation between chorus and solo was appropriate.

Mme. Bridgman has already questioned the connection between the canto carnascialesco and the madrigal; I should like to add another question here. At one point you compared "Hora è di Maggio" [84] to a carnival song. I think that while this piece may be related to the madrigal, it has no relation at all to the carnival song. It starts with a beautiful imitation, and is almost always contrapuntal in style, except for a few passages. This is almost the opposite of the carnival song. In the latter there are occasional short bits of imitation, but homophonic texture prevails. One of your examples, the *Trionfo de' diavoli* of Coppinus,[85] has imitation on the words "Donne, fuggiti," but this is a superficial madrigalism. At any rate pieces like this are not directly behind the madrigal.

To return to the question of vocal and instrumental part-writing, I feel that what is called "frottola literature," a very loose term, is mainly soloistic. I base this not on examination of the voice parts, but mainly on contemporary evidence, which always speaks of poems being sung by *citaredi*. One even hears of poetry being published by being released to a *citaredo* to be sung. Calmeta, when the collection of Tebaldeo's poems was published, remarked [86] on the difference between reading the poems one every few weeks—as given out to a *citaredo*—and reading them as published all together in a book. One saw, when the poems were all together, how repetitious they were, a fact not noticed when they were circulated a few at a time. If I examine the parts, I think that just those features which bring you to

---

[84] See text at note 30.
[85] See text at note 34.
[86] V. Calmeta, "La poesia di Tebaldeo," *Prose e lettere edite e inedite,* ed. C. Grayson (Bologna, 1959), p. 16.

think of a fully vocal performance are those indicating performance with lute—or viol, any single string instrument—accompaniment. The pieces you think of as instrumental, on the other hand, seem to me to have been written for performance by solo singer and a group of instruments each taking a single line. This is the reason for all the imitations and thick textures: not imitation for its own sake, but the attempt to create a background of sonority for the solo singer. This type of frottola was published in great numbers by Petrucci; he also published a certain number of frottole in chordal style. In some cases there may be fully vocal pieces; but are these really frottole? They may be theatrical pieces, or refrains, such as "D'un bel matin d'a-more," of which you mention the version by Zesso.[87] This same material is found two or three times as the refrain at the end of another piece. In these pieces the "popular" refrain, full-voiced, would follow a soloistic verse—another example of solo-chorus alternation. Many of the pieces which may be thought of as fully vocal are mascherate or canti carnascialeschi texts, so perhaps meant for theatrical performance of some kind. They may have been used in *intermedi,* for instance.

MR. RUBSAMEN: I had also noticed that pieces with villotistic undertones are likely to be vocally conceived throughout. I had not, however, noticed any connection with the theater.

MR. PIRROTTA: We may perhaps turn once more from texting to text, to the literary side of things. If we are to be concerned with the "goûts réunis," this side is important. You spoke, Mr. Rubsamen, of Isabella d'Este; but I should think that in this matter of literary change of taste Pietro Bembo was the important figure. Isabella may well have been the link between Bembo and musicians, but the ideas were those of Bembo. His general conception was a humanistic one, although not quite that of the fifteenth century. Early humanists admired ingenuity in music; they praised Leone Battista Alberti because without any training he could compose songs as well as professional musicians. Fifteenth-century humanists favored popular musical production, and the frottola is actually a late fruit of this tendency. Bembo's ideas lay in the direction of learned humanism—or, rather, classicism. Latin was admired to such an extent that it was

---

[87] See Example 27. Other pieces using the popular textual refrain of this piece include "D'un bel matin," in Petrucci's *Frottole Libro VI,* fol. 55ᵛ, and "E d'un bel matin," *Frottole Libro XI,* fol. 35ᵛ.

thought necessary to write in it, to use classical prosody and forms. Bembo tried to extend this admiration to Greek, Provençal, and Trecento Italian poets, so that one could have a modern classicism not directly in imitation of ancient patterns. This is important because a wider concept of classicism made room for developments such as the madrigal. Italian, then, had to be dignified to the stage where it could express as well as, even better, since more contemporary, than Latin, humanistic sentiments. Resurrection of the Italian past accounts for the renewed use of the word "madrigal" as well as for the return to the old ballata forms and performance methods, which had been more or less obliterated by lesser forms such as the frottola. There was a literary return to the old ballata, including a return from eight-syllable lines to seven- or eleven-syllable lines.

Then there is the question of supplying music for these newly resuscitated forms. There are two trends here; let me state the first in connection with Calmeta, since I have recently come across a reference to a newly discovered manuscript of Calmeta in Spain,[88] one which has very interesting passages. Calmeta explains, in giving advice to young poets, that if they are good singers as well as poets they might write simple things in frottola style, imitating Tebaldeo, since their singing will cover up the words, and they can make their points without being particularly distinguished poets. But if they want to set a literary standard they must imitate jewelers who, in mounting a beautiful stone, display it not against a busy background but against a simple black cloth. Good poetry, then, should be simply written; and Calmeta adds—a century before Monteverdi—that the music should be the servant of the poetry. I think that the line of development, literary development, in Tromboncino, in Sebastian Festa, even in some early madrigalists, led in the direction of simplicity, with the aim of making the text appear prominent. The other trend is one followed by the Florentine group, for instance, Pisano: music was to have as high a standard as poetry, and this led to elaboration of style. We should try to determine whether the sources of this musical elaboration were Italian, French, Flemish, or what have you. This is the way in which I see the madrigal-origins problem in general.

[88] Published in Calmeta, "La poesia di Tebaldeo." The passage referred to here is on pp. 21–25, in the section called "Qual stile tra volgari poeti sia da imitare."

MME. BRIDGMAN: This question of language is of great importance. I should, however, like to turn from it to two additional points concerning Italian music of the turn of the century. First, a new trend in secular music is seen; contrary to medieval practice, secular music could now be used as a serious thing, not a mere diversion. Second, the frottola may well have been sung by amateurs, such as those in Isabella d'Este's court; but the madrigal was almost from the beginning the province of professional musicians.

MR. RUBSAMEN: What leads you to believe that the madrigal was performed by professionals?

MME. BRIDGMAN: It was too difficult for amateurs to perform.

MR. REESE: But some of the early madrigals are really rather easy.

MR. RUBSAMEN: And as for the frottola, the solo voice part was not really too easy.

MR. D'ACCONE: In any event the level of musical culture among amateurs was often very high. If one reads contemporary letters, such, for example, as one from Niccolò Machiavelli's son, who writes that he has been to his lesson in three-part counterpoint,[89] one sees that in the sixteenth century cultivated amateurs in Italy, as in France, were trained in music and could conceivably sing anything put before them.

MME. BRIDGMAN: Yes, but some study was necessary—more for the madrigal than for the frottola.

MR. RUBSAMEN: Then you mean that not so much professional singers as educated amateurs were necessary for madrigal performance. There were of course a good many such amateurs.

MR. REESE: Professionalism may have been very important later— for Marenzio, or Gesualdo. But I wonder whether this is as true for earlier stages of the madrigal.

MR. D'ACCONE: The matter of chronology in Italian composers of this period might be brought up here, if we may change the subject slightly. Mr. Rubsamen, you spoke of Bernardo Pisano's early works as dating from the 1490's. I have looked at Pisano's birth certificate,[90]

[89] See Niccolò Machiavelli, *Lettere,* ed. G. Lesca (Florence, 1929), p. 244, a letter from Guido Machiavelli to his father dated April 17, 1527: "comincerò questa Pasqua . . . a sonare e cantare e fare contrappunto a tre."

[90] For new biographical information on Pisano see Frank D'Accone, "Bernardo Pisano—An Introduction to his Life and Works" (to be published in *Musica Disciplina*).

and he was born in 1490; his early works cannot therefore come before, say, 1506. Pisano's works were published in some number by Petrucci in 1520, as we know; this brings up a question: you said that Pisano's works, published by Petrucci, were composed over a long period of time, and you cited several examples. How does one know when Bernardo composed these works, there being as you say certain contradictions in style within his work?

MR. RUBSAMEN: I assumed that pieces with a good deal of frottolistic repetition might be earlier than pieces of more madrigalian character, without such repetitions.

MR. PIRROTTA: Or it might be that these were two different genres, and therefore a different style applied to each.

MR. D'ACCONE: That is exactly the point I would like to make: Pisano, when writing in his "older" style, follows a tradition handed down to him by, say, Coppinus, and Bartholomaeus, and particularly by Isaac, who was *maestro di cappella* when these composers were growing up. Here is where the question of Netherlandish influence re-enters. As for the Florentine composers' chronology, my research [91] shows that Coppinus was the earliest, born about 1465, since he was a choirboy in 1477; Bartholomaeus was born in 1477, Pisano in 1490, and Layolle in 1491; so here we have three half-generations.

MR. RUBSAMEN: Could there have been two Bernardo Pisanos?

MR. D'ACCONE: I think not; he was simply a many-sided personality. Layolle is another example of a composer who wrote in several styles at once. I have found an early account, dated 1589,[92] of Layolle, which states that he wrote all his madrigals before he left Florence around 1530—he was, you know, an opponent of the Medici. Here, then, is a way of dating madrigals, written before 1530, by a man who was also writing in a deliberately older style. This was one man, not three, as Einstein would have had it. The problem of chronology is a difficult one.

[91] See Frank D'Accone, "A Documentary History of Music at the Florentine Cathedral and Baptistry during the 15th Century," unpubl. diss., Harvard University, 1960, pp. 67–68, 48–49, 262–263.

[92] Michele Pocciantio, *Catalogus scriptorum fiorentinorum omni generis* (Florence, 1589), p. 70; "Ajolle, celebratissimo musico, il quale dopo aver dato alla luce alcuni bellissimi madrigali portatosi in Francia, circa l'anno 1530, qui menò il rimanente della sua vita in gran posto e reputazione."

MR. HEARTZ: May I ask a few questions about chronology? First of all, there is a discrepancy between your statement, Mr. Rubsamen, that Layolle left Florence about 1520 and Mr. D'Accone's that he left about 1530.

MR. D'ACCONE: I think 1530 is the generally accepted date.

MR. HEARTZ: But he published in a large religious collection in Lyons in 1528.[93]

MR. LESURE: Yes, Layolle left Florence in 1522.[94] Einstein, as has been said, "divided" Layolle, as he tended to do with a musician who had to some extent changed his style. It was hard for Einstein to believe that Layolle's pieces represented in Florentine manuscripts, pieces written in extreme youth, could be by a man who later, around 1540, wrote madrigals. There is of course no reason why a composer should not have a marked difference of style between his youth and his mature period; however, I can give no precise biographical information which could "put back together the pieces" of Layolle.

MR. RUBSAMEN: Did you not give a political reason for his having left Florence?

MR. LESURE: He left Florence before anti-Medici plots had gotten very far; later he was able to receive an agitator (Luigi Alamanni) at Lyons.

MR. HEARTZ: That answers my first question. The second concerns Verdelot. How can one know that he composed his first madrigals early in the decade of 1520 to 1530?

MR. RUBSAMEN: They appear in Bologna Conservatory Cod. Q 21, the date of which is apparently 1523 or 1524, from what Claudio Gallico says in his book on the subject.[95]

MR. HEARTZ: Why is it, then, that Verdelot is not represented in the few prints of the period which contain music to Italian texts? I am searching for tangible evidence to support your assumption that Verdelot was writing madrigals at this early date.

MR. RUBSAMEN: The few part-music prints of the period—the Pisano, for instance, and the *Motetti e canzoni Libro I*,[96] are of 1520-21, perhaps a year or two before Verdelot's works began to appear.

---

[93] *RISM* 1528[1].

[94] Lesure, "Layolle," *MGG*, VIII, 398.

[95] Gallico, *Un canzoniere musicale,* p. 8. Gallico actually puts the date at "verso o intorno il 1526."

[96] *RISM* [c. 1521][6]. The Pisano print is of course Petrucci's 1520 publication of the *Musica sopra le Canzone del petrarcha.*

MR. HEARTZ: Would you not expect to find such a prominent composer in a 1526 publication?

MR. RUBSAMEN: You mean the *Libro I. De la Croce?* [97] That is not so much a madrigal source as it is a frottolistic collection. As for tangible evidence, I think the date of Bologna Q 21 is quite definitely established. Also there is the information given by Anne-Marie Bragard that Verdelot was in Italy in the early 1520's. [98]

MR. HEARTZ: Do you think that Willaert and Arcadelt were also writing madrigals at this time? If Verdelot did, so might they.

MR. RUBSAMEN: But Willaert and Arcadelt are not represented in collections of the early 1520's at all, whereas Q 21 does contain Verdelot pieces.

MR. HEARTZ: Florence, Biblioteca Nazionale, MS. Magl. XIX, 164–167, on the other hand, does not contain any Verdelot pieces.

MR. D'ACCONE: Florence 164–167 is not dependable, since it was probably copied quite late.

MR. HEARTZ: This point is important in connection with the history of the chanson as well as of the madrigal, since one would want to know when the Frenchman Verdelot wrote his first madrigals.

MR. PIRROTTA: The 1530 prints of madrigals show Verdelot occupying an important place. His reputation as the most important of the madrigal composers was established by this time.

MR. D'ACCONE: In support of Mr. Rubsamen I should like to point out that when Pisano left the chapel at Florence, Verdelot succeeded him directly. This is in 1520. [99] We know that Pisano wrote his early madrigals before 1520, since they were published then. It seems reasonable to suppose that if a vogue for madrigals was setting in, and Verdelot remained in Florence for three years, he could have composed his first madrigals then.

MR. HEARTZ: It is of course probable; but I find it strange that these madrigals are not represented in printed sources of the 1520's.

MR. PIRROTTA: But it is a decade in which there are very few prints.

MR. RUBSAMEN: Exactly. Where are the sources, other than manuscript, of the 1520's?

MR. HEARTZ: But some composers, such as Sebastian Festa, are rep-

---

[97] *RISM* 1526[6].

[98] Bragard, "Verdelot en Italie," pp. 109–124.

[99] According to Bragard, p. 115, Verdelot was not at S. Giovanni until sometime after August, 1522.

resented then by their secular music. And Verdelot is not represented even by sacred music until 1526.

MR. PIRROTTA: One point that puzzled me was the reference to repetition in the frottola as being an "economical" procedure. Why? The repetitions, it seems to me, are intended to reflect the metrical form of the poems. This, in fact, is a basic aspect of the frottola.

MR. RUBSAMEN: I tried to make a distinction between repetition to illustrate rhyming lines of text, which is repetition for the sake of the poetry, and those repetitions which do not spring from poetic rhyme but are independent of the text, which are done simply to save musical material.

MR. REESE: There is of course a distinction between repetitions which are structural and those within a through-composed phrase. In the barzelletta, for instance, there is repetition within the scheme, then the complete scheme repeated for each stanza; the latter would be a structural repetition, having nothing to do with musical economy. But a repetition within the stanza would be the type you refer to.

MR. RUBSAMEN: Yes, if it is independent of poetical rhyme, if the music for one line of text is repeated for a following, unrelated line.

MR. PIRROTTA: I am inclined to think that most of the repetitions are structural ones. This does not mean that the two lines concerned in a repetition need rhyme; they might occupy corresponding positions in the stanza without actually rhyming.

MR. RUBSAMEN: As an example I cited Tromboncino's "Si è debile il filo"; [100] two or three of its repetitions are explainable because of the rhyming lines of text; but in other instances Tromboncino waits for some ten measures, then repeats something he had used earlier— for no rhyme nor reason! And I have seen this sort of thing in hundreds of compositions.

MR. D'ACCONE: One of the things that I have noticed particularly in the works of these transitional people is that the liking even for structural repetitions begins to disappear; in Pisano's pieces there are examples in which musical repetition is absent though the poem would still give room for it. This may perhaps be taken as evidence of a changing attitude of composers toward poetry.

MR. PIRROTTA: Yes; there is a movement from set forms toward free

[100] Published in Rubsamen, *Literary Sources*, p. 53.

forms in Italian music, while in French music the opposite trend seems to have been working.

MR. REESE: I am inclined to take issue with that. It seems to me that the frottolistic forms, *formes fixes* of a kind, became fashionable just when the French formes fixes died out. The French actually found, or worked toward, free forms before the Italians did.

MR. PIRROTTA: What I meant was that in the new (Parisian) chanson there is a certain return to symmetrically repeated phrases, although not in the same way as in the old formes fixes.

MR. REESE: But I thought of this as evidence that although sixteenth-century chanson composers desired freedom from the past, they had not yet made a complete break, and some of the old repetition ideas persisted. The past offered models of organization, of form, and these were used, but in a freer way and with remarkable imagination.

MR. PIRROTTA: This return takes place, however, after a movement toward complete freedom has occurred.

MR. REESE: I don't see this. If I may oversimplify here, one has the Dufay-Binchois generation using the formes fixes, the Ockeghem-Busnois generation largely retaining them; more free pieces are found here, of course. Then the Josquin-La Rue generation practically abandons the formes fixes, writing very few pieces in those moulds. These men use repetition forms of their own invention, but they don't go so far as "complete freedom." Josquin and Pierre de la Rue have their own schemes, interesting ones; the ingenuity and originality of these schemes is part of the reason for the charm of their music.

MR. PIRROTTA: But this sort of thing corresponds to freely repetitive schemes like those of the canzone and the madrigal. This is just what Bembo wanted: an open scheme having a certain amount of structural combinations of material, but no pre-established forms. In every case there was to be a new poetic structure invented, to be followed or modified by the musician.

MR. RUBSAMEN: Perhaps the clue to this whole argument is that repetition in the formes fixes has to do with the poem, whereas repetition of sections in the Josquin-La Rue generation has to do with the musical structure only. For example, there is repetition of the music of the last line, done in order to give a sense of climax, musically, rather than to follow anything in the poetic structure. The repetitions exist, it is true, but for different reasons.

MR. PIRROTTA: But sometimes this still has a connection with a re-frain or with something repeated in the poem.

MR. RUBSAMEN: That would be rather exceptional in the Josquin-La Rue era.

MR. PIRROTTA: I was really referring, however, to Févin and to the early Claudin.

MR. BROWN: It seems to me that all the Josquin repetition schemes are closely connected with the structure of the poems they set. The examples I used, I think, showed typical musical structures closely related to poetic ones. There are, on the other hand, chansons like "Mille regretz," free pieces without any repetition scheme at all.

MR. REESE: But one sees enormous variety in this generation: free pieces, chansons with freely invented repetition schemes, and even some formes fixes.

MR. BROWN: That is true, but the newly invented repetition schemes almost always have a direct relation to the structure of the poem.

MR. PIRROTTA: To know the reasons for abandonment of fixed forms and change to freer ones one would have to have been inside the minds of the men who did it; but it is revealing that at the turn of the sixteenth century there were a certain number of people—lit-erary men such as Sannazzaro and Tebaldeo—publishing chanson-niers whose contents clearly reflect the influence of Petrarch's *Can-zoniere*. They contain a great number of sonnets, a certain number of canzoni, and, since Petrarch had a few madrigals, three or four or five texts which are called madrigals. On the other hand there is ev-idence that as early as 1500—the reasons for this date would take too long to tell—Bembo gave the name of madrigal to a metrical scheme which is no longer that of the old madrigal; and actually all of Bembo's writings tend to identify the madrigal with a poem of a sin-gle strophe, whatever form this single strophe may take. A canzone of a single strophe can be a madrigal; a ballata of a single strophe (Mr. D'Accone has shown me some examples in poems by Strozzi,[101] in the old ballata form but consisting of a single strophe) can be a madrigal. So there were two trends: first, to stay with the old mean-ing of the term "madrigal," and second, to give it a new definition. The general movement, however, was toward a loosening of fixed repetitive schemes in favor of freely invented repetition patterns; and

[101] In a manuscript in the Biblioteca Mediceo-Laurenziana in Florence. Fuller information is to be had in the article mentioned in note 90, above.

although the musician might disregard or add repetitive elements, there was a more or less parallel trend in music, in the direction of free repetitions.

MR. D'ACCONE: This is exemplified by the collaboration of Strozzi and Pisano, who set the poetry as it was written.

MR. PIRROTTA: One finds this freedom in Pisano, in a certain number of madrigals by Verdelot, in Arcadelt, and in Willaert, although in these last three the subtle changes in harmony, registration, note values, and so forth, make the repetitions harder to perceive. But one nevertheless sees that the musician was stimulated by the form of the text to create his own musical forms.

MR. REESE: You made some point, Mr. Rubsamen, of asymmetry in the strambotto, as having a relation to the development of the madrigal. I wonder whether this asymmetry was not cultivated deliberately because of the extreme simplicity of the strambotto, with its many repetitions. A simple musical style if there were only two phrases could have been pretty deadly.

MR. RUBSAMEN: Composers didn't mind being deadly in the barzelletta and the oda.

MR. PIRROTTA: Settings of the oda were always very short, of course.

MR. RUBSAMEN: Although I didn't go into reasons for this asymmetry in the strambotto, it probably had something to do with a soloistic manner of performance. The solo performances of the improvisators who performed these pieces may have been suited to rhapsodic, irregular treatment.

MR. REESE: You also mentioned the ottava rima. Are you thinking of it as different from the strambotto?

MR. RUBSAMEN: My view of the ottava rima is that it looks very much like a strambotto in form, but that its literary quality is higher.

MR. PIRROTTA: One could perhaps say that ottava rima was a form in which long poems were set, while the strambotto was usually a single poem, although one could have chains of strambotti fitted together. In other words, the strambotto is a lyric poem, whereas the ottava rima is a poetic structure used for narrative poems.

MR. RUBSAMEN: Of a more philosophic nature, perhaps.

MR. PIRROTTA: Consider Pulci's *Morgante maggiore;* is it more philosophic? More amusing, yes.

MR. REESE: I have one or two details to mention. You referred to the ternary section at the end of Compère's "Scaramella."[102] That is a sophisticated little piece; although the mensuration is binary in the first sections, in performance it comes out as being quite ternary. One more small point, perhaps rather a conjectural one: you mentioned "Dal lecto me levava"[103] as forecasting the madrigal. I have always thought of that piece as so French in style that if one substituted a French text it could be mistaken for a chanson of the Claudin generation. This is perhaps a matter of taste not to be discussed, but I wish to place it on record that it sounds French to me.

MR. RUBSAMEN: Let me say that I consider the madrigal to be a combination of various stylistic elements; the one that I was here trying to trace was that in which all voices are melodic in a vocal sense and are fitted to the texts. I do not maintain that, in quality of text or in expressive content, "Dal lecto" is a madrigal; only in one respect, that the voices are all melodically conceived, can it be thus described.

MR. REESE: One could of course say the same thing of the chanson.

MR. PIRROTTA: One remark may be made here about the term "madrigal," which term itself has some importance. There is one strange sideline for which I have no logical explanation; but it exists, and it might explain some of Pesenti's settings. Alongside the madrigal as a literary form (a resurrection of the fourteenth-century madrigal) there is a popular connotation of the word as well. There exists a text speaking of a company of singers performing, at a banquet, madrigals in "Paduan dialect."[104] Many villotistic pieces—in fact, the villotta itself—have strong Venetian connections; but the only explanation I can think of is that in 1509 the old treatise by Antonio da Tempo[105] was published. He is the one to advance the explanation of the madrigal as coming from *mandria*, saying that orig-

[102] Published in Schwartz, *Petrucci*, p. 92; Riemann, *Handbuch*, vol. II, pt. 1, p. 349; Torrefranca, *Il segreto*, p. 522.

[103] Published in Torrefranca, p. 434; Riemann, vol. II, pt. 1, p. 360; Cesari and Monterossi, *Le frottole di Ottaviano Petrucci*, I, 22; *Das Chorwerk*, XLIII, 7.

[104] See Cristoforo di Messiburgo, *Libro novo nel qual s'insegna a far d'ogni sorta di vivanda* (Venice, 1564), pp. 18a–b, where in the course of a Ferrarese banquet held in 1529 it is said that "a questa sesta vivanda cantarono Ruzante et cinque compagni et due femine canzoni et *madrigali alla Pavana* bellissimi et andavano intorno la tavola contendendo insieme di cose contadinesche."

[105] The fourteenth-century treatise of Antonio da Tempo, given various titles, was first printed in 1509. See Einstein, *Italian Madrigal*, I, 117. The treatise has been reprinted; see G. Grion, ed., *Antonio da Tempo: Delle rime volgari* (Bologna, 1869).

inally madrigals were shepherds' songs, only later turned into literary poems. This may be an explanation for those madrigal texts which are, so to speak, antiliterary, in dialect.

MR. RUBSAMEN: Among these would be Verdelot's piece "Ohime che la brunetta mia," [106] certainly not a very elegant specimen of literature.

MR. PIRROTTA: But on the other hand these villotistic texts often get a much more sophisticated setting than the clearly "literary" madrigals. And Pesenti in just this type of piece showed that he was a contrapuntist, and an elegant one. This is still another paradox in the early history of the madrigal.

[106] Published by Gardane in his collection of Verdelot's six-part madrigals (*RISM* 1541[18]). The text is reprinted in Einstein, *Italian Madrigal,* I, 257.

III

LES GOÛTS RÉUNIS or
THE WORLDS OF THE MADRIGAL
AND THE CHANSON CONFRONTED

DANIEL HEARTZ[*]

THE AFTERMATH OF THE FRENCH CAMPAIGNS IN ITALY, 1494–1525

SEVERAL times within the span of a generation Italy witnessed the descent of armies led by Charles VIII, Louis XII, or Francis I in pursuit of claims to the Angevin succession in Naples or the Visconti succession in Milan. Conquest was easy but colonization could be enforced only with arms or money, and the lack of one or the other soon turned the Italian schemes of the Valois to chimera. Yet Lombardy was under French rule from 1500 to 1512 and from 1515 to 1521. Naples and Genoa were occupied for shorter periods of time and the peninsula as a whole was swarming with French agents, while France in turn saw a tremendous influx of Italians. In order to measure some of the results of this prolonged and tumultuous contact between North and South, we can do no better than call to witness a few of the outstanding figures who lived through it.

Francesco Guicciardini, the great historian of Florence, writes in his *Storia d'Italia:* "Before the year 1494 wars were protracted, battles bloodless, the methods followed in besieging towns slow and uncertain; and although artillery was already in use, it was managed with such want of skill that it caused little hurt. Hence it came about that the ruler of a state could hardly be dispossessed. But the French, on their invasion of Italy, infused so much liveliness into our wars, that up until the year 1521, whenever the open country was lost, the state

* The author is indebted to the University of California, Berkeley, for a 1961 Summer Faculty Fellowship and wishes to express his thanks for being allowed to put aside his official project—an Attaingnant bibliography—during the month of August, while the present study was undertaken.

was lost with it." Old-style war and politics were revolutionized; a new age of steel, of battles in earnest—a grim and terrible age—had opened with the dawn of the sixteenth century. Machiavelli drew the lesson for all Italy when he adjured unity and strength, concluding testily, and in no very flattering terms for the foreign invaders, that a strong monarchy had made a fighting power even out of the fickle and light-minded French. Ever since Dante Itàlians had remarked the frivolity of the French; a Venetian ambassador traveling with the French court in 1529 reported that "the people in this country are very gay and both men and women spend their time laughing, joking and dancing." [1] Was the Italian impression of Gallic light-mindedness derived in any part from the very chansons at issue here? It would be agreeable to think so. A mixture of admiration—for French arms—and scorn is quite characteristic. It emerges from the pages of Castiglione's *The Booke of the Courtier,* which we quote in the 1561 translation of Sir Thomas Hoby. During the first day of discussion Count Lewis is led to comment: "Beside goodnesse the true and principall ornament of the minde in every man I believe are letters, although the French men know onely the noblenes of armes, and passe for nothing beside: so that they doe not only set by letters, but they rather abhorre them, and all learned men they doe count very rascalles, and they thinke it a great villany when any of them is called a clarke . . . I would not now some one of the contrarie parte should alledge unto mee the contrarie effectes to confute mine opinion with all; and tell mee how the Italians with their knowledge of letters have shewed small prowesse in armes from a certaine time hetherto, the which neverthelesse is too true." Castiglione is confident of intellectual superiority, but running alongside this as an undercurrent is a kind of envy, not only of French arms, but of the other trappings of an older feudal society, considered more noble because more ancient, militaristic though it was. This is quite understandable in an Italy where yesterday's merchants and hired assassins—the Medici, the Gonzagas, the Sforzas, to mention a few—were struggling to become today's noble families and to establish hereditary principalities on the ruins of former city-states. Isabella d'Este frequently praised the chivalrous behavior of the northerners, and she could be carried

[1] Niccolò Tommaseo, *Relations des ambassadeurs venitiens sur les affaires de France* (Paris, 1838), I, 14. Further, see Leo Moulin, "Ce que l'Italie du XVIe siècle pensait de la France," *Revue de l'Université de Bruxelles,* XLI (1936), 345–364.

away with the idea of royalty to the extent of writing to Elisabeth Gonzaga after a visit to Louis XII at Milan: "I have been to the first and noblest court in Christendom" (letter of July 7, 1507); and again, upon being asked to serve as godparent to the expected child of Louis and Anne of Brittany, she writes: "What greater honor could there be in this world than to be sponsor to a King of France! Oh what splendor, pomp and glory will be mine! I shall not only visit Paris, the most flourishing University and populous city of the universe, but the whole of France" (letter of September 25, 1507). Even the best minds in Italy were not exempt from a certain deference toward their longer-pedigreed invaders, a deference which comes close to snobbery. Rightly understood, it goes far to explain Isabella's—and Italy's—love for medieval French romances, and perhaps helps to explain also what otherwise might seem a very precious and artificial cultivation of the chanson at the little Italian courts.

Italian artists had little use for what they saw in France. Benvenuto Cellini, given the task of making over the old gate at Fontainebleau, disdainfully called it "grande e nana" ("big and tiny," all out of proportion) "di quella lor mala maniera franciosa" ("in the bad French taste").[2] But with the artists' patrons it was different. The world of courtly manners owed much to the North. When the Burgundian court was at its height in the fifteenth century, Italians looked to it for modes of dress, courtly deportment, and such chivalrous pastimes as the art of the dance, where several traces of Burgundian influence are to be noted. One passage in the *Courtier* suggests that for many Italians the model had merely switched to the new breed of northerner in their midst; the Marquess Phebus says in the Second Book: "Looke what good things the Italians have in their garments, in feasting, in banketing, in feates of armes and in every other thing that belongeth to a Courtier, they have it all of the Frenchmen." Some took too much from the French to suit Castiglione's taste, for he has Sir Frederick respond by inveighing against those who imitate "the quicke livelinesse that is perceived in the French nation almost in everie gesture," saying "there are many Italians that would faine counterfaite their fashion, and can doe nought els but shake the heade in speaking, and make a legge with an ill grace, and when they come out of their doores into the Citie, goe so fast that good foote-

---

[2] *La vita*, bk. 2, chap. xxi.

men can scant overtake them, and with these manners they weene themselves good Frenchmen."

French reactions to Italy found no spokesmen of Castiglione's eloquence; they may be deduced quite readily, however, by turning the coin to the other side: scorn for what was considered a want of chivalry and nobility (narrowly tied up with small skill at arms), but at the same time a slowly dawning awareness of Italy's artistic and intellectual advance. The earliest campaigns penetrated but slightly into the French consciousness. What is considered today the true Renaissance—the refined and classical purity of Brunelleschi's Florence—apparently did not impress the northerners at all. In his memoirs, Philippe de Commynes is lavish in his praise of the richly ornamented Venetian palaces, and for him the finest building in Italy was the Certosa of Pavia, an example of that Milanese style which, by Florentine standards, would be thought hardly less barbarous than the flamboyant Gothic surroundings in which the French knights had been weaned. In other words, the French responded to those elements that were congenial to them in Italy, at least in the early years. The artistic harvest of the first Italian campaign was well summed up in the little troupe of Italians who followed Charles VIII back to France. It consisted of five tailors, four men skilled in various handicrafts, two sculptors, two architects, a gardener, an organ maker (Giovanni da Grana), a *parfumeur,* an *inventeur subtil a faire couver et naistre poulets,* and a man who kept parrots, which assemblage was hardly capable of dethroning overnight a deeply rooted and vigorous late medieval tradition among French artists. Pierre Du Colombier calls this first period of Italian contact an invasion of ornamentists and points out that what we witness in the Amboise of Charles VIII and the Blois of Louis XII are Gothic buildings onto which a few classical motifs and ornaments have been tacked.[3] Similarly, in Jean le Maire de Belges, the leading court poet until about 1515, we see a man who still belongs to the medieval past; the tortuous elocutions of *les grands rhétoriqueurs* are his mainstay, even if he does interlard an occasional idea from Petrarch.

Things began to happen at a rapid pace only after 1515. Less timid spirits came to the fore, pushing France ever further in the direction Italy led. A large share in the quickening tempo by which the Renais-

[3] *L'art renaissance en France* (Paris, 1945), p. 8.

sance overwhelmed France may be laid directly at the door of the singular personality of *le roi chevalier* himself, Francis I. Castiglione had already predicted great things of him in the *Courtier,* where Giuliano de' Medici says: "If Monseigneur de Angoulesme have so good luke that he may (as men hope) succede in the Crowne, the glory of armes in France doth not so florish nor is had in such estimation as letters will be, I believe. For it is not long sins I was in France, and saw this Prince in the Court there, who seemed unto mee beside the handsomenesse of person and bewtie of visage, to have in his countenance so great a majestie, accompanied neverthelesse with a certaine lovely courtesie, that the realme of France should ever seeme unto him a small matter. I understood afterwarde by many gentlemen both French and Italian, verie much of the most noble conditions, of the greatnesse of courage, prowesse and liberalitie that was in him: and among other things, it was tolde me that hee highly loved and esteemed letters, and had in very great reputation all learned men, and blamed the Frenchmen themselves that their mindes were so far wide from this profession, especially having at their doores so noble an universitie as Paris is, where all the world resorteth."

It seems almost as if Francis, who knew the *Courtier* well and was responsible through his urgings for Castiglione's eventually publishing it, set out deliberately to live up to this flattering picture. On February 5, 1517, Guillaume Budé wrote to Erasmus that the king had proclaimed his intention of establishing a seminary of learned men in France—a project which was to culminate in the Collège Royal. Erasmus declined his invitation to Paris and in his stead came Agostino Giustiniani, the first of a great many Italian humanists attracted by the new Maecenas of letters. Francis was intent on creating an intellectual and artistic milieu which would form a suitable backdrop for so spectacular a prince. The attitude in itself is redolent of Italy and the kind of society painted by Castiglione from his idealized Urbino. To whom should the king turn but to Italian artists? Nothing was more natural, since he considered himself an Italian prince, as well as the head of the noblest of royal houses. He called to France Michelangelo, who did not go, but Andrea del Sarto and Leonardo da Vinci did. After them went the younger artists Primaticcio and Rosso, who were responsible for the decoration of Fontainebleau, a full-blooded creation of the Renaissance. The theme given for their decor is significant—how Francis I introduced the arts into the realm.

King Francis patronized Italian poets too, most notably Luigi Alamanni, whose *Opere Toscane,* in fulsome praise of the royal person, were printed in Lyons in 1532. Alamanni became a kind of laureate in the Italian language, sharing this role with the French poets Clément Marot and Mellin de Saint-Gelais, Marot a good deal better versed in Italian letters than was Jean le Maire, and Saint-Gelais a thorough-going *français italianisant,* of whom there will be more to say.

As the reign of Francis I continued, Italian influence increased in scope and depth. There is perhaps no better way to underscore the extent of the contact than to refer to the extensive treatment of the subject by the great twentieth-century scholar Emile Picot: *Les Italiens en France au XVI*ᵉ *siècle,* and *Les Français italianisants.*

EXCHANGES OF PERSONNEL AND MUSIC

French musicians in Italy and Italian musicians in France represent a small part of the exchanges which took place constantly and at every level in the first part of the sixteenth century. At the highest social level Francis I did not hesitate to engineer some political marriages between members of his own house and Italians of considerably lesser station. Of the greatest significance to our subject is the marriage in 1528 of Princess Renée, last surviving child of Louis XII and Anne of Brittany, with Hercules II of Ferrara, heir to the small duchy ruled by the Estes. Five years later an alliance with Florence brought to France as a spouse for the king's second son, the Duc d'Orléans, Catherine de' Medici, only child of Lorenzo de' Medici, duke of Urbino, and Madeleine de la Tour d'Auvergne. Their wedding on May 2, 1518, represented an earlier stage in the king's nuptial diplomacy, and is of particular interest as the event which engendered the Medici Codex.[4] Musical exchanges were already intense during this decade, which saw a whole group of French singers sent to serve the music-loving Medici pope, Leo X; among them were Elzéar Genet, alias Carpentras, Hilaire Penet, Antoine Bruhier, Jean Conseil (or Consilium), Michot, Levasseur, Gomont, Bonnevin, alias Beausseron, Fochier, Jonauld, alias Brule, and Milleville, who was later to turn up at the Este court. Numerous musical traces of this pacific invasion are left in Italian prints and manuscripts of around

[4] Edward E. Lowinsky, "The Medici Codex: A Document of Music, Art and Politics in the Renaissance," *Annales musicologiques,* V (1957), 61–178.

1520. As for Italians in France, it has been assumed that the Noli, Porchi, and Albi encountered on a list of singers in the Chapelle Royale in 1515 were from Italy; caution is due here, however, because Noli could be French as well as Italian on the basis of his name, and Albi is, after all, the name as well of a French city within the confines of the royal domain. With another group of musicians serving Francis I there can be no question. The roster of the royal *écurie* between 1517 and 1530 reveals these players of shawms and sackbuts: Bartolomeo da Firenze, Pietro Pagano, Cristoforo da Piacenza, Masone da Milano, Francesco da Birago, Nicolo da Brescia, Simone da Piacenza, and Francesco da Cremona. Besides these, several Italian soloists on the *cornetto* served in the *musique de chambre,* not to mention the *valet de chambre* and royal lutenist, Albert de Rippe of Mantua. The Italian wind band is particularly interesting because it formed an ensemble apart, which Prunières believes came to France as a unit.[5] There is a parallel to be drawn here with the troupe of Italian comedians in the king's service which had arrived in the 1520's and was playing a leading role by 1531 in the festivities for Queen Eléonore's entry into Paris.

For a gauge of the effect which such exchanges of personnel had upon musical life, we may turn to the products of the music printers in both lands. To a certain extent these businessmen led the musical taste of their customers, but they also had to follow, for otherwise it could be difficult, conceivably, to sell the thousand or twelve hundred copies which constituted an average press run. With prints we are thus on safer ground than with manuscripts, which possibly reflected the tastes of but one music lover.

Petrucci set the example in 1501 of course, when he chose to begin publication with hundreds of chansons by the *oltremontani*. For our purposes it will be useful to survey the French-texted pieces printed in Italy during the two decades after 1520, in the full awareness that a survey of Latin sacred music by French composers printed in Italy would be equally long and equally instructive. At the beginning of this period stand Andrea Antico's two Venetian prints of 1520, *Chansons à troys,* with 41 pieces, and the collection of canons *Motetti novi e chanzoni franciose,* with 22 pieces on French texts. The following decade is more confused than any other in the annals of Italian music

[5] Henry Prunières, "La Musique de la Chambre et de l'Ecurie," *L'Année musicale,* I (1911), 215-251.

printing, but it is generally agreed now to place within its confines the *Libro primo de la fortuna,* which ends with a three-part chanson, "J'ai bien nourri sept ans ung papegay," and a piece labeled as a duo, "Je le lerray puisqu'il me bat." This print is found at Bologna together with another of *Motetti* and *Carmina gallica* (as its index says, there is no title), the latter comprised of four old-fashioned imitative chansons. According to the catalogue of the Colombina at Seville, the year 1530 saw the publication of *Madrigali de diversi musici libro primo,* probably printed at Rome by Valerio Dorico, and adopting the format of separate part books, each texted, like Attaingnant's chansonniers, which began to appear in 1528. Represented beside Verdelot, Costanzo and Sebastiano Festa, Maître Jhan, "Carlo," and Jacopo da Thoscana was Clément Janequin, whose program chanson "Le Chant des oiseaux" occupied the last eight pages. In the second edition of this collection, three years later and signed by Dorico, the Janequin piece was joined by two of the most famous chansons by Claudin de Sermisy, "Languir me fait" and "Tous mes amis." But meanwhile, in 1531, Dorico had included in the *Libro II de la Croce* an even more famous program piece of Janequin, "La Guerre." The name Antico appears again in 1536 on another Venetian print with French title: *La Couronne et fleur des chansons à troys,* containing 41 pieces not perceptibly different in style from his *Chansons à troys* of sixteen years earlier. A year previous to this the publisher Ottaviano Scotto, with Antico as his printer, brought out two collections of a much more up-to-date and Parisian cast, *Il primo libro de le canzoni franzese,* with 23 pieces, succeeded by a second book, with 21 pieces. Their success must have been great, because a year did not go by before both were reprinted, in 1536.[6] The same year saw Francesco Marcolini's print *Intabolatura di liuto de diversi, con la bataglia e altre cose bellisime de Messer Francesco da Milano,* in which the Janequin favorite is joined by two chansons of Josquin and two of Claudin. Finally there was Antonio Gardano, "musico francese," as he called himself, who printed in Venice a collection of *Canzoni francese nu-*

[6] Superius parts are preserved in the Harding Library in Chicago. There was probably another and earlier edition of the first book, to judge from the numerical correspondence of a now lost collection, *Vingt trois chansons amoureuses et gaillardes* (Venice: Luc Antonio Giunta, 1520), cited in the sale of the Bancel library in Paris at the end of the last century; see Paule Chaillon, "Les Musiciens du nord à la cour de Louis XII," *La Renaissance dans les provinces du nord* (Paris, 1956), p. 69.

mero trenta,[7] devoted overwhelmingly to Claudin, *Venticinque canzoni francese a quatro di Clement Iannequin e di altri eccellentissimi authori* in 1538, and 28 *Canzoni francese a due voci* in 1539, with many of the arrangements attributed to the printer himself. Rather than draw an arbitrary line at 1540, it will be instructive to advance at least two years further, because 1541 saw Gardano's curious publication *Di Constantio Festa il primo libro de madrigali a tre voci . . . aggiuntovi similmente trenta canzoni francese di Janequin,* in which Festa appears to be represented by only one piece, and Janequin by none.[8] Obviously, the name Janequin, like Festa, was good for "selling" a collection, and Gardano was none too scrupulous with names. Note also the technique of including chansons and madrigals in equal proportions, to which Gardano resorted again in *Il primo libro de madrigali italiani et canzoni francese a due voce di Jhan Gero* (1541), where 26 chansons alternate page by page with a comparable number of madrigals, and in the 1542 *Primo libro di madrigali d'Archadelt a tre voci . . . con la gionta di dodese canzoni francese.* The chansons printed in Italy in the collections just mentioned total 325 different pieces. A significant statistic to place beside this would be the number of Italian-texted pieces printed during the same two decades. Surprising as it may seem, their number probably did not exceed twice that total—that is, one chanson for every two Italian pieces.

Next it is the turn of the French music publishers. Attaingnant went through six active years and approximately fifty collections before printing some pieces with texts in Italian. Then, in April 1533 he placed two settings of Petrarch by Sebastiano Festa, "O passi sparsi" and "Perche al viso d'amor," at the beginning of a collection.[9] The following year saw an anonymous madrigal, "Dite di non amor, quanto vi piace," included in *Vingt et huyt chansons* (March 1534), and in another collection of the same title (October 1534), Claudin's

---

[7] A print which seems to be unrecorded and is found in the Accademia Filarmonica in Verona, bound with the *Primo libro di madrigali d'Archadelt a tre voci* (Venice: Antonio Gardano, 1542; *RISM* 1542[18]).

[8] François Lesure, "Les Chansons à trois voix de Clément Janequin," *Revue de musicologie,* XLIV (1959), 193–198.

[9] *Chansons musicales a quatre parties desquelles les plus convenables a la fleuste.* See Daniel Heartz, "La Chronologie des recueils imprimés par Pierre Attaingnant," *Revue de musicologie,* XLIV (1959), 176–193, on the dating of this work. The signature there conjectured, and the resultant date of April 1533, not 1534, have since been confirmed by the copy in the Bibliothèque A. Cortot in Lausanne.

"Altro non e il mio amor," on the superius of a madrigal of Festa which Dorico had first published in Rome six months earlier. There is something very much in need of explanation regarding this flurry of Italian pieces. It stops as suddenly as it began, and the last piece on an Italian text which Attaingnant was to print was Janequin's "Si come il chiaro," in 1540. That is, in all, five Italian-texted pieces printed in Paris in the first half of the century, out of a total of about 2000 chansons.

In Lyons, a city half Italian in character, with its Florentine bankers and merchants and its Italian-language printers, we should certainly expect to find a higher proportion of madrigals in the musical collections. Jacques Moderne, an Italian himself in origin, brought out the ten large volumes of his *Parangon des chansons,* starting in 1538; he included only six pieces on Italian texts, two by De Villiers, the rest by Francesco L'Ayolle, and it is almost as if the printer took special care to place these pieces inconspicuously, for in general he included only one in each collection, and that was placed at the end. Moderne concentrated his Italian pieces instead in special volumes, two devoted to the *Canzoni* of L'Ayolle, the Florentine republican permanently exiled to Lyons, and one devoted to the settings of Petrarch by another Florentine, Mateo Rampolini.

Everyone may draw his own conclusions from this lengthy bibliographical enumeration. But no one, surely, will claim that the favor which the chanson enjoyed in Italy was returned by anything approaching a similar interest in the madrigal in France. The evidence of the chanson's diffusion in Italy is overwhelming. In his *Italian Madrigal* Alfred Einstein, taking this into account, was led to ascribe what he termed the "artistic pause" between frottola and madrigal in part to the attractions of the chansonniers of Attaingnant. The figures just cited do nothing to contradict such a view, which may still serve us well as a working hypothesis. But there are pitfalls here for those unfamiliar with the book trade of the time. The temptation is to think that any Venetian, or Florentine, or Roman, could, by stopping at his bookseller's, purchase this or that chansonnier of Attaingnant. This was never the case. French music prints were extremely scarce in Italy, and it cannot be a coincidence that very few from the period survive today in Italian libraries. An avid collector like Antonfrancesco Doni wrote in 1550 to the Fleming Jacques Buus, who was organist at San Marco, "It would please me if you could write to some musician in France to have him send us a list of all the musical works printed there, for I do not have these in my library." [10] A generation later the Florentine courtier Jacopo Corbinelli, resident in Paris, saw to the needs of Fulvio Orsini at Rome and other Italian bibliophiles by procuring French books.[11] Once purchased, there were many hazards to overcome before the books could reach their destination. Should they safely make their way through French territory and across the Alps, every additional little state on the peninsula through which they had to pass decreased the chance of arrival. A certain Francesco d'Asola, a Venetian printer, in a request for a privilege, protested that a package of books which he had sent from France with the intention of reprinting them, was confiscated at Turin by some Gascons. Among the prints seized was one described as "uno libretto di canto canzon' venti nove di Paris," which can be nothing other than Attaingnant's *Vingt et neuf chansons,* printed in 1530.[12] Thus not even professionals in the book business could be sure of surmounting the difficulties which geography and politics imposed.

The number of Italian books in French collections of the time is surprisingly small.[13] And it did not become easier for books to travel between France and Italy as the century continued, but increasingly difficult. The normal market for the Parisian printers lay not to the south in any case, but to the north and west, and especially in England. Aside from this, what commercial trade there was with Italy declined steadily after 1515, as the Hapsburgs tightened their grip on the peninsula.[14] France's love affair with everything Italian waxed more intense in spite of worsening trade relations. Italy's infatuation with the chanson surmounted the same obstacles and resulted in a

---

[10] "V.S. mi fara un piacere scrivere a qualche musico in Francia, che ci mandi una lista di tutte l'opere di musica che sono stampate la, perche nella mia libraria non ho" (Doni, *La Libraria,* Venice, 1550; the letter is quoted at the beginning of the section "La Musica Stampata, Madrigali, Motteti, messe e canzoni").

[11] Gabriel Maugain, *Ronsard en Italie* (Paris, 1926), p. 11.

[12] Geneviève Thibault, "De la vogue de quelque documents français à Venise," *Bibliothèque d'humanisme et renaissance,* II (1935), 61-65.

[13] A. H. Schutz, *Vernacular Books in Parisian Private Libraries of the Sixteenth Century according to the Notarial Inventories,* University of North Carolina, Studies in Romance Languages and Literatures, 25 (Chapel Hill, 1955). Italian authors in French translation or printed in France were, on the other hand, very numerous.

[14] John S. C. Bridge, *A History of France from the Death of Louis XI, Vol. V: France in 1515* (Oxford, 1936), p. 280.

flourishing native industry in chanson prints. The mere fact of being printed did not guarantee music passage across national frontiers. Music traveled by way of musicians. Our next line of inquiry becomes clear. Who were the key figures who might have brought the new forms from one country to another?

Summing up the musical exchanges just discussed, we saw that French singers abounded in Italy, while Italy exported instrumental musicians to France. The astounding vogue of the chanson south of the Alps in the years after 1520 suggests that a newer school, no longer Burgundian, but truly French, had inherited to some degree the position of arbiters of musical taste so long occupied by Franco-Flemish composers. And there lies an interesting parallel with the Gallophile courtiers censured by Castiglione.

SOME KEY FIGURES

Willaert. Like thousands of students from every corner of Europe, Adrian Willaert left his home in Flanders as a young man and went to Paris to study at the university. After trying jurisprudence he turned to music under the tutelage of Jean Mouton, who, as chapel master of Francis I, was the leading personality in the musical world of the French capital around 1515.[15] These studies may have been completed by 1517, the year of Glarean's arrival in Paris; the Swiss humanist mentions meeting Mouton, for whom he has great praise, but not Willaert.[16] The young Fleming was at any rate a skillful composer by 1518, the date of the Medici Codex and the manuscript of Diane de Poitiers (Bologna, Biblioteca del Conservatorio, Cod. Q 19), in both of which he is represented by several motets, including the variety of double canon which was to make him the leading contributor to Antico's *Motetti novi* of two years later. From Paris he did not go directly to Italy, but returned first to the Low Countries. One of Zarlino's anecdotes places him in Rome before the end of Leo X's pontificate, when the papal choir sang his "Verbum bonum" under the impression that it was by Josquin. Another link with Rome is Adrian's "chromatic duo" (in reality a chromatic quartet, as Lowin-

[15] For an up-to-date biographical sketch see the article of Walter Gerstenberg in *Encyclopédie de la musique Fasquelle,* vol. III (Paris: Fasquelle, 1961).

[16] *Dodecachordon* (Basel, 1547), p. 320: "Ioannis Mouton . . . qui cum ego quondam Luteciae in Parisiis collocutus, sed per Interpretem, in aula Francisci Francorum Regis eius nominis primi." Whose spoken Latin was insufficient?

sky has shown [17]), purportedly sent to Leo in 1520 or 1521. A sojourn
at the Este court in Ferrara from 1522 to 1525 was followed by two
years in the service of Ippolito d'Este, the young cardinal of Milan
who was later to pass from the Imperial to the French camp. There-
upon Willaert went to Venice, replacing Pierre de Fossis as chapel
master at San Marco, where he remained for the final thirty-five years
of his life, becoming a virtual pope of Italian music.

As a composer of chansons, Willaert was especially disposed to
three-part imitative settings of chanson rustique melodies after the
style of Févin, specimens of which he contributed to Antico's prints
of both 1520 and 1536. This type of piece has sometimes been considered as having mainly a didactic function. But even in these lusty
pre-Tridentine years it is difficult to imagine that choirboys were
given for practice such suggestive ditties as "Au joly bois" (Example
34). Willaert contributed two different imitative settings of this piece
to Antico's *Chansons à troys* of 1536. It appears that he had not lost
touch with Paris, where the tune was a great favorite, having been
published by Attaingnant in various arrangements in 1529, 1530, and
1531, and set later by Pierre Certon, Adrian le Roy, Guillaume Morlaye, and Albert de Rippe.[18] The case for a specifically Parisian tune
is good.

[17] "Adrian Willaert's Chromatic 'Duo' Re-examined," *Tijdschrift voor Muziek-
wetenschap,* XVIII (1956), 1–36.

[18] *Quarante et deux chansons musicales a troys parties* (1529), fol. 17; *Six gaillardes et six pavanes* (1530), no. 9; *Vingt et cinq chansons musicales reduictes en
la tabulature des orgues espinettes manicordions* (1531), no. 13 (in Albert Seay, ed.,
Pierre Attaingnant. Transcriptions of Chansons for Keyboard, American Institute
of Musicology, 1961, p. 105). Certon's setting, from the *Premier livre de chansons*
(Paris: Le Roy and Ballard, 1552), is published by François Lesure in *Anthologie
de la chanson parisienne* (Monaco, 1953), no. 18. In it the old text is replaced by a
colorless contrafactum, "J'ai le rebours de ce que je souhaite," in which "Baisez
moy tant tant" becomes "J'ay du mal tant tant." Other settings: "Paduane-gaillarde,"
fol. 30ᵛ in Guillaume Morlaye's *Premier livre de tabulature de leut* (Paris, 1552);
"Paduane au Joly bois," fol. 20 in the same author's *Quatriesme livre . . . en
tabulature de guyterne* (Paris, 1552); "Chanson-Pavanne J'ay le rebours," fol. 2ᵛ in
Le Roy's *Second livre de guiterre* (1555); "Pavane J'ay du mal tant tant–Gaillarde,"
in Le Roy's *Tiers livre de tabulature de guiterre* (1552); "Pavane J'ay du mal tant
tant," fol. 23 in Albert de Rippe's *Quart livre de tabulature de luth* (Paris: Le Roy and
Ballard, 1553); "Pavane J'ay du mal tant tant–Gaillarde," fol. 6ᵛ in Le Roy's *Second
livre de cistre* (1564); "Pavane J'ay du mal tant tant–Gaillarde," fol. 5ᵛ in the
Premier livre de danseries (Louvain: Phalèse, 1571); "J'ai le rebours," in Le Roy's
Premier livre de chansons en forme de vau de ville composés à quatre parties (Paris,
1573), fol. 2ᵛ; "J'ai le rebours" (tune only) in Chardavoine's *Le Recueil des plus*

Willaert also wrote many-voiced chansons which fully reveal his Franco-Flemish musical ancestry, as well as a few four-part chansons for Attaingnant of a more homophonic and Parisian cast. He was a master of the chanson in several of its guises before coming to the madrigal. His contribution to the madrigal appears to be late from the printed sources, although it should be remembered that Marcolini announced a whole volume of Willaert madrigals in May 1536. Great as was his fame and fortune as first musician of Venice, he did not consider it demeaning to arrange a colleague's madrigals for voice and lute—the Verdelot lute songs printed in 1536. Such a service bespeaks a special admiration for Verdelot. Did the two become personally acquainted? And if so, was it in Venice, or in Rome? In Florence, or in Paris?

Verdelot. Philippe Verdelot's career was almost totally obscure until the quite recent researches of Edward Lowinsky and Anne-Marie Bragard. On the basis of the Vallicelliana Motet Codex, Lowinsky has established the composer as being in Florence from 1527 to 1529, during the last Republic.[19] Bragard has found documents to show his service from 1523 as chapel master of the Baptistry in Florence, whence he made trips to Rome to sing for Clement VII as early as January 1524.[20] Both scholars associate the Vallicelliana Codex with Verdelot, but they diverge slightly on its interpretation. Lowinsky stresses its republican, pro-Savonarola elements. Bragard sees it not as a document of solely republican sentiment but as a wider collection having to do with Florence, including as it does some texts in sympathy with the Medici. Her conclusions in this regard are startling: Verdelot must have been in Rome from about 1529 to 1533, at which time he supervised the redaction of the lavish motet codex, which she believes was prepared for Pope Clement on the occasion of the Medici return to Florence in 1533. In addition, she sees Verdelot in

---

belles et excellentes chansons en forme de voix de villes (Paris, 1576 and 1588), p. 96 in the 1588 edition.

[19] "A Newly Discovered Sixteenth-Century Motet Manuscript in the Biblioteca Vallicelliana in Rome," *JAMS,* III (1950), 173–232. For the French locutions in the manuscript (such as "a troys" and "tournes"), Lowinsky proposes in explanation that the scribe copied from Verdelot's originals (p. 195). Since the page turns would most likely come in places different from the originals, it seems more likely that the scribe who wrote "tournes" was a French musician.

[20] "Verdelot en Italie," *Revue belge de musicologie,* XI (1957), 107–124; "Détails nouveaux sur les musiciens de la cour du pape Clément VII," *ibid.,* (1959), 5–18; s.v. "Verdelot" in vol. III of the *Encyclopédie de la musique Fasquelle.*

contact with the pope's French singers under Jean Conseil, and in close connection with another papal musician, Costanzo Festa, adducing here their appearance together in the Vallicelliana manuscript and in the *Madrigali* of 1530. Not a single document illuminates Verdelot's whereabouts after this period. Nothing yet has turned up to clarify his origins. Because Antonfrancesco Doni, in his *Marmi,* has the composer narrate a tale which is set in the town of Carpentras, it has been assumed that Verdelot came from southern France. Greater confidence could well be placed in the more responsible Florentine writer Lodovico Guicciardini, whose *Descrizione de' Paesi Bassi* (1565) includes Verdelot among many other Netherlanders responsible for the illustrious school of composition flourishing there. Moderne prints five Verdelot motets in his *Primus liber* of 1532, which fact could be used as an argument in favor of a southern French connection. But three years previous to this Attaingnant had already printed two motets unquestionably by Verdelot. They are ascribed however to Ph.[ilippe] Deslouges (Bragard unaccountably reads "Deslonges"). Have we a case here of a Philippe Deslouges, alias Verdelot? The fashion for aliases was quite current among composers in France, as we have seen. Earlier Jean Ghiselin, alias Verbonnet, had provided a precedent. And the most striking example was Pierre Regnault, a leading contributor to the Parisian chansonniers about 1540, and later in the service of Ippolito d'Este. Regnault, alias Sandrin, took his pseudonym from a celebrated farce character of the late fifteenth century.[21] As a name, Verdelot has the ring of a pseudonym quite as much as Sandrin. However the composer came

[21] François Lesure, "Un Musicien d'Hippolyte d'Este: Pierre Sandrin," *Collectanea historiae musicae,* II (1956), 245-250. Names like that of the composer in question were not uncommon in musical circles. In 1509 a person connected with the Parisian farce troupe Enfants-sans-Soucy left his mark on the ballade literature in the form of a "chanson nouvelle composée par un condamné à mort nommé Verdelet." See Emile Picot, *Chants historiques français du seizième siècle* (Paris, 1903), pp. 5-6. This is perhaps the "Verdelet" cited as a tune for a noël in *S'ensuivent plusieurs chansons de nouelz nouveaulx* of Lucas le Moigne (Paris, 1520). André Pirro, in his *Histoire de la musique de la fin du XIVᵉ siècle à la fin du XVIᵉ* (Paris, 1940), p. 148, links a fifteenth-century *ménétrier* named Verdelet and cited by Martin Le Franc with "La Verdelete" in the Brussels basse danse manuscript (Bibl. royale, MS. 9085). Edmond Van der Straeten cites a "Jean Torret, dit Verdeloot," *ménestrel* of Bruges in 1534, and a "Gilles de May, dit Verdelot," a member of the household of Charles V, in *La Musique aux Pays-Bas avant le XIXᵉ siècle* (Brussels, 1867-1888), IV, 97; VI, 322. The several instances work together to tie the name in with the region of the Low Countries.

to be called Verdelot, the fact remains that Attaingnant first printed his music by another name, hinting at some special relation between the composer and Paris. If Willaert's itinerary is any indication, the route whch took Verdelot from a probable origin in the Low Countries to Italy, where both composers turned up at about the same time, lay by way of Paris.

Not very many chansons of Verdelot survive, and Einstein cautions against the three printed by Le Roy and Ballard as being somewhat suspect because of their late publication (*Italian Madrigal,* p. 264). The chanson "E dont venez vous Madame Lucette," ascribed to Verdelot in Scotto's *Secondo libro delle canzone franzese* of 1535 should be beyond any suspicion. It is based on a *chanson rustique* also set by Pierre Moulu, by Gascongne, and arranged as an *allemande* in an ensemble collection of Attaingnant.[22] Thus the tune itself is a link with Paris and can be traced there at least as early as 1520, when Lucas le Moigne cited it as a *timbre* for one of his noëls in *S'ensuivent plusieurs chansons de nouelz nouveaulx.* Also to be considered is the very somber "Seule demeure et desporveue," signed "Deslouges," in Attaingnant's *Trente et une chansons* of November 1529. As a composer of Italian secular music, Verdelot first appears in the *Madrigali* of 1530, where his share of eight pieces is by far the largest. His own first book of madrigals, formerly thought to date from 1535, can now be pushed back two years because of the bass part dated 1533 in the Bibliothèque G. Thibault, giving the composer even stronger claim to precedence in the domain of the madrigal. Of the masters of the chanson, Janequin and Claudin, who slip into Dorico's *Madrigali* alongside his own pieces, Verdelot was quite cognizant. He paid

---

[22] Moulu's setting is found in *La Couronne et fleur des chansons a trois* (1536), fol. 11ᵛ. The connection of this composer with the French court around 1517 is established by his motet "Mater floreat," in the Medici Codex, as Lowinsky has shown ("Medici Codex," p. 112). Gascongne's setting succeeds that of Verdelot in the *Secondo libro delle canzoni francese;* François Lesure, in his article "Gascongne," *MGG,* IV, 1404, claims the piece for Mathieu Gascongne, whose motets connected with Francis I place him likewise in the circle of the French court. The three masters treat the tune in a similar imitative style, and each differently. In "Et d'ou venez vous madame Lucette. Almande VIII," from Attaingnant's *Troisieme livre de danceries* (1530), fol. 20ᵛ, the same tune, in the soprano, is treated homophonically, and this version probably gives us the best idea of what the learned composers took as their point of departure. Lassus later set the same text, without recourse to the common tune; see his *Sämtliche Werke,* ed. F. X. Haberl and A. Sandberger (Leipzig, 1894–1953), XIV, 68.

Janequin the compliment of adding a skillful fifth voice to "La Bataille"; concerning his relation to Claudin more will be said below.

Costanzo Festa. Costanzo Festa's early life has taken on a completely new aspect in the light of recent research. It has long been known that he entered the papal chapel in November 1517, to remain until his death in 1545. That he was a Piedmontese—papal documents refer to him as a priest from the diocese of Turin—is also common knowledge, although this fact has never been pursued as to its ramifications. Being a native of the mountainous border province between France and Italy, Festa was born a subject of the house of Savoy, whose territories, falling on both sides of the Alps, stretched from the Sâone River, north of Lyons, all the way to Nice, on the Mediterranean. Even Geneva, which was theoretically a free bishopric, came under increasing Savoyard domination, and a good indication of this was the sumptuous entrée accorded to Margaret of Austria there in 1501 as wife of Duke Philibert. With the death of Philibert in 1504, Margaret returned to the Low Countries, but the ducal chapel continued to be dominated by northerners, and a list of singers serving Duke Charles II at Turin in 1526 reveals no Italians, only Flemings and Frenchmen. Turin was a stopping place along the route during the comings and goings of Charles VIII, Louis XII, and Francis I into Italy, and it is probably in this light that the Stribaldi manuscript of French *basses danses,* dated December 26, 1517, in the Archives of Turin, should be viewed.[23] Costanzo Festa's origins in Savoy territory point to a family relationship with the other Festa, Sebastiano, for as Lowinsky has shown, the latter can also be traced there, having served in 1520 the bishop of Mondovì, a town in southern Piedmont. Mention of this town calls to mind another early madrigalist, Eustachius, Gallus, de Monte Regali.

The earliest traces of Costanzo's activity situate him as music tutor to some children sometime between 1510 and 1517, located on, of all places, the island of Ischia. This fact must be reconciled with his four motets in the Medici Codex, his lament for the death of Anne of Brittany in 1514, and another motet which Lowinsky has ingeniously linked with the death of Louis XII the following year. We quote Lowinsky's conclusions directly: "A little island remote from the mainstream of music is not the nursery of a composer of Festa's

[23] Transcribed by P. Meyer, "Rôle de chansons à danser du XVIe siècle," *Romania,* XXIII (1894), 156–160.

stature; Paris is. Festa may very well have been in Ischia in 1509 or 1510; he may have stayed there for a year or two. Then he may have left for Paris. The presence of the greatest composers of the age, Josquin, Mouton, and others in France must have exercised a magnetic attraction on the young composer" ("Medici Codex," p. 96). He goes on to suggest that it was Mouton from whom Festa learned his contrapuntal mastery, mentioning particular passages to support this view. Mouton would have been in a good position to secure a Vatican post for a pupil. Leo X is known to have had a predilection for Mouton's art, and the master wrote his "Christus vincet, Christus regnat" especially for the pope. When Francis I met Leo at Bologna in December 1515, the royal and papal chapels vied with each other in San Petronio, and unless some exceptional circumstance such as illness intervened, it can be assumed that the pope heard Mouton sing on this occasion.

Festa's French connections do not leave many obvious souvenirs in his secular output, unlike the case of Willaert. His "Amor che mi consigli," printed in the *Libro II de la Croce* of 1531, Einstein wished to read as a double canon, and thus establish a relationship with the double-canon chansons of 1520 (*Italian Madrigal,* p. 143). It is not a double canon, but be that as it may, the model for such duos is not Italian, and it is symptomatic that the same collection should revive the anonymous duo "Je le lerray puisqu'il me bat." In the 1541 volume of Jean Ghero entirely devoted to duos, "Amor che mi consigli" reappears without Festa's name; but another piece in the collection offers an arrangement *a* 2 of a great favorite among chansons, "Amy souffrez que je vous aime," and it is signed "Costantio Festa." In preferring a texture of three melodious voices for his madrigals, Festa turned his back on the frottola with its animated yet sham four-voiced writing, which Einstein amusingly calls "a bag filled with straw" (p. 114). If Festa was following French models here, they were not so much Févin's three-part chanson on a cantus prius factus, beloved of Willaert, but the rhythmically smoother and less complex style of a younger Frenchman, Claudin de Sermisy, who also cultivated three-part writing in the 1520's. But before turning to Claudin it will be opportune to mention two colleagues of Festa in papal service.

Jacques Arcadelt was admitted to the Julian Chapel in January 1539. As a master of both the madrigal and the chanson he offers in himself abundant material for a comparative study. Einstein points out (*Italian Madrigal,* p. 267) one case of a piece doubling as both— "I vaghi fiori" in Italy, which is "Quand je me trouve" in France. But Arcadelt did not participate in the mainstream of madrigal or chanson until after 1535. He offers less of interest to our immediate subject than does a comparatively minor figure, Jean Conseil. Born in Paris in 1498, and a choirboy in the Sainte Chapelle in 1509, the same time that Claudin was there, Conseil was sent to Leo X in 1513 or 1514, receiving instruction thenceforth from Elzéar Genet.[24] He remained at the Vatican after the accession of the second Medici pope, Clement VII, who sent him to France in 1526 and again in the latter part of 1528 to procure singers. Returning to Rome early in 1529 with Vermond, Yvo Barry, and Philippe de Fontaine, all of the Sainte Chapelle, could Conseil have failed to notice that his native city now had its own music printer? Already off Attaingnant's presses by the end of Conseil's visit were the two chansonniers of 1528 devoted to Claudin and Janequin respectively, and in all probability the printer's imitation of Antico's *Motetti novi* as well.[25] Another trip to secure singers took Conseil to Cambrai in 1531. By an act of September 7, 1534, we learn that he was "Maestro di cappella secreta di N.S."; his requiem was sung in Rome on January 11, 1535. Conseil's participation in the chanson is known—his style is homophonic, "Parisian," and like so many of Attaingnant's composers, resembles Claudin in everything except genius. In January 1529, near the time of his departure from Paris, Attaingnant placed one of Conseil's pieces in *Trente et quatre chansons,* to be followed by four more in the course of 1530 and one more in 1532. He is also represented in the 1534–35 series of motet volumes. A madrigal is attributed to him posthumously in Gardano's book of five-part madrigals of 1541, which Einstein says (p. 262) the publisher had a difficult time filling, and for this reason resorted to Conseil and other Frenchmen. Yet Conseil vied with Festa in setting a text of Michelangelo; both settings are lost, unfortunately. Michelangelo wrote to Sebastiano del Piombo: "I have received the two madrigals and Giovan Francesco

[24] Geneviève Thibault summarizes recent discoveries about the composer in her article "Conseil," *MGG,* II, 1634–35.

[25] See Daniel Heartz, "A New Attaingnant Book and the Beginnings of French Music Printing," *JAMS,* XIV (1961), 9–23.

[Jean Conseil] has had them sung several times." [26] Paris and Rome were closely linked through the person of Jean Conseil. A musician in immediate contact with the first madrigalists, he was not only in touch with the latest style of chanson, but wrote them himself.

Claudin. Claudin de Sermisy entered the Sainte Chapelle as a youth in 1508, passing subsequently to the Chapelle Royale, where he served beside Mouton until Mouton's death in 1522. He became *sous-maître* in his own turn before 1532. What Claudin owes to the older master is most clearly apparent in Mouton's "De tous regretz," a piece whose shorter and more polyphonic middle phrases—the second of which modulates—are framed by a more homophonic main phrase. Lacking only is Claudin's terseness and greater vocality. The success of the younger master with the public is apparent from Attaingnant's first chansonnier of April 1528, devoted overwhelmingly to him. It was Claudin who dominated the collections in 1529 and 1530, and whose chansons prevail in the lute and keyboard books of 1529 and 1531, almost to the exclusion of anyone else. In one piece printed by Attaingnant in 1530, "Allez souspirs" (Example 35), Claudin set a French paraphrase of the first four lines of Petrarch's sonnet "Ite calde sospiri":

> Allez souspirs enflammez au froit cueur
> Tant que la glace de rigueur soit fondue
> Et si priere est au ciel entendue
> Mort ou mercy soit fin a ma douleur.

This chanson is often cited as an example of Claudin's indebtedness to Italian literary art. But can we claim an indebtedness to Italian musical art?

Those well acquainted with Claudin will recognize here many features familiar from their use in hundreds of chansons: agreement of prosody and musical form (an *abba* quatrain uses the same music for first and last lines); repetition of the final phrase; balance of the middle phrases in length (both being shorter than the main phrase) and in their nontonic cadences—in this way musical rhyme supports the verse rhyme; an advanced degree of tonal planning,

---

[26] "Io ho ricevuto i due Madrigali e ser Giovan Francesco [Jean Conseil] gli a fatti cantare piu volte" (in H. W. Frey, "Michelangiolo und die Komponisten seiner Madrigale," *Acta Musicologica*, XXIV, 1952, 147–197).

here expressed in the sequence of cadences—tonic, relative major, dominant, leading to the reprise. Smaller details of style are the syllabic and homophonic beginning, broadening into a slight fioritura before the cadence; the rhetorical pause after the first four syllables, deriving from the typical 4-plus-6 caesura of French decasyllabic verse (here mistakenly applied because it separates the noun "souspirs" from the qualifying word "enflammez"); hints of imitation in the subsidiary phrases, restricted in this piece to the rising fourth in bass and soprano at the beginning of the third line. One little device often used by Claudin that is missing here is the diminution and repetition of the opening motto at the point of reprise. Here described is a formula used so often and so convincingly by Claudin that it can be regarded as his own, although others frequently imitate it, and as we have seen, Mouton provided a model for it. There is no musical Italianism in this piece, unless it be admitted that, in a general sense, all Claudin chansons owe something to Italy in their concision, their syllabic writing, or their approach to textual-musical form. But the composer did not change his style when he came to use verses of the poet of Madonna Laura, if indeed he realized at all that the text was by Petrarch. There lies an interesting problem in itself, because 1530 is some years before the first French translations of Petrarchan sonnets, according to literary historians.[27] Who provided Claudin with this text? Bear in mind that no composer was closer to the immediate circle around the king and his brilliant literary sister, Marguerite de Navarre; this is apparent from Claudin's frequent collaborations with Clément Marot, who was both servant and intimate of the royal pair, and his settings of lyrics by the king himself. Petrarch was already a cult at the French court, so much so that Francis in 1533 ordered a tomb to commemorate the burial place of Laura in Provence; Saint-Gelais celebrated the occasion in verse.

As the leading composer at the French court, Claudin would quite naturally be a choice to represent the king abroad. It is hardly surprising to learn that he traveled to the little outpost of France that the king's sister-in-law had created at Ferrara. Renée de France made a point of retaining her native tongue and habits. At a banquet in Belfiore palace on May 20, 1529, the guests, among whom Isabella d'Este figured, were entertained by the singing of chansons by chil-

[27] Henri Weber, *La Création poétique au XVIe siècle en France* (Paris, 1956), p. 234.

dren: "Cantarono quattro putti francesi Canzoni di gorgo sopra modo belle" and by French dances like the *branle* and the *basse danse commune,* played by Renée's pipe and tabor.[28] Claudin's visit to this circle is known from an undated letter which he wrote to the Duke of Ferrara, quoted here after the transcription of Prunières from the original in the Archives at Modena:

My lord, I received a few days ago the letters you were pleased to write me through your *chantre* the Sr. de Milleville, for which I humbly thank you. To explain fully: I retired from your city because of the colic which has tormented me for a long time, and so much that I wasn't able to follow my [planned] route. My lord, it pains me not to have served you better in this business. It is very difficult just now to find good children [singers] in France. I believe their mothers must all be dead. Nonetheless Sr. de Mille-ville has brought back two of them, with the help of the lord Cardinals, as he will tell you. Please hold me excused for not having done my duty to you any better. My lord, I have delivered to Milleville a little motet begin-ning "Este merci," to present to you. I hope you will like it, and with this, my lord, I beg God to keep you in the best of health and to grant you long life. From Paris, the 1st of July.

Your very humble and obedient servant,
Claudin de Sermisy [29]

The year of the composer's sojourn at the Este court, like that of the letter, is unstated. A *terminus ante quem* of 1530 is provided by Milleville's engagement at Ferrara. It is tempting to posit as a *ter-minus post quem* the little group of four Italian pieces printed by Attaingnant in 1533–34, and culminating with Claudin's reharmoni-

---

[28] Christoforo di Messisbugo, *Banchetti compositioni di vivande et apparecchio generale* (Ferrara, 1549), fol. 2.

[29] "Monseigneur, j'ay receu ces jours passez les lettres qu'il vous a pleu m'escrire par votre chantre li s^r de Milleville, dont tres humblement vous remercye. Pour lors m'estoys retiré de vostre ville a raison d'une colicque qui m'a tourmenté long temps et tourmente souvent, par quoy n'ay pu suyvre la route. Monseigneur, il me desplaist que ne vous ay mieulx servy en ceste affaire. Il est fort difficile de trouver bons enfans pour le present en France. Je croy que la mere en est morte. Touttefoys ledit sr. de Milleville en a ramené deux, a l'ayde de Messeigneurs les Cardinaulx, comme il vous dira; s'il vous plaist me tiendrez pour excusé que n'ay mieulx faict mon debvoir envers vous. Monseigneur, j'ay baillé aud. Milleville ung petit motet qui se comence *Este merci,* pour vous presenter. Il vous plaira prendre en grâce et sur ce, Monseigneur, je prie le Createur vous tenir en saincte très bonne, et très longue vie. De Paris, le 1er jour de juillet. / Votre très humble et très obeissant servi-teur / Claudin de Sermisy" (Henry Prunières, *L'Opéra italien en France avant Lulli,* Paris, 1913, p. xv).

zation *a 4* of the three-part madrigal "Altro non e il mio amor." Intended perhaps as a tribute to Festa, the new version becomes an impressive tribute indeed to Claudin's restrained and subtle polyphonic writing, which replaced Festa's rather stiff accompanying parts, in which surprisingly archaic octave leaps occur at the cadences. The royal chapel master was more implicated in Attaingnant's Italian group than attributions, or the lack of them, would lead us to believe. How well Claudin appreciated "O passi sparsi" his parody mass on the same demonstrates. This tune of Sebastian Festa, moreover, with its gently falling minor strains, seems to pervade the tenor which Claudin wrote under Costanzo Festa's "Altro non e." A reunion of the two Festas by their Parisian colleague? The idea, extraordinary to us, would hardly appear so to their age. Finally, the anonymous "Dite di non, amor," although a true madrigal in its diffuse form, unequal line lengths, and concluding pedal in the top voice, is in its turn haunted by the melody of "O passi sparsi," and on this account, as well as for its excellence, suggests Claudin (see Example 36).

Posterity has linked the names of Claudin and Janequin in one of those pairings which too often encourage us to overlook stylistic differences. Some precedent for this appears in Jean Daniel's charming noël, where a whole roster of famous composers, some living, some not, come forth to praise the new-born Child. Last of all, in a stanza by themselves:

> Janequin vint au roolet
> Bien jouant son personnaige
> Claudin monstra son collet
> Autant que nul de son age
> Chascun a si bien joué
> Que Jesus en est loué
> En mainte façon congrue
> Je lui presente ma grue. Noel.

The two masters were the youngest of all mentioned, when Daniel's noëls were published about 1524, and reference is made to Claudin's voice being surpassed by not one "of his age."

Janequin. With Claudin a splendid career was the complement of a rather inward musical speech. Quite the contrary with Janequin, whose chansons, on account of the outward brilliance and show of some, have been more studied than those of any other composer in the period. Largely unencumbered by documents on Janequin the man, scholars have given free reign to their charitable instincts by sending the composer to Italy at different dates and for varying lengths of time. Torrefranca is perhaps the most generous of all when he states that Janequin was in Italy from 1507 to 1515.[30] Recent years have brought to light a few inhibiting facts about Janequin: he was a Poitevin, probably born in Chatelerault; he occupied a series of minor posts in this corner of France and in Bordeaux from 1526 on, for a period of two decades. Was he a court musician at any time before 1528, when Attaingnant devoted a volume to his work? Not unless we invent some happening which gave his career a drastic downward turn, sending him back to the provinces. The composer does appear in Paris about 1548 and there he lived the final decade of his life in poverty. He died in the early part of 1558. The theories of Janequin's Italian sojourn are constructed solely on his battle piece, "La Guerre," and for the present generation of musicological skepticism this constitutes scant evidence. Indeed, François Lesure, by pointing out that only later did "La Guerre" come to be called "La Bataille de Marignan," seems to doubt whether the battle in question is really that of 1515. On the basis of the text there can be no doubt about this, however: mentioned are "le noble roy François," his actual presence at the scene, "la fleur de lis y est en personne," an enemy which talks in Swiss dialect, and finally, victory for the king, which last consideration alone greatly limits the possibilities. Janequin need not have been present at Marignano, however, because all France quickly learned the electrifying news in one way or another. The popular press made a specialty of battles portrayed in gruesome detail, and the one at Marignano did not fail to elicit a pamphlet of this type, *La terrible et merveilleuse bataille qui a esté veue nouvellement en la duché de Milan*.[31] "La Bataille" does not constitute in itself proof of the place or the time of composition. Some scholars, too

[30] F. Torrefranca, *Il segreto del quattrocento* (Milan, 1939), pp. 260 and 346. Note in this connection that Einstein (*Italian Madrigal*, p. 319) donates "occasional stays in Venice" to Mouton, which would seem to indicate that he believed the composer was there whenever the Venetian presses turned out a volume of his music.

[31] Jean-Pierre Seguin, *L'Information en France de Louis XII à Henri II*, Travaux d'Humanisme et Renaissance, 44 (Geneva, 1961), p. 79. Besides this Francis I wrote from the battlefield a famous descriptive letter to his mother, Louise of Savoy, and it was widely circulated, if not printed, as is shown by a paraphrase in the *Journal d'un bourgeois de Paris* (for the year 1515), ed. V. L. Bourrilly (Paris, 1910), pp. 21–23.

cautious to consider it an eyewitness account, assert that it must belong to the period before 1525, the year of the battle of Pavia, which would have overshadowed any celebration of Marignano, they argue. Why not argue the reverse? That precisely after the defeat, truly worthy of *le roi chevalier* in its magnitude, would the idea occur to celebrate his greatest victory. The piece was sung with great effect at court and enjoyed a continuing favor long after Pavia. Noel du Fail, in his *Contes d'Eutrapel* (1585), testifies to this: "Quant l'on chantait la chanson de la guerre faite par Janequin devant ce grand François, pour la victoire qu'il avait eue sur les Suisses, il n'y avait celui qui ne regardast si son espee tenoit au fourreau et qui ne se haussast sur les orteils pour se rendre plus bragard et de la riche taille."

Another musical souvenir of Marignano was recorded by a composer who was in fact a member of the royal entourage in 1515: Mouton celebrated the event in the style of his generation, composing the Latin motet that is preserved for us in the Medici Codex.

Janequin's enigmatic relation with Italy resides less in "La Bataille" than in a shorter and more old-fashioned piece, "Or sus vous dormez trop," or "L'Alouette," printed by Attaingnant as a four-part piece along with "La Guerre," "Le Chant des oiseaux," and others in *Chansons de maistre Clement Janequin* of 1528. An "Or sus" minus the countertenor but otherwise nearly identical was printed anonymously in *Chansons à troys,* the volume of Antico brought out in Venice in 1520—eight years before the Parisian print. The text derives from a virelai dating back a century or more.[32] Its first lines are:

> Or sus vous dormez trop, Madame joliete.
> Il est jour, levez vous, Escoutez l'allouette.

For these lines the two outer voices imitate a tenor melody indistinguishable in character from numerous other chansons rustiques in

[32] Modern edition in Willi Apel, *French Secular Music of the Late Fourteenth Century* (Cambridge, Mass., 1950), no. 70. For an up-to-date concordance see Gilbert Reaney, "The MS. Paris Bibliothèque Nationale, Fonds Italien 568," *Musica Disciplina,* XIV (1960), no. 181. Sebastiano Festa uses the same tenor as Janequin in his "L'ultimo dì di Mazo un bel mattino," found in Florence, Bibl. Cons., MS. B 2440, and printed in *Libro I. De la Croce* (Rome, 1526); it is transcribed by Torrefranca, *Il segreto,* pp. 486ff. As might be expected, Torrefranca uses the Festa piece as an argument to support his contention that Janequin's program style was learned in Italy, from Italian models. Before him the same argument had been advanced by G. Cesari, *Istituzione e monumenti dell' arte musicale italiana,* II (Milan, 1932), xxx–xxxi. The model, it appears now, was much older than either Janequin or Festa, and was French.

the collection. In this sense is the piece "old-fashioned"; there is no musical relation to the old virelai, however. With the injunction "listen to the lark," the imitative texture gives way and the bird speaks. A series of melodic ostinati in rapid declamation gradually engulf all the parts. "Il est jour, il est jour, il est jour," sings one voice over and over in triple figures which run counter to the duple tactus. "Ferelire ly ti ty pi ti re ly" and "Coqu, coqu, coqu," sings another. Some of the melodic motives of the bird music are the same as in the old virelai. But they are worked out at a length and with an ingenuity which make this piece a genuine example, the first, of the program style for which Janequin was to become famous. The *chaces, caccie,* and descriptive bird pieces of an earlier day produced a belated and worthy offspring! If Janequin's contribution to "Or sus" was no more than an added countertenor, then we are forced to invent, after the manner of the art historian, a "master of 1520" who was responsible for the revival.

The question is complicated further by two manuscript sources. One is St. Gall, Stiftsbibliothek, MS. 463, an extensive compilation written by Aegidius Tschudi, who was a pupil of Glarean and accompanied him to Paris in 1517.[33] As a source for Parisian music before and around 1520, the manuscript of this Swiss musician rivals in importance the Medici Codex and Bologna Q 19. Tschudi's copy of "Or sus" survives only as a superius, part of his book being lost. This anonymous superius agrees in details with the 1520 printing of Antico, including the use of a mezzosoprano clef instead of the soprano clef found in the 1528 Paris version. In the Medicean manuscript (Florence, Bibl. Naz., MS. Magl. XIX, 117) a choirbook whose repertory is anterior to 1528 and includes such composers as L'Ayolle, Lafage, and Mouton, "Or sus" appears as an anonymous three-part piece lacking the 1528 countertenor, but otherwise agreeing in detail with the Paris version. Thus this Florentine copy stems not from Antico but from another source closer to the Paris circle. Assuming that the piece is by Janequin, Antico's 1520 version does not prove that the composer was in Venice; it does tend to show that, from an early date, that is, before 1520, Janequin had connections with Paris, whence came the main body of Antico's *Chansons à troys* and double-canon chansons. The two manuscript versions corroborate this be-

[33] Clement Miller, "The *Dodecachordon:* Its Origins and Influence on Renaissance Musical Thought," *Musica Disciplina,* XV (1961), 155–156.

cause each stands close to Parisian sources, although for different reasons. What did Janequin have to do with Paris before 1520? Like his great contemporaries, he must have learned his craft from some master. And unless the provincial archives can furnish additional documents on his formation, all circumstances point to an apprenticeship in the capital. The net which drew together the creators of the new chanson and the madrigal is tightening.

From 1528 on, while serving in distant posts, Janequin kept an unceasing flow of chansons coming to Attaingnant. His life long, he never was in want of texts, it appears. Many that he set are of a consummate obscenity—a taste not at all characteristic of the gentle Claudin—suggesting that the good priest wrote them himself.[34] Janequin was at any rate a more "secular" musician than most, for, if Latin church music still forms the center in the production of Willaert, Verdelot, Festa, and Claudin, Janequin's output includes but one book of motets (lost) and two masses, one a parody on his own "Bataille."

In the two decades following the *Chansons de maistre Clement Janequin* of 1528, we look in vain for any change in style which could be interpreted as an awareness of the madrigal. That Janequin knew the madrigal is apparent from his "Si come il chiaro" of 1540. But like Claudin's "Altro non e," the impression this piece gives is of an amusing pastime, just as Josquin and Compère had amused themselves earlier with writing an occasional frottola. The situation changed by the time Janequin settled in Paris, however. De Rore had made of the madrigal something which commanded more attention than did the species cultivated by the chansonesque and too one-sided Verdelot. Chromaticism began to make inroads in the chansons of Sandrin and the elderly Janequin. But this takes us into a different period. Attaingnant's twenty-second book marked the beginning of a new Italian influence. The year of its appearance, 1547, was also the last in the reign of Francis I. His son and successor, Henry II, played the guitar instead of the rebec; the new queen was Catherine de' Medici.

[34] Cf. François Lesure, *Poets and Musicians of the French Renaissance* (New York, 1955), p. 25.

SOME TRACES OF RECIPROCAL MUSICAL INFLUENCE

By the time the reign of Francis I got under way in 1515, the frottola was nearing the end of its life span. There is no question but that this kind of music was known in certain French circles. To the Marquis of Mantua, residing at the French court in August 1516, Marchetto Cara sent "Quattro libri di canti, frottole, e altre cose nuove" that he had been composing, according to Einstein (*Italian Madrigal,* p. 52). Doubtless the husband of Isabella d'Este was eager to show his French overlords what "his" composer could do. André Pirro first pointed out the mention of a particular frottola by Marguerite de Navarre in *nouvelle* 19 of the *Heptaméron* (1558), Michele Pesenti's "Che fara la che dira la," which had been printed in Petrucci's eleventh book and is a simple, dancelike piece in triple meter. The case has been cited ever since as an example of the frottola's diffusion in France, but no one seems to have looked at the passage itself, where an interesting comment on the music is to be found. *Nouvelle* 19 concerns a young man at the court of Isabella d'Este who, despairing of the love of the fair Poline, takes religious orders and sings the complaint "Che fara la"; Marguerite translates the whole poem, which begins now:

> Que dira-elle
> Que fera-elle
> Quant me verra de ses oeilz
> Religeux?

Of the music, that is, Pesenti's setting, she says, "Le chant est italien et assez commun, mais j'en ay voulu traduire les motz en francoys le plus pres qu'il m'a esté possible." Given the speaker and the context, "chant assez commun" can best be rendered in English as "rather banal music." Where and how such music influenced the chanson is going to be debated for a long time to come. In attempting to find traces of an Italian influence in Claudin and Janequin, we have heretofore been quite blind to some obvious traces left by the frottola in France. For example, there is a highly curious souvenir of Italy, "Quoando dormy ve" (Example 37), which turns up in Attaingnant's *Trente et six chansons* of 1530, a little piece with a macaronic text, half Italian, half French: [35]

[35] Another Franco-Italian *macaroné* is pointed out by Nanie Bridgman, "Un Manuscrit italien du début du XVIe siècle," *Annales musicologiques,* I (1953), 187.

> Quoando dormy ve come la mya seignore
> Sempre me la voules la couchy couchy qui
> La couchy couchy qui la couchy coucha.

Although the syntax and vocabulary may be a trifle obscure, the point is clear, as is the form—terza rima. Understand for "come" in the first line the Latin "cum," separate the more Italian beginning from the more French conclusion, and we have:

> Quando dormiva con la mia signora
> Sempre me la voulait coucher, coucher, coucher, etc.

The musical garb of the first line has nothing of the chanson about it, being simply a declamation in near monotones, chordally supported below, with the typically frottolistic cadence of two notes on the same pitch for the feminine rhyme "Sei-gnó-re." But the second part, with its rapid patter in ostinato repetition, seems to "talk French," following the suggestion of the text, and we are not so far from Janequin (despite the repeated parallel octaves between alto and bass). Compare Janequin's "Au joly jeu du pousse avant" (Example 38), with its repeated "laissez, laissez, laissez trut avant."

"Quoando dormy ve" is not the sole reminiscence of frottolistic monody to issue from Attaingnant's presses in 1530. Others are to be found in the two ensemble books *Six gaillardes* and *Neuf basses dances*. Before them, in February of 1530, the lute tablature *Dixhuit basses dances* had first brought before the Parisian public in printed form a new dance out of Italy, the pavane, and also the group of characteristically Italian harmonic progressions later to be called the *passamezzo antico, moderno, romanesca,* and so forth. Both ensemble books contain pavanes. The first pavane from *Six gaillardes* (Example 39) will make it clear what kind of music we have to deal with. Repeated notes at the cadences from strong to weak beat, the monotone declamatory character of the second strain, these are things which speak clearly enough for themselves, or rather, they shout. This is an Italian piece, and it would be unmistakable as such even if it were not called in other sources by such names as "Pavana sguizera," "Danza di Bologna," or "Balleto Amor costante." [36] Italian currents are not restricted to the pavanes in the Attaingnant ensemble

---

[36] The titles are found, respectively, in British Museum, Add. MS. 31389, fol. 4; Munich, Bavarian State Library, Mus. MS. 1512, fol. 58ᵛ; and in Fabritio Caroso, *Il ballarino* (Venice, 1581), fol. 27.

books; even the basse danse, long established in France, was affected in a few cases, as may be seen by two pieces in *Neuf basses dances,* called "La gatta en italien," and "La scarpa my faict mal" (Example 40). "La gatta" reveals one of the frottola's favorite rhythmic patterns:

a pattern almost never found in French music, dances or otherwise. Who was this Italian "cat" who set Paris dancing? The answer may be found with the appearance of a similar melodic motive in the quodlibet by Ludovico Fogliano printed in Petrucci's *Frottole Libro VIII;* the text is

> O gatto selvatico
> Quando sara tu
> Domestico?

Another quodlibet, in Bologna Q 21, provides the text and tune of "La scarpa my faict mal":

> La scarpe mi fa mal s'io non la taglio un trat'

alluding to a distress perhaps the result of excessive terpsichorean activity.[37]

What is the source of this Italian current in Paris around 1530? Attaingnant's chansonniers and publications of sacred music rely heavily on the singers in royal service, so that in a very real sense he is a printer of the court. At that same court we find a band of Italian oboists and trombonists whose main function was to play at tournaments, mascarades, banquets, and balls, and whose main repertory must have consisted of dance music. These instrumentalists are the most obvious source for the Italian tunes. To consider the printed ensemble books as a document of the art brought to France by the Italian band would be going entirely too far, however, first because the professional dance musician did not rely on scores, and second because many pieces are provably French in derivation—for example the branles, a type of dance untouched by Italy, the majority of basses danses, and several dances derived from courtly chansons (Claudin here again was the favorite model). Even pavanes could be written on French tunes; one example, the innocuously labeled

[37] For transcriptions of the two quodlibets, see Torrefranca, *Il segreto,* pp. 462 and 504; see also Claudio Gallico, *Un canzoniere musicale del cinquecento: Bologna, Conservatorio di musica G. B. Martini, MS. Q 21* (Florence, 1961).

"Pavane 3" in *Six gaillardes,* turns out to be a setting of the risqué "Au joly bois" (see Example 34). It cannot be argued that the instrumental dance preceded the chanson, because the words alone explain the odd phrase structure. The first cadence of descending second from strong to weak beat "m'a—mý—e" can be considered a typically French device—it had been in use a long while in the chanson rustique—to be opposed to the frottola's repeated notes.

There was at the French court another center of Italianism operating in a different and much higher sphere than the Italian band. In the thick of courtly life was a poet and singer who matched and perhaps surpassed Marot in popularity as a purveyor of gallantries, epigrams, mascarades, cartels—in short, whatever was needed at the moment by court and courtier. Mellin de Saint-Gelais, sent to Italy in 1508 as a young man to study law at the University of Bologna, was seduced instead, like another young student of law at Paris, by the enchantments of the Muses. He returned to France after a decade on the peninsula, to become the man of whom Gabrieli Simeoni said, "He understands and speaks the Tuscan language better than anyone else in France," the man who introduced the sonnet into France, according to Du Bellay, who had the *Courtier* translated and published, the translator of Ariosto, Trissino, and Petrarch, the plagiarizer of Bembo, Sannazzaro, and Petrarch. Saint-Gelais wrote in Italian as well as French, and it was he who polished the verses of Francis I, if indeed he did not actually write them, as some believe. The mainspring of his poetic art was not the academic Petrarchism of Bembo, but the school of courtly improvisers, whose theme was "Carpe diem" and whose chief was Serafino dall' Aquila, the leading poet of *strambotti.* Under his influence Mellin became, according to his biographer Molinier, "Le premier des strambotistes français," or, to put it another way, the leading inventor of "poesia per musica." [38] Like Serafino, he put his verses to music, sang them himself to the accompaniment of the lute, and was careful never to publish them, so that they might pass continually for improvisations. In regard to the lute, Pontus de Tyard does not hesitate to put him in a category with Albert de Rippe:

[38] H. J. Molinier, *Mellin de Saint-Gelays (1490?–1558)* (Rodez, 1910). See also Joseph Vianey, "L'Influence italienne chez les précurseurs de la Pléiade," *Bulletin italien* (University of Bordeaux), III (1903), 86–117, and Ph. Auguste Becker, *Melin de Saint-Gelais: Eine kritischer Studie,* Akademie der Wissenschaften in Wien, philos.-hist. Klasse, vol. 200, pt. 4 (1924).

Chante mon leut
Y employant la mieux parlante corde
Que touche Albert
Ou que Saint-Gelais sonne.

What his verses owe in form and content to Italian poetry, their musical setting often owes to Italian music. As an example of this the "Complainte amoureuse pour dire au luth en chant italien" (Example 41) may serve. The verse was printed in the *Saingelais* brought out at Lyons in 1547 without the author's consent, and is a *capitolo* consisting of eleven stanzas in terza rima, of which the first is:

Helas mon Dieu y'a-t-il en ce monde
Dueil ou ennuy, dont on ait congnoissance
Qui soit egal a ma doleur profonde.

Two musical settings of the text survive, or rather, one *voix de ville* melody arranged by Adrian le Roy for four voices, and for voice and guitar, because the tune and its accompaniment are the same in both. Perhaps no one will object to crediting the poet himself with this melody; all ten subsequent stanzas were sung to the same tune, which in Le Roy's settings is supported by only four different chords: tonic, dominant, mediant, and its dominant. This is a typical example of Saint-Gelais' verse and of the kind of musical setting it received; many more could be cited but they would only confirm the point that, in this style, Italian patterns ride roughshod over the French language, with results often as appalling as the cadence between lines 1 and 2:

♩. ♩ ♩ ♩♩ ♩
mon - de. Dueil ou en - nuy.

The late and surreptitious publication of Mellin's verses and their subsequent appearance in music books as the mainstay of the strophic voix de ville suggest that this practice was something introduced around the middle of the century. Thus Einstein (*Italian Madrigal,* p. 268) was led to speak of a revival of the frottola in France during the second half of the century. But the whole career of Saint-Gelais argues against this—his youthful years in Italy when the frottola still flourished, his position as a favorite of Francis I, and his reputation built on pseudo-improvisations for the lute. At least one musical piece connected with him survives from the first third of the century. His poem "Si j'aime ou non, je n'en dy rien" (Example 42) is a sixaine of several stanzas, apparently written to order for some particular situation in which a courtly patron found himself. It has a musical setting in Le Roy's book of *Voix de Villes* of 1573, and also in the book of arrangements for voice and guitar of the same pieces (1555). The tune used is a straightforward gaillarde, for which Arbeau included a choreography in his *Orchésographie*. The identical gaillarde tune appears in Attaingnant's books of lute songs, *Très brève et familière introduction* of October 1529, long before Adrian le Roy was heard of. Only an incipit, "Fortune a bien couru sur moi," is printed in the way of a text, but inasmuch as this line commences the last stanza of "Si j'aime ou non," the bond with Saint-Gelais is forged. His verses were indeed sung to strophic dance tunes —and what is more, sung to the lute—in the early years of Francis I. Such pieces give us some idea of what was meant in France by "le chant italien," to use the phrase of Saint-Gelais himself, or as Marguerite de Navarre would have it, "le chant assez commun." It stemmed from the lightest kind of frottola and left its mark on both strophic air and dance—the two can hardly be separated. The frottola was not revived in France around 1550. With its dancelike rhythms, its stereotyped, or improvisatory, declamation patterns, it led a continuous existence at the French court, just as, but slightly transformed, it kept on living in the lighter Italian vocal forms. Its primitive simplicity of melody and harmony throws into bolder relief the subtlety of the true chanson in the hands of a Claudin or a Janequin. From this kind of Italian music the masters of the chanson had little to learn. What the earliest madrigalists learned from them is another question, and unfortunately, one still more difficult of discussion.

Considering again the origins, the similar formation, and the contemporaneous activity of Verdelot and Festa, Claudin and Janequin, it would be surprising not to find numerous points of contact between the nascent madrigal and the new chanson. Both forms can claim the same Franco-Flemish grandparents, and in particular considerable evidence points to Mouton as the mentor of the chief creators. Both forms represent a precarious balance: on the one hand, breaking away from the international Netherlandish art of 1500 in the direction of, if not nationalism, at least a greater sensitivity to the diction and prosody of the particular language and to the qualities of the human voice; on the other hand, coming to terms with the high technique and seriousness of the old international and universal art, reacting thereby to some extent against the too facile attractions of frottolistic monody. In 1530 the madrigal and the chanson are still recognizable as two dialects of the same mother tongue.

Since so much depends on textual form in the style of 1530, the two dialects should approach most nearly wherever the texts have most in common. This would seem to be in the strambotto, whose ottava rima provided the model for the French epigrams of Saint-Gelais and Marot, those of the latter being a particular favorite with composers. But these pieces account for but a small portion of the total musical output on either the French or Italian side, and much more is to be learned from the archetypal French quatrain, the musical product of which is the *ABCA* or reprise chanson. The quatrains of Italian sonnets furnish a close textual parallel; the literary *ballata,* with its *ripresa* after intervening *piedi,* furnishes a looser one. Most instructive, however, are the Italian approximations of the reprise chanson which are not motivated by the prosody. Hans Engel has already pointed out that the early madrigal often assumes some kind of *AB . . . A* form *in spite of* the text, as for example, when ending rhyme and initial rhyme do not agree. He stresses also that the repetition of the final phrase, which became a common feature of the madrigal, must stem from the influence of the chanson composers, who applied the same device even in their motets.[39]

In detailing briefly some of the more obvious resemblances, it will be useful to bear in mind the components of a typical chanson of Claudin, as outlined above in connection with "Allez souspirs." Festa's "Bramo morir" (Example 43a) begins chordally, makes the rhetorical pause after the fourth syllable, and then picks up again with a group of three upbeats—another cliché of the chanson. But here the resemblance of "Bramo morir" to the chanson ceases, because the cadence is quite un-Claudinian, lacking as it does any kind of melismatic extension. With Festa's madrigal is the beginning of Claudin's "Contre raison" (Example 43b), which happens to offer, besides the usual rhythmic figuration for a decasyllabic line of four plus six syllables, parallels in melody and harmony as well. Not very

[39] "Die Entstehung des italienischen Madrigals und die Niederländer," *Kongress-Bericht der I.G.M., Utrecht, 1952* (Amsterdam, 1953), pp. 166–180.

much store should be set by melodic resemblances like this. But harmony and tonality offer a potentially more rewarding field of comparison. For example, Verdelot's madrigals in the major mode show a remarkable preponderance of F, the key which, under the name of "Ionian on F," Edward Lowinsky calls "the French mode par excellence." [40]

What the Festa example lacks in the way of a chansonesque cadence may be easily found elsewhere; we need look no further than the first two pieces of the *Madrigali* of 1530. Festa's "Lieti fior," which opened the collection in the most radiant F major, is quoted in excerpt, with the beginning and final line of the superius, in order to show the florid cadence at the end (Example 44a). The second piece in the *Madrigali*, "Con lacrime sospir," introduced an Italian public to the secular music of Verdelot in print; first and final phrases are quoted in Example 44b. The cadence is similar to Festa in its *fioriture,* and quite similar in its rhythmic pattern:

$$\text{♩.♪♩ ♩.♪♩ ♩ ♩, or } 3 + 3 + 2.$$

This is a rhythmic cliché, usually accompanied harmonically by a progression I IV V I, or variants thereof. It might well be objected that we have here a pan-European cadential figure (although this does not gainsay it as a stylistic property common to chanson and madrigal). And it is true that the figure is older than 1530—the frottola displays it, and so do some chansons of Compère in the *Odhecaton.*[41] Who is to say where it came from?

Disregarding the previous word of caution on the subject of "tune-detecting," we note that the opening motive of "Con lacrime sospir" recurs in two other madrigals of the same collection, "Madonna io mi pensa," by "Carlo," and Verdelot's "Se gli occhi." By coincidence, or perhaps not entirely by coincidence, one of Claudin's chansons chosen for inclusion in the second edition of the *Madrigali,* "Tous mes amis" (Example 45), displays the same melodic figure. The rising-third motive was a favorite of chanson and madrigal alike at this time, a kind of motto which, a few years later, was to launch Arcadelt's "Bianco e dolce cigno" on its songful voyage.

[40] *Tonality and Atonality in Sixteenth-Century Music* (Berkeley and Los Angeles, 1961), p. 27.

[41] Cf. Compère's "Allons ferons barbe," in Helen Hewitt and Isabel Pope, eds., *Harmonice Musices Odhecaton A* (Cambridge, Mass., 1942), no. 26, mm. 15–17 and 46–48.

Claudin's "Tous mes amis" may also serve as an example of his characteristic shortening and repeating the motto at the point of reprise. Verdelot does something quite similar at the reprise in his "Se del mio amor temete" (Example 46), also from the 1530 *Madrigali.*

Moving from these details to the scale of the whole piece, it might be instructive to approach the madrigalists with a measuring rod, so to speak, and compare the dimensions of phrases and sections. Differentiation of phrases by length goes hand in hand with careful tonal planning in Claudin, as we have seen. Example 47 presents a diagram of section lengths in Verdelot's "Madonna qual certezza," from his *Libro primo* of 1533 (transcribed in Einstein, *Italian Madrigal,* no. 16). The text of this piece is unusual in the many short lines and the return to the opening which the music imposes, suggesting the ripresa of a ballata. Verdelot combines three or four lines into a unit— the equivalent of Claudin's line-phrase. Of the four units, the first and last are the same, while the shorter second and third are of comparable length. For these proportions there is no textual explanation. In fact, the shorter musical sections have more text to traverse than the longer. Musical considerations would appear to be uppermost in Verdelot's mind. Can it be a coincidence that the proportions between sections are so chansonesque? (Compare Example 35, by Claudin.)

Our aim has been to suggest some avenues of approach to a comparative study of the chanson and the madrigal. To harry the question of priority and derivation further would be less than prudent. What should be apparent to anyone who will take the trouble to sing, one after another, "Tous mes amis" and "Con lacrime sospir," is the closeness of the chanson and the madrigal in 1530. For a brief moment in history, the leading musicians in Italy and in France were pursuing similar aims, using similar means. Of no other period is it more appropriate to speak of "les goûts réunis."

DISCUSSION

PANELISTS: MR. HERTZMANN, MR. JOHNSON, MR. PALISCA

MR. JOHNSON: Mr. Heartz's paper having posed a confrontation of French and Italian styles, we might now attempt to take a view of the general problem. Mr. Heartz spoke, rather casually, about an international style, and about his unwillingness to talk of separate, nationalistic French and Italian trends, particularly with regard to prosody. What happened in this admittedly transitional period is hard to determine. But if one selects a point before the period and one after it, he sees that from the fifteenth-century attitude, in which a composer sees his text perhaps primarily from the standpoint of its formal structure, a profound change takes place by the time of the mature madrigalists, for whom the content of the text acts along with the form as stimulus—indeed it seems almost in the forefront. This change is not only a musical one, but is connected with changing literary attitudes as well. I wonder whether the analogies between French and Italian developments here suggested cannot be viewed as the result of a cultural foundation common to both nations.

MR. HERTZMANN: I think that in the madrigal it is not a question of interpreting the text, but rather of interpreting individual words and phrases. Could one tell the meaning of a madrigal from its music alone?

MR. JOHNSON: Perhaps not; but it is just this connotative value of the individual word that I am speaking of in the madrigal.

MR. HERTZMANN: Of course that already existed to some extent in the fifteenth century. It is a matter of degree, of importance; word painting became very important for the madrigalists.

MR. JOHNSON: It became almost a new structural procedure, then.

MR. HEARTZ: I did not really offer any general conclusions; it is hard to arrive at generalizations, which in the light of new details are constantly changing. If one goes forward to 1540, Italian influence is stronger; by 1560 it is very strong. In the sixteenth century one sees Italian influence almost everywhere; but it seems to me there is less of it in the Claudin chanson than almost anywhere else— even though that is the place where we have been trying hard to find it.

MR. HERTZMANN: It is probably true that some relationship between chanson and madrigal did exist even at the outset of madrigal composition. But later on things took a different course. Whether the chanson was circulated in Italy by French composers, instrumental players, and others, or whether the circulation was that of printed chansons, may be immaterial. The main point is that there was an intercourse at this time. Having dealt with Willaert, who was part of this process, I find that it is difficult to see him as either a Flemish or an Italian composer, but rather as a combination. You spoke, Mr. Heartz, of Willaert's output as a chanson composer, mentioning his three-voice chansons. I should think that these, although not published early, are early pieces—especially the rustic pieces, containing folk tunes or quasi-folk tunes (but I don't want to get into that matter again). As for Willaert's canonic chansons in Antico's *Motetti novi e chanzoni franciose* of 1520,[42] these double canons of his strike me as rather naïve, in fact best considered as schoolwork or preparatory work, compared with other works in the volume. So I would not consider these as pieces by an accomplished master. It was quite customary for composers to write double canons at this time, and these pieces could be considered as, so to speak, Willaert's "Master's essay." I would put them before the *Verbum bonum*,[43] for example, even though they are published later. The Willaert chansons mentioned above are, then, early; so are the madrigals—the *Musica nova* of 1559 should have been called *Musica antica*.

If I may, I should like to comment on one or two other points. I want to ask about "Or sus, vous dormez trop," which was set early, in a publication of Antico, then by Janequin.[44] Do you assume that Janequin wrote the three-part version?

MR. HEARTZ: I do.

MR. HERTZMANN: This piece has puzzled me for some time. It is based on the text of an anonymous virelai found in Paris, Bibliothèque Nationale, fonds ital. 568, fol. 122[v].[45] There one sees the same approach to onomatopoetic devices as here. Of course the programmatic element is not as extensive as in the fourteenth-century caccia, but there is too much resemblance for the early virelai to be omitted from a discussion of the program chanson. How Janequin got hold of this text, an anonymous virelai of about 1390, is beyond me. If Paris 568 was in Paris, in the royal possession at Janequin's time, his

---

[42] *RISM* 1520[3]. This volume contains nine double canons by Willaert.

[43] Published by Petrucci in 1519 in the *Motetti de la corona, Libro IV* (*RISM* 1519[4]).

[44] The three-voiced version published by Antico is in *RISM* 1520[6]; another version of the piece was printed by Attaingnant around 1528, in the *Chansons de maistre Clement Janequin.*

[45] The virelai "Or sus, vous dormez trop" is printed in Apel, *French Secular Music of the late Fourteenth Century,* no. 70, after this Paris manuscript.

knowledge of this text might perhaps be evidence of a Parisian connection.

With regard to the "classic" chanson, that of the Attaingnant period, I am of the opinion that its composers were much more strongly influenced by ideas about prosody than the madrigalists were. The early Verdelot, Festa, and Willaert madrigals are declaimed well enough, but the liberties taken with matters of prosody are much greater than any chanson composer would dare. The increasing expansiveness of the madrigal as it developed was of course almost diametrically opposed to the prosodic as well as the musical ideals of the chanson.

MR. HEARTZ: In my paper I tried to keep to the period before 1530, not going much beyond that point.

MR. HERTZMANN: Of course. Earlier we broached the subject of organization within the madrigal. The madrigals of the early 1530's are, it seems to me, highly organized, even patterned. There may well be a connection here with the older Févin-Mouton chanson. The developed madrigal departs from this. There is then some question as to whether the early madrigals actually deserve the name of madrigal. In some respects they are neither fish nor flesh.

MR. HEARTZ: One might perhaps call them chanson-madrigals.

MR. HERTZMANN: At this period there are, on the other hand, a number of chansons with some madrigalistic leanings. Things are not definitely set as yet. By the period of Ronsard there is of course no longer a bridge between the two. But earlier there was no such thing as "the" madrigal; composers simply used techniques really belonging to the Mouton school. Perhaps here more credit should be given to Josquin. Mouton as a musical personality is not as clear to me as Josquin is; I wonder whether Mouton could not be considered as the bearer, the teacher, of a tradition actually created by Josquin.

MR. PALISCA: If possible I should like here to try to restore the balance in favor of Italy by throwing in one or two counterweights to Mr. Heartz's admirably learned and eloquent paper. One concerns the lack of tangible evidence for Italian influence on the chanson. It is difficult to speak of the influence of one genre on another; the force of tradition on a composer's mind is not always appreciated. A composer about to write a chanson had in mind the tradition of the chanson and was not likely to borrow formal ideas, indeed any obvious traits, from, say, the frottola or the incipient madrigal. If there were influences they were likely to be of a more subtle kind. There may not have been, in the early stages, "a" madrigal tradition; but there was one for the chanson, one which almost forced composers to work from it. Among the subtle changes one might look for in the way of Italian influence on the chanson we might list the nature of the harmony used; the interpolation of sections in triple meter in the midst of duple pieces; declamatory passages; and, perhaps, traces of an expressive use of text. I shall return to this after adding my second counterweight, which is concerned with tracing Italian musicians, and prints and manuscripts of Italian music, in France.

The evidence seems all in favor of French influence in Italy, because so many French pieces were printed there, so much French music circulated there. But perhaps we underestimate the ability of musicians to pick up and assimilate new styles simply by hearing music. I was surprised to hear, in 1949, an equivalent of progressive jazz in France and Switzerland. Here there was no exchange of prints and manuscripts (there may of course have been recordings). Mr. Heartz did mention Alberto de Ripa,[46] who certainly made the French acquainted with new styles.

To return to my first point: one stylistic aspect in which a subtle influence of Italy on France might be suspected is harmony, the particular kind of homophonic harmony which one finds in the chansons of Claudin and Conseil. Before citing anything of this kind I should like to distinguish between several types of homophonic style. There is the isometric style in which the parts simply go together, leaving a chordal impression. Actually if this is the result of part-writing the bass may have roots, thirds, almost anything. A second type is the fauxbourdon harmony still found in chansons of Josquin; this has nothing to do with Italian styles. A third type—and here I suspect one might find Italian influence—is the style in which one sees almost entirely root-position chords. This is very prevalent first in the frottola, the carnival song, and Italian music in general.

MR. HEARTZ: By "first" do you mean earlier than in France?

MR. PALISCA: Perhaps; it is at any rate very much evident in Italian music. I should like to refer to Mr. Pirrotta's earlier remark that the frottola was often a solo song meant to be accompanied by the lute.

[46] For Alberto de Ripa, a Mantuan lutenist in the service of Francis I, see the bibliography in Gustave Reese, *Music in the Renaissance* (New York, 1954), p. 554n.

Lutenists are not likely to care about a smooth bass line; they are more apt to want to use root chords; so the style often found in French pieces, in which the bass progresses smoothly, forming many sixth chords, and creating dissonances with the other parts, is not very characteristic of the frottola. Many examples could be found; for instance, "Contre raison," [47] which you compared to an early madrigal, has nothing but root chords. This kind of harmony is very characteristic of the frottola, of dance songs in general, and I think it must have crept into the chanson; it would not have violated the tradition of the genre in the way that some of the points you have mentioned would—such as repetition schemes, and so forth.

MR. HERTZMANN: A point on which chanson and madrigal might be compared is the role of the tenor. I think the tenor part always, or nearly always, plays a more important role in the chanson than in any Italian madrigalistic composition. I know that there are some early "madrigals" in which the tenor is important, perhaps the basis of the composition. In these pieces the repeat of the last phrase is, for example, clearer in the tenor than in the discant. But apart from these the tenor in the madrigal plays a minor role. It does seem to me that in the chanson the tenor, whether a cantus prius factus or a tune fabricated by the composer, is made to meet the prosodic specifications of the verse. There are many of Claudin's chansons, for example, where one can see that the tenor is the mainstay of the composition.

MR. HEARTZ: I don't know that I can agree with that. In a chanson of Claudin it is characteristic that the contratenor is as melodic and as well conceived as the tenor; the two inner voices are in many ways equal. I think there are many melodies that, if one simply heard them, would be hard to label as tenor or contratenor.

MME. THIBAULT: The lutenists prove that the superius is the important part. It is always the superius which is for the voice, the lower voices being taken by the lute. In the case of settings of psalms, it is in fact sometimes the tenor which is sung, the other parts being played. But this is quite a different technique; in the chanson it is the superius that is important.

MR. HERTZMANN: I agree, but my point is this: the composer writes the top part as a free melodic flow, whereas the tenor is the constructive element, the matching of the poem's requirements.

[47] See Example 43.

MR. REESE: In a composition in which the superius "takes over," the tenor may lose its significance. If I may for a moment turn to Germany, there is a striking example in Schlick, in the collection which includes "Maria zart." [48] There are two versions of "Maria zart": one is a keyboard version in which the melody is intact and the piece a sort of early example of a chorale prelude; the other is a lute version in which the melody has nothing whatever to do with "Maria zart," which is in the lute accompaniment and can't be heard at all.

MR. HERTZMANN: On the other hand there is the example of the basse danse, where the tenor of some song is used, even though this tenor was the compositional skeleton only of a superius-dominated piece. Although I agree with Mme. Thibault as to the importance of the superius, I do think that composers, even in free compositions of the sixteenth century, sketched out a tenor first, as a kind of basis over which to write the melody. The theorists still tell us that this was the practice.

MME. THIBAULT: But I think the theorists say that in *religious* works the tenor is the first conceived, with the cantilena then written out. As for the basse danse, I don't quite agree. Some early ones, such as "Triste plaisir" and the Fontaine chanson "Sans faire de vous departie," [49] use chanson tenors. But in most later basses danses, the superius is used.

MR. REESE: What you say about the theorists is doubtless correct for most of the repertory. But there are exceptions, such as "La belle se siet au pié de la tour." [50]

MME. THIBAULT: But the tenor there is pre-existent. We are here speaking of original composition, quite another thing.

MR. RUBSAMEN: The problem of influences on the Parisian chanson concerns me very much. In the discussion of the origins of the Claudin style no mention has been made, except in my own paper, of the composers who wrote chansons, about 1500, in a way different

[48] Arnolt Schlick, *Tabulaturen etlicher Lobgesang und Lidlein uff die Orgeln und Lauten* (1512), ed. G. Harms, 2d ed. (Hamburg, 1957). The organ version of "Maria zart" is on pp. 32–33; that for lute is on pp. 50–51.

[49] Two tenors in the Brussels basse danse manuscript (Bibl. royale, MS. 9085), nos. 23 and 31.

[50] "La belle se siet" is in Oxford, Bodleian Library, Canonici Misc. MS. 213, fol. 31; it is printed in Sir J. Stainer, ed., *Dufay and His Contemporaries* (London, 1898), p. 122.

from that of the Netherlanders—the kind of chanson that Helen Hewitt refers to as the "new trend" [51] in the Petrucci publications. It seems to me that the Claudin chanson, except for its structural pattern, the symmetrical patterning of sections, is definitely foreshadowed by the works of Ninot le Petit and Bruhier. There are chansons by these men which if we were to hear without knowing their authors, we would think sounded remarkably like Claudin, in their texture at any rate. If this is admitted, it seems quite logical for Claudin to have worked in the tradition of the chanson rather than from foreign compositions. The point has been made that Claudin did not have very definite connections with Italy; and we can't prove that the frottola had an influence upon him. But the relation between Ninot le Petit and Claudin is so obvious—and the pieces printed in *Canti C* (1504) come long before Claudin—that I then ask, where did the style of Ninot and Bruhier come from? It is not from the Netherlanders, but from some other place. The chanson "Et levez vous" [52] in *Canti C* is in clearly distinct sections; there are purely homophonic parts, with all voices starting and ending phrases nearly simultaneously, and there are of course alternating sections in more imitative counterpoint. There is even a section in triple meter, a feature mentioned earlier by Mr. Palisca. I would maintain that there is a likelihood of Italian influence on Ninot, and that therefore the Italian influence upon Claudin may have been secondhand.

MR. HEARTZ: The similarity you speak of has to do with texture; that is one element, but only one of a number which have to be considered.

MR. RUBSAMEN: But texture is very important; it must not be neglected. Then there is the "Parisian" sound of the opening theme, very like "Allez souspirs" [53] of Claudin, which you showed to us.

MME. THIBAULT: We have been stopping at Ninot and Bruhier, members of a transitional generation. I agree with Mr. Rubsamen that they are very important in the development of a certain style of French chanson. I think, however, that we must go back further. When Mr. Brown spoke of predecessors of the Parisian chanson, I

---

[51] *Odhecaton*, p. 9.

[52] See Example 25. The chanson, which is anonymous in *Canti C,* is attributed to Ninot in Florence, Bibl. Cons., MS. B 2442, p. 23.

[53] See Example 35.

was rather sorry he chose Ockeghem, for I felt that other authors would have been more suitable for demonstrating that precise, "thematic" chanson in which the music follows the words with great exactness. I find much more of this in Busnois, for example, than in Ockeghem. I think that perhaps the ancestors of Ninot and Bruhier are here rather than in Ockeghem. The last part of the Dijon manuscript, for example, containing pieces which are almost all polytextual, or at least on two texts, newly written, and on "popular" themes, has a chanson of Busnois, "Vous marchez du bout du Marionnette," [54] which is very close to Bruhier and Ninot—closer, I would say, than Mouton, because for me Mouton, like Josquin, belongs to the Northerners, in quite another tradition.

MR. RUBSAMEN: There are exceptions; these men wrote some pieces of a lighter, more homorhythmic variety.

MME. THIBAULT: But even in their lighter moments Josquin and Mouton wrote more complicated inner parts. And not only in compositional details, but in spirit as well Josquin and Mouton, even when bowing to the popular style, are Northern polyphonists, whereas a man like Busnois, primarily a writer of chansons, wrote in the light style naturally. In "Vous marchez" only a little melisma at the end of the phrase tells us that the date is 1465 and not later.

MR. RUBSAMEN: Are you speaking of one voice or all of them? And do you refer to homorhythmic patterns?

MME. THIBAULT: I mean the whole complex, which of course is not always homorhythmic; sometimes there is imitation. All of the last group of chansons in the Dijon manuscript are examples. In French music of the fifteenth and early sixteenth centuries there are two very different traditions: one purely polyphonic, aiming toward the North, with Josquin and then later Gombert as representatives. Then there is music based on popular themes—itself "learned" music, but related to popular melodic style. Of this other extreme Bruhier and Ninot are links, men who rather than create something new develop an old tradition, one which leads to the typical Parisian chanson of the 1530's. And this, if I may say so, is really the chanson of Janequin and Passereau rather than that of Claudin, who I maintain has qualities which make him stand apart.

[54] Dijon, Bibl. de la Ville, MS. 517, fol. 182; Trent, Castello del buon consiglio, Cod. 91, fols. 42ᵛ–43. Printed in *DTO* VII, 236.

MR. HEARTZ: Nonetheless it seems to me that the study of Claudin will be most fruitful in offering links with Verdelot and Festa.

MME. THIBAULT: I quite agree with you as to connections with the madrigal. But in trying to answer the question of where the style of Ninot and Bruhier comes from, I should say that it is from Busnois, and if I were to go back further, even from Dufay. We must of course distinguish between the young Dufay—of "La belle se siet au pié de la tour"—and the old Dufay, of "Je vous pri, mon très cher ami," [55] which is of quite another style.

MR. RUBSAMEN: But Dufay was in Italy when he was young.

MME. THIBAULT: Yes; but "La belle se siet" is an old French theme which he took up, and is not Italian at all in style. Dufay's early Italian pieces, such as "Questa fronte signorile" or "Donna gentile" are another matter. But when Dufay in his later years wrote "Je vous pri" in four-voice style he anticipated the trend of which you, Mr. Rubsamen, were speaking. On the other side of the question there are possible French connections with the frottola. Mr. Brown has given us some French pieces rather like the frottola in style, such as "Il est de bonne heure né." [56] I think that not only are there French pieces of the same style as the early frottola, but that this connection goes much further back; in the Montecassino and the Pixérécourt manuscripts there are pieces with both French and Italian texts, and the contact there is quite plain. How these contacts accord with stylistic currents in both national genres remains to be studied in detail. But "Il est de bonne heure né" is at any rate of the same type as the Busnois "Vous marchez au pied," or as the Ninot-Bruhier type, or as certain chanson types of the 1530's, to give a rough picture of the whole.

MR. REESE: It is certainly true that Busnois was enormously influential. Busnois' music rewards investigation; one finds in him, for example, the paired imitation that we think of as characteristic of Josquin, as well as other stylistic features important in the develop-

[55] "Je vous pri" is found in Florence, Bibl. Naz., MS. Magl. XIX, 178, fols. 74ᵛ–75.
[56] An anonymous four-voiced chanson, in Dijon, Bibl. de la Ville, MS. 517, fols. 177ᵛ–178. This, and a four-part chanson of the same name, attributed to Japart. which uses the tenor melody of the Dijon piece, are in Howard M. Brown, *Theatrical Chansons of the Fifteenth and Early Sixteenth Centuries* (Cambridge, Mass., 1963), nos. 25 and 26. For a discussion of "Il est de bonne heure né" see Howard M. Brown, *Music in the French Secular Theater, 1400–1550* (Cambridge, Mass., 1963), pp. 121–122.

ment of the kind of chanson that we have been discussing. The work of Miss Catherine V. Brooks [57] on Busnois deals with many of these things.

MR. BROWN: I agree that Ninot's chanson, as well as that of Mouton, does come from the Busnois type. Mouton's "Resjouissez" typifies this kind of chanson, and perhaps half of Mouton's chansons are of this sort.

MME. THIBAULT: But for Mouton it was occasional, whereas Ninot apparently always wrote in this style; or at least we do not know him for anything else.

MR. RUBSAMEN: One point puzzles me. If the syllabic style of Ninot comes, as some of you say, from Busnois, where does the alternation of sections in duple and triple time come from? I don't find this in the Netherlandish chanson; does one see it in Busnois?

MR. REESE: Yes, in "L'autrier qui passa," [58] for instance. The change is made occasionally even within a single section.

MR. RUBSAMEN: Are the Busnois chansons for solo voice with instruments, or for voices throughout? I speak not so much of performance as of the composer's conception.

MME. THIBAULT: The composer knew that in writing a piece he only gave an outline; with Italian *giustiniane* or *arie veneziane,* for instance, when Lodovico Sforza [59] asked for them to be sent, he asked also for a young boy who knew how to sing them. The singer who performed the top part in a frottola knew the words, certainly; he may have sung the melody in a different way in each stanza, knowing the accompaniment under him; and perhaps there was even more than one accompaniment for the same melody. This music was made for pleasure; and all accounts of its performance contribute to give us the idea that there were many ways of performing it. The same thing is true of the chanson.

MR. REESE: This seems very true to me. I might add that with regard to Busnois, if one drops the question of whether the parts were performed by voices or instruments, the style of the individual parts is very often "vocal," in all parts. There is great variety in Busnois'

[57] "Antoine Busnois as a Composer of Chansons," unpubl. diss., New York University, 1951. See also Miss Brooks's article "Antoine Busnois, Chanson Composer," *JAMS,* VI (1953), 111–135.

[58] In *Canti B,* fol. 12

[59] See E. Motta, "Musica alla corte degli Sforza," *Archivio storico lombardo,* ser. II, vol. iv, no. 14 (1887), pp. 542–543.

·chansons, and many of them do have parts that one would term "instrumental." The same chanson may be found in one source with text only for the upper part, in another with text underlay for two parts; and the text can quite easily be added for the third.

MR. RUBSAMEN: Do you know of any of Busnois' chansons which begin homorhythmically, with syllabic treatment in all the voices? The point is crucial, you see; does this homorhythmic style come from France or from Italy? I know that Mme. Thibault believes it comes from France.

MME. THIBAULT: I can in fact think of at least two examples of Busnois: "Vous marchez" and "Ma plus qu'assez." [60] But this is not to say that France deserves all the credit. I think that there were parallel trends, Italian and French music developing in similar ways. The homorhythmic style, which we identify with "popular" pieces, is really used in very much the same way by both French and Italian musicians. Here there is no question of influence, but rather of simultaneous use of a current way of treating themes and of writing melodies.

MR. PALISCA: With regard to the "popular" style which culminated in the Janequin-Claudin chanson, I think one might speak of a survival of the fittest. At this time society wanted frivolity, and these men could supply the kind of music desired. It is as much as anything a change of taste which accounts for the development; and this change of taste may have been influenced by importations to France of Italian culture. At the same moment in Italy there was a trend toward seriousness and lyricism, a trend in the opposite direction.

MR. PIRROTTA: I should like to say something in payment of the debt owed by Italian music to that of France. Mr. Heartz spoke of influence caused by the French invasion of Italy, and it is true that this meant contact with a new world for the French who entered. But for Italians, at least in the field of music, there was nothing new here, because Italy had nourished itself for a century on French music. Perhaps the fifteenth-century style was partly Flemish, partly German, in a sense international—still, it was mainly French

[60] For "Vous marchez" see above, note 53; "Ma plus qu'assez" is printed in Eugénie Droz, Geneviève Thibault, and Yvonne Rokseth, eds., *Trois chansonniers français du XVᵉ siècle* (Paris, 1927), no. 28.

in origin. All music was basically French, in spite of the fact that in some places there may have been local preferences fostered by local musicians; these were but modifications of a fundamentally French style. As for the trend toward seriousness and an improved musical level in the madrigal, when Italians wished to improve their style they turned to the learned tradition, again essentially a French one. So the madrigal is really French in many aspects, many techniques.

As for the frottola, it was often considered as a minor genre, an opinion supported by sixteenth-century French judgments of it as "très commun," and so on. I am not convinced that this is fair. There are frottole which are poor music; but there are some which while simple are highly refined, of a cultivated simplicity; here the frottola takes advantage, as did Italian music of the fourteenth century, of its very provinciality in order to obtain an individual flavor. In the frottola, taken as a generic term, there is an enormous variety of verse forms and of patterns in the music, greater than in the chanson. This offered musicians of a later time many choices and antecedents, for use in the madrigal or even in the chanson.

Then, I believe that the "economical" repetition of phrases in the frottola had a real meaning, a formal meaning, for Italian composers. Repetition could be subtle, skillful. I have prepared an example of this, a frottola by Marchetto Cara, which I give in its lute version (Example 48), although it appears first in Petrucci's *Frottole Libro V* (1505).[61] The great flexibility in rhythmic patterns within this piece is indicated in my transcription, which changes from measures of 2/2 to 3/2 (often to be taken as 6/4). The skip of a seventh at the beginning may be thought daring, but it fits the exclamation "O bon, egli e bon!" very well. Note particularly the subtle repetition in this piece, a kind of repetition that may have been suggestive to later composers who could apply it to madrigal or to chanson. And of course one finds here root chords, which as Mr. Palisca pointed out are a very strong characteristic.

To sum up my opinion: while the French had nothing to learn from Italians in techniques, they might have learned to value this

[61] The frottola is on folio 5 of Petrucci's fifth book. The intabulation for voice and lute after which Mr. Pirrotta's example is taken appears in the *Tenori e contrabassi intabulati . . . Libro II* of Bossinensis (1511), fol. 23.

simplicity, and to use it, not directly but in a translated form suiting them, in the chanson. The favor which the chanson rustique enjoyed may be in part the result of the French seeing the similar favor which the frottola enjoyed in Italian courts.

MR. HEARTZ: It is certainly possible that the frottola was attractive, in its simplicity and its elegance, to the French court. It might have been more attractive to Claudin, for example, than to Verdelot, who was so close to things Italian that he could hardly imitate. Although I agree also about the continuity of French influence I feel that in the period we are discussing one has for the first time to separate general French influence from the influence of a dialect—what was popular in Paris, or at the court, in the 1520's. We might do better to think of this material as a very special local dialect, when trying to link it with the protomadrigal of the 1520's.

MR. PIRROTTA: Yes; and here the Italian influence may have been strong, since the court went to Italy. Court musicians went there, and Italian musicians came to the French court. Tromboncino, so called because he must have been a wind player (he was the son of Niccolò Piffaro) is an example of an Italian instrumentalist-composer.

MR. BROWN: Perhaps we should have met earlier to decide what we mean by "influence." It may mean what Mr. Heartz pointed out, specific imitation of things such as Italian wind bands; or it may mean subtler things such as what Mr. Pirrotta has just been talking about. We should be careful not to be trapped by merely semantic relations—we may describe one kind of music in terms which also fit another kind without these two being much alike in sound. Chronology can be of help if stuck to; for instance, Mr. Heartz has pointed out that Italian influence in France was strong later, after Attaingnant's twenty-second book. We have perhaps confused a bit the questions of influences at different times—say at 1520, then earlier, at 1500.

MR. LESURE: I should like to take a minute to speak of Janequin. Did I really say, or write, that "La Guerre" was not about Marignano?

MR. HEARTZ: Although I cannot remember just where, I think that you did question the connection with Marignano.[62]

[62] See François Lesure, "Chanson: III. Chanson in der 1. Hälfte des 16. Jahrhunderts," *MGG*, II 1060: ". . . war der grösste Erfolg des 16. Jh. wohl *La Guerre*

MR. LESURE: It is true that when the piece first appeared in print it was called "La Guerre" rather than specifically "The Battle of Marignano." But this is understandable, since some years had elapsed since the battle, and it was no longer such a topical subject.

Here I might touch on another topic raised in this panel: Janequin's early years, and the question of influences on him. There are documents newly discovered tracing him back to 1505 in the region of Bordeaux; he there served two patrons, Lancelot Du Fau, bishop of Luçon, and especially the archbishop of Bordeaux himself, Jean de Foix. Neither of these two personages had any relationship with Italy, however; chances for an early visit of Janequin to Italy do not therefore seem great, since we know more about his activities from, say, 1515.

As for Franco-Italian interconnections, we have found them to be marked in textual relations. I think that as far as the Parisian chanson is concerned, these are more real than any relationships of musical style. Although of course French musicians were not ignorant of what was going on in Italy, I think that in three quarters of the pieces one might examine, if the text were removed, one could still distinguish quite precisely between chanson and madrigal, between French and Italian styles.

MR. PIRROTTA: This proves that if the madrigal sprang from French techniques and styles, still it had individuality, even if this is subtle and difficult to define.

One aspect of relations between the two genres we may never know much about: French and Italian ways of singing, which could be another area for mutual influences and interconnections.

MR. REESE: There is a small footnote to the discussion of Mr. Heartz's paper that I might offer here. We heard something about Costanzo Festa's presence in France, along with the fact that there was very little trace of French influence in his secular music. Festa wrote a mass, a *Missa diversorum tenorum,* which includes several French melodies, such as "Adieu mes amours" and "Si congie pris." The mass is not unknown to scholars such as Jeppesen; but one of my students, who did a thesis on Festa, made a transcription of the whole work and has traced down melodies in addition to those al-

---

oder *La bataille,* die eine alte Tradition mit dem Waffengang von Marignano (1515) verknüpft."

ready identified.[63] This is a mass very much in the Franco-Netherlandish style, so much so that one wonders if Festa did not have a few lessons with Josquin when he was in France.

MR. HEARTZ: I think I suggested that the place to look for Festa's origins is probably Savoy, connected with Marguerite d'Autriche; here is a link which has never been investigated.

MR. REESE. We seem now to have come to the end of our sessions. It would of course be pleasing if we could have arrived at some sort of conclusion, but it might be disappointing as well. We all want to go on thinking about the problems raised; and I suppose there are as many conclusions as there have been participants in this conference—or as many inconclusions! Most of us can agree, however, on a few major points: it does seem obvious that each of these two great countries influenced the other in various ways; that the Franco-Netherlanders influenced the early madrigal, in fact came close in the early period to creating the musical part of it; that the Italians influenced the French at the beginning of the sixteenth century, with regard to texture at any rate. Many of us perhaps already felt this; what we have really gained is some enormously helpful detail, for which we are greatly indebted to our three authors and also to the members of the panels.

[63] The mass to which Mr. Reese refers is in Rome, Vatican Library, Cappella Giulia, Cod. XII, 2. It uses, among other tunes, "L'homme armé," "Adieu mes amours," and "De tous biens plaine." "Si congie pris" is used as the cantus firmus of another Festa work, a five-voiced mass in Wolfenbüttel, Landesbibliothek, Cod. A. Aug. Folio. See Jeppesen, "Costanzo Festa," *MGG,* IV, 98. The thesis referred to is that of Alexander Main, "Costanzo Festa: The Masses and Motets," unpubl. diss., New York University, 1960.

MUSICAL EXAMPLES

INDEX

Example 1

Les desleaulx ont la saison

Johannes Ockeghem

(Droz, Thibault, and Rokseth, *Trois chansonniers,* no. 9)

Les des - le - aulx ___ ont ___ la sai - -

- - son Et des bons nes - sun ne ___

tient ___ comp - - -

te Mais bon droit de ___ trop ___ se

mes — con - — — - — te

De — souf - — frir — si grant des.-

rai - — - — - — - — -

- — - — - — - — son.

Example 2

Mille regretz

Josquin des Prez
(*Werken,* chanson no. 24)

[143]

- - - - ger vo - stre fa - che a-mou - reu -

ger vo - stre fa - che a-mou - reu -

ger

vo - stre fa - che a-mou - reu -

se, Jay

se, vo - stre fa - che a - mou - reu - se, Jay

vo - stre fa - che a - mou - reu - se, Jay

se, vo - stre fa - che a - mou - reu - se, Jay

si grand dueil et pai - ne dou - lou - reu -

si grand dueil et pai - ne dou - lou - reu -

si grand dueil et

si grand dueil et

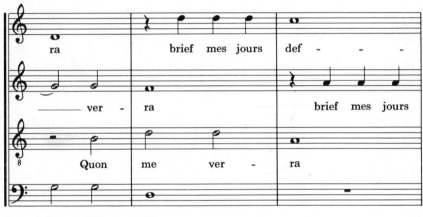

Example 3

Cadences in "Plus nulz regretz"

Josquin des Prez
(*Werken*, chanson no. 29)

Example 4

Beginnings of four monophonic chansons in the Bayeux Manuscript
(pr. in Gérold, *Le Manuscrit de Bayeux*)

Example 5

J'ay veu la beauté

Antoine de Févin
(Cambridge, Magdalene College, MS. Pepys 1760, fol. 65ᵛ)

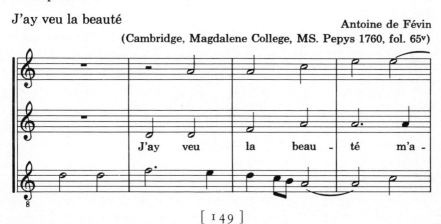

Que j'en fus — — se — le sei - gneur

Et le

so - leil fust cou - ché Et le

jour n'a - iour - nast pas Et je

fus - se_a - vec m'a - my - e Nu à

nu en - tre ces bras, Com - pain que di - ras

tu, ton ar - gent est per - du,

Example 6

En amours n'a sinon que bien

Antoine de Févin
(Brown, *Theatrical Chansons,* no. 17)

Example 7

Il fait bon aimer l'oyselet

Antoine de Févin
(Brown, *Theatrical Chansons,* no. 27)

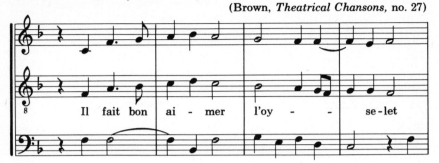

Il fait bon   ai - mer   l'oy -   -   se - let

Qui chan -   te par ———— na - tu -   - re   etc.

Example 8

Resjouissez vous bourgeoises

Jean Mouton
(Florence, Bibl. Naz., MS. Magl. XIX, 117, fol. 45ᵛ)

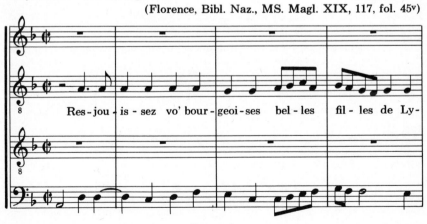

Res - jou - is - sez vo' bour - geoi - ses   bel - les   fil - les de Ly-

qui s'en va en A - vi-gnon,

miè - re c'est la Rho-ne   qui s'en va en A - vi-

L'aut-re cho -se   c'est la Sao-ne

gnon,   L'aut-re cho -se   c'est   la   Sao - ne

qui por - te   le   grand pois - son, ——

qui por - te   le   grand pois-

don - ner aux mar - chans, quant au four - nir vien -

C'est pour don - ner aux mar-chans, quant au

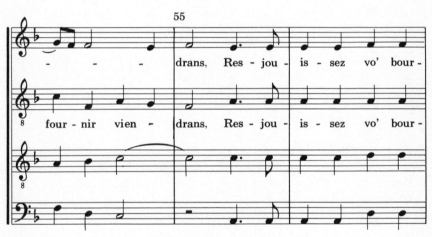

55

- - - drans, Res - jou - is - sez vo' bour-

four - nir vien - drans, Res - jou - is - sez vo' bour-

geoi - ses bel - les fil - les de Ly - on.

geoi - ses bel - les fil - les de Ly - on.

Example 9

Adieu soulas

Antoine de Févin
(Cambridge, Magdalene College, MS. Pepys 1760, fol. 63ᵛ)

Example 10

Si j'ay pour vous

Claudin de Sermisy
(Attaingnant, *Trente et sept chansons*, 1529, fol. 5ᵛ)

Example 11

J'attens secours

Claudin de Sermisy

(Attaingnant, *Trente et sept chansons*, 1529, fol. 12ᵛ)

Example 12

Summaries of some chansons in Attaingnant, *Chansons nouvelles* **(1528)**

3. *Dont vient cela*
Musical form	A	A	B	A			
Rhyme scheme	a	b	a	b	b	c	c
Cadences	F	d	F	d	F	F	d

4. *Vivray-je tousjours en soucy*
Musical form	A		A		B			B′		
Rhyme scheme	a	b	a	b	c	c	d	c	c	d
Cadences	C	F	C	F			d			F

5. *Jouyssance vous donneray*
Musical Form	A	B	C		B	
Rhyme scheme	a	a	b	a	a	b
Cadences		B♭	g		B♭	g

8. *Le content est riche*
Musical form	A		A		B		A	
Rhyme scheme	a	b	a	b	b	c	b	c
Cadences	d	g	d	g	(B♭)	d		g

10. *Quand chanteras*
Musical form	A		A		B	C	
Rhyme scheme	a	b	a	b	b	c	c
Cadences		F		F	d		F

14. *Mon cueur en souvent bien marry*
Musical form	A		A		B		C	
Rhyme scheme	a	b	a	b	c	c	d	d
Cadences		F		F		F		F

1. *Secourez moy madame par amours*
Musical form	A	B	C	A	B	C	D	B	C	E	C
Rhyme scheme	a		b	a		b	b		c	c	
Cadences		F	d		F	d		F	d		d

Example 13

Some superius parts from Attaingnant, *Chansons nouvelles* **(1528)**

9. *De resjouyr*

De res - jou - yr mon pau - vre cueur

Veu sa dou - leur

— qui est si ter - ri - - - ble, Hé - las ma -

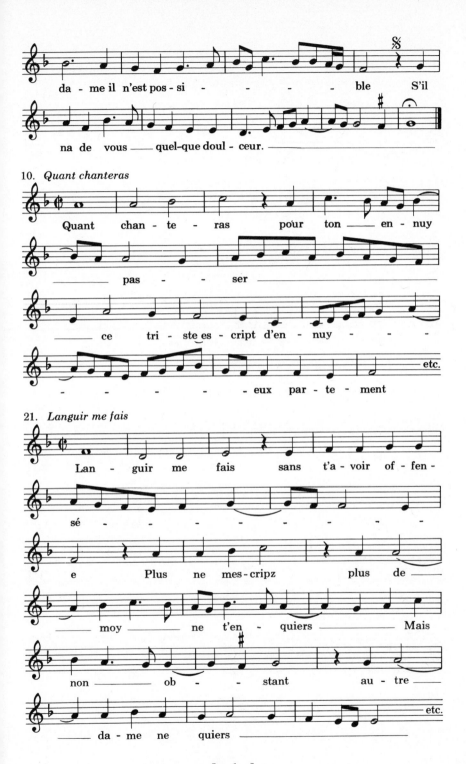

10. *Quant chanteras*

21. *Languir me fais*

Example 14

Some superius parts from Attaingnant, *Chansons nouvelles* (1528)

2. *Tant que vivray*

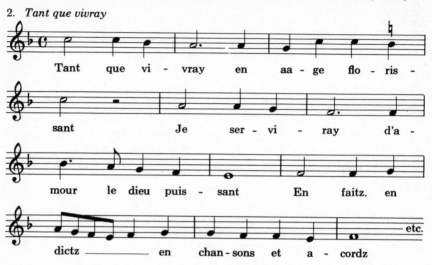

Tant que vi - vray en aa - ge flo - ris -
sant Je ser - vi - ray d'a -
mour le dieu puis - sant En faitz, en
dictz _____ en chan - sons et a - cordz

etc.

3. *Dont vient cela*

Dont vient ce - la bel - le je vo' sup -
jours se - ray de tris - tes - se rem -

- ply _____ que plus à moy ne vo' re -
- ply _____ Jus - ques à tant que au moy le

1.

com - - - man - dez. Tous
me _____ man -

2.

dez, Je croy que plus da - my ne
de - - - - man - dez

etc.

4. *Vivray-je tousjours en soucy*

Vi - vray je tous - jours en sou - - cy Pour vous ma très loy - al - le a - my - e Si vous n'a - vez de moy mer - - - cy Je lan - gui - ray tou - te ma vi - - e Vo - stre beau - té m'a ar - res - té pour ⸺ son ser - vant

Example 15

Changeons propos

Claudin de Sermisy

(Attaingnant, *Trente et sept chansons*, 1529, fol. 12)

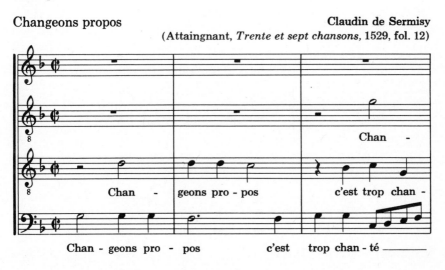

Chan - geons pro - pos c'est trop chan - té

Chan - geons pro - pos c'est trop chan - té ⸺

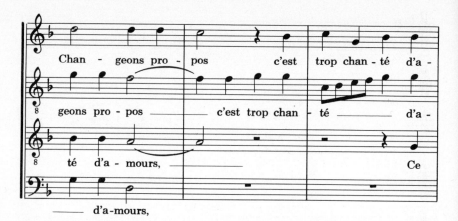

Example 16
Merce te chiamo

Text by Leonardo Giustiniani

Anon.

(Bologna, Bibl. Univ., MS. 2216, pp. 54-55; ca. 1430)

moro, e sol per trop - - po a-

ma - - re. Oy - me che mo-

ro, e non my voy ve - de - re.

Oy - me che mo - ro,

an - cho - ra non my voy par - la -

- - - - - re.

Example 17

Perla mia cara

Text by Leonardo Giustiniani

Anon.

(Paris, Bibl. Nat., Chansonnier Cordiforme, fol. 11ᵛ-12)

che dir non ———— say; So - la re -

gi - na del mio cor, re - gi - na del mio —— core.

Tu sey, madona, la mente mya,
Car e le gran tempo dolce per la mya bella
Per te languisco he languiroye.

Io sono ung servo tho servitore,
Ne tu sey, madona, daltro myo parere
De altro grando regno et grando seignore.[1]

[1]This text is a corrupt version of lines 1-6 and 64-66 of the poem printed as no. xiv in *Poesie edite ed inedite di Lionardo Guistiniani, ed.* B. Wiese, Scelta di curiosità letterarie inedite o rare, disp. 193 (Bologna, 1883).

Example 18

Chon tutta gentileça

Antoine Busnois

(Florence, Bibl. Naz., MS. Magl. **XIX**, 59, fols. 52ᵛ-53, anon.; Paris, Bibl. Nat., MS. fonds fr. 15123, fols. 13ᵛ-14)

*From here through m. 22 the bass notes missing in Florence are supplied from Paris.

Col bel viso giocondo
et gli ochi vaghi et begli,
Isguardando con quegli
a guisa di due stelle,
Colle sue luce belle, piene d'amore.

(Chon tutta . . . Paris manuscript only)

Example 19

La nocte è curta

Text by Marchesini Stanghe[1]

Anon.
(Paris, Bibl. Nat., Dépt. Mus.,
Rés. MS. Vm.[7] 676, no. 105)

*The rest is lacking in the manuscript.

El giorno è breve a Chi non ha Tempesta;
Il sol è chiaro a Chi lo mira in facia;

La fede e la speranza è manifesta
a Chi ad aspectare non segui Tracia;

la morte è morte oh fin d'ogne grameza;
la vita è vita oh fin d'ogne Tristeza.

¹Rome, Vatican Library, MS. Urb. 729, fol. 13ᵛ. Published by G. Zannoni, "Gli strambotti inediti del Cod. Vat. Urb. 729," *Rendiconti della R. Accademia dei Lincei,* Classe di scienze morali, storiche e filologiche, ser. V, vol. i, (Rome, 1892), p. 632.

Example 20

Iti, suspiri, la dove amore

Text by Serafino Aquilano[1]

Anon.
(Paris, Bibl. Nat., Dépt. Mus.,
Rés. MS. Vm.7 676, fols. 74v-75)

che per le - i la mia vi - ta, la mia vi - ta, la mia vi - ta ha tol - - - to.

*In the manuscript as

Ch'ogni dolzeza me ha di dolori piena
per suo dipartire in pianto e volta.

Ma prima serà il mar senza aqua o rena
Che del mio core lei sia privata e sciolta;

Che spero ancor per lei soffrire gran guerra
Fin che ogne membro sia converso in terra.

[1]*Opere dello elegantissimo poeta Seraphino Aquilano . . . (Florence, 1516), fol. 178ᵛ; "Seraphini," in Rome, Vatican Library. MS. Urb. 729, fol. 56.

Example 21

De che te pasci, Amore

Johannes Ghiselin
(Rome, Bibl. Casanatense, MS. 2856, fols. 138v-139)

*Longa in the manuscript

Example 22

Una donna l'altrier fixo mirai

Text by Lorenzo Strozzi

Bernardo Pisano

(Florence, Bibl. Cons., MS. B 2440, pp. 100-103)

- - re den - tro a — suo' ra - -

- - - - - - - i, — den-

- tro a — suo' ra - - - j.

[Una donna l'altrier fixo miraj . . .]

2. Ne lingua exprimerebbe
   Una belleça tale,
   Ne intender la potrebbe
   Intellecto mortale;
   Che allei, donna, equale
   Non fu vista da noj;
   O ciel, sol dir ne puoi, che fatta l'haj.

3. Quanto è ciascun felice
   Che nato è in questo etate,
   In la qual' veder lice
   Una immensa beltate.
   O voi che in cielo state,
   Tal ben non ci togliete
   Che'l mondo lassarete in pianto he in guaj.

[Una donna l'altrier fixo miraj . . .]   [Una donna l'altrier fixo miraj . . .]

Example 23

Questo mostrarsi lieta a tutte l'hore

Text by Lorenzo Strozzi

Bartholomaeus Florentinus Organista
(Florence, Bibl. Cons., MS. B 2440, pp. 26-29)

sol non ba - sta

a chi ar - de et mo - - - -

re. a chi ar - de et mo - - re.[1]

[1]The text of three additional strophes appears in the manuscript.

Example 24

Forestieri a la ventura

Anon.

(Petrucci, *Frottole Libro VI*, 1505, fol. 44)

gran me - su - ra   Gior - no e   no - te hor al - to hor

ge - gno e gran me - su - ra Gior - no e   no - te hor al-to hor

ge - gno e gran me - su - ra Gior - no e   no - te hor al - to hor

gran me - su - ra   Gior - no e   no - te hor al-to hor

bas - so,   Ch'o-gni cor af - flic - to e las - so

bas - so,   Ch'o-gni cor af - flic - to e las - so

bas - so,   Ch'o-gni cor af - flic - to e las - so

bas - so,   Ch'o-gni cor af - flic - to e las - so

Le - va - rem d'o - gni al - tra   cu - ra.[1]

Le - va - rem d'o - gni al - tra   cu - ra.]

Le - va - rem d'o - gni al - tra   cu - ra.]

Le - va - rem d'o - gni al - tra   cu - ra.]

[D.C.]

*The single note value in Petrucci has been divided

[1]Three further strophes are printed by Federico Ghisi in *I canti carnascialeschi nelle fonti musicali del XV e XVI secolo* (Florence, 1937), p. 131.

Example 25

Et levez vous hau, Guillemette

Ninot le Petit

(Florence, Bibl. Cons., MS. B 2442, discant p. 23;
Petrucci, *Canti C*, 1504, fols. 81ᵛ-83)

Example 26

Tous les regretz

Antoine Brumel
(Florence, Bibl. Cons., MS. B 2442, discant pp. 130-131;
Brussels, Bibl. Royale, MS. 11239, fols. 8ᵛ-9)

[205]

Example 27

D'un bel matin d'amore

Ioannes B. Zesso
(Petrucci, *Frottole Libro VII*, 1507, fol. 27ᵛ)

mor che me — le - va - va. — Me - tì la sel - la al

mor — che me le - va - va, — Me - tì la sel - la al

mor che me le - va - va, Me - tì la sel - la al

mor che me le - va - va. — Me - tì la sel - la al

vos - tro bon — ron - zin, e do' fu la

vos - tro bon ron - zin, e do' fu la

vos - tro bon ron - zin, e do' fu la

vos - tro bon ron - zin, e do' fu la

Gran zo - gli-a tra - di - to - ra, Me -

Gran - *de* zo - glia tra - di - to - ra, Me -

Gran - *de* zo - glia tra - di - to - ra, Me -

Gran - *de* zo - glia tra - di - to - ra, Me -

Example 28

Ben mille volte: Modus dicendi capitula

Micha [Don Michele Pesenti]
(Petrucci, *Frottole Libro I*, 1504, fol. 46)

1Five additional strophes appear in the print.

Example 29

Alma gentil

Don Michele Pesenti
(*Motetti e canzone libro I* [1521?], no. 20)

Example 30

Amor, se vuoi ch'i torni al giogho antico

Text by Petrarch

Bernardo Pisano

(Pisano, *Musica sopra le Canzone del petrarcha,* 1520)

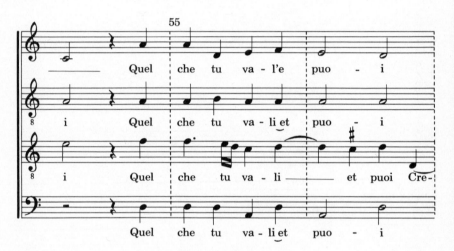

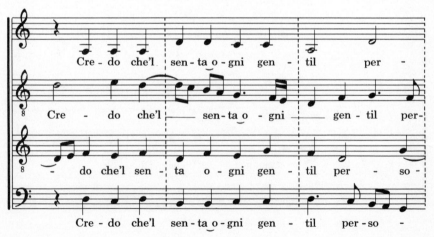

Example 31

Occhi suavi et chiari

Jacopo Fogliano

(*Canzone sonetti strambotti et frottole libro I,* Siena: P. Sambonetti, 1515)

[227]

¹Seven additional strophes appear in the print.

Example 32

O passi sparsi

Text by Petrarch

Sebastian Festa

(*Canzoni frottole et capitoli... Libro I. De la Croce*, 1526)

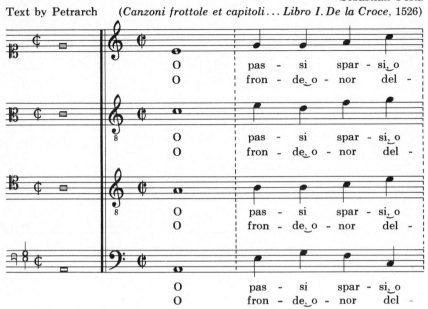

[229]

ce me-mo — ria o fier ar - do - re, O
se - gna al ge — mi - no va - lo - re; O

na - ce me-mo - ria o fier——— ar - do - re, O
la in - se-gna al ge — mi - no——— va - lo - re; O

ce me-mo — ria o fier ar - do - re, O
se - gna al ge — mi - no va - lo - re; O

ce me-mo — ria o fier ar - do - re, O
se - gna al ge — mi - no va - lo - re; O

pos - sen - te de - sir, o de - bil co - re,
fa - ti - co - sa vi - ta o dol - ce er-ro - re,

pos - sen-te de - sir, o de - bil co - re,
fa - ti-co-sa vi - ta o dol - ce er-ro - re,

pos - sen - te —— de- sir, o de - bil co - re,
fa - ti - co - sa vi - ta o dol - ce er - ro - re,

pos - sen - te de - sir, o de - bil co - re,
fa - ti - co - sa vi - ta o dol - ce er - ro - re,

O o-chi mei, o-chi non già, ma fon - ti;
Che me fat' ir cer-can - do pia - gge e mon- ti;

O o - chi mei, o-chi non già, ma fon - - ti;
Che me fat' ir cer-can-do pia-gge e mon - - ti;

O o - chi mei, o-chi non già, —— ma —— fon - ti;
Che me fat' ir cer-can-do pia - gge e —— mon- ti;

O o-chi mei, o-chi non già, ma fon - ti;
Che me fat' ir cer-can- do pia - gge e mon- ti;

O bel vi - so, o-ve a - mo - re in-sie - me po -

O bel vi - so, o-ve a - mo-re in-sie - me po -

O —— bel vi - so, o-ve a - mo-re in-sie - me po - se

O bel vi - so, o-ve a - mo-re in-sie - me po - se

Example 33

Tanto mi trovo

Anon.

(Venice, Bibl. Marciana, MS. Cl. It. IV, 1795-98, no. 25)

[235]

gion - ta et sgom-br'o-gni mar - ty -

ta et sgom- br'o-gni mar-ty -

gion - ta et sgom - br'o - gni mar - ty -

gion - ta et sgom - bra o - gni mar - ty -

45

re. Co - sì de - sio et ti -

re. Co - sì de - sio et ti - mo - re

re. Co - sì de - sio et ti -

re. Co - sì de - sio et ti - mo - re

50

mo - re Mi — spo - glia et da vi -

Mi — spo - glia et da vi -

mo - re Mi spo - glia et da vi - go -

Mi spo - glia — et da vi - go -

Example 34

Au joly bois

Anon.

(Attaingnant, *Quarante et deux chansons,* 1529, fol. 17)

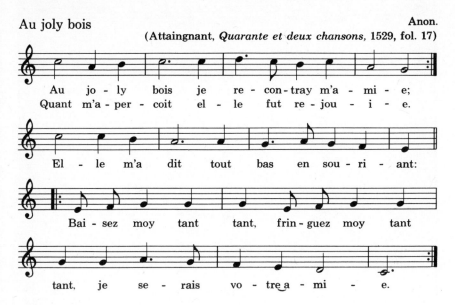

Au jo - ly bois je re - con-tray m'a - mi - e;
Quant m'a - per - coit el - le fut re - jou - i - e.

El - le m'a dit tout bas en sou - ri - ant:

Bai - sez moy tant tant, frin - guez moy tant

tant, je se - rais vo - tre_a - mi - e.

Example 35

Allez souspirs

Claudin de Sermisy

Text by [Petrarch]   (Attaingnant, *Vingt et neuf chansons,* 1530, fol. 10ᵛ)

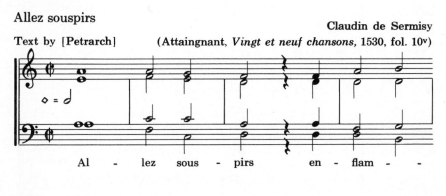

Al - lez sous - pirs en - flam - -

- - - - mez au froit cueur

[243]

Tant que la gla - ce de ri - geur soit fon -

du - - - - - e, Et si pri -

e - re est au ci - el en - ten -

- du - - e, Mort ou mer - cy soit

fin a ma dou - - - - leur.

Example 36

Comparison of Sebastian Festa's "O passi sparsi" with the anonymous "Dite di non"

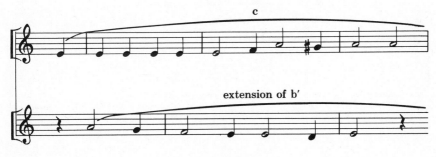

Example 37

Quoando dormy ve
Anon.
(Attaingnant, *Trente et six chansons*, 1530, fol. 14ᵛ)

Quoan - do dor - my ve co - me la ____

my - a Sei - gno - re sem-pre me la vou - les la

cou - chy cou - chy qui la cou - chy cou - chy qui la

cou - chy cou - chy qui la cou - chy cou - cha.

Example 38

Au joly jeu du pousse avant (excerpt)

Clément Janequin

(Attaingnant, *Trente et une chansons,* 1529, fol. 12ᵛ)

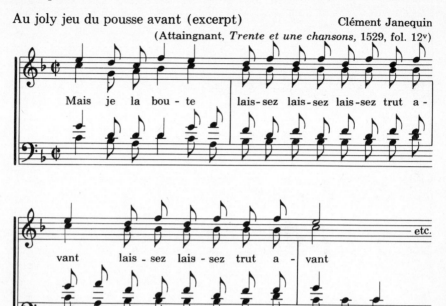

Example 39

Pavane 1

Anon.

(Attaingnant. *Six gaillardes.* 1530, fol. 3ᵛ)

Example 40

Basse dance 4: La gatta en italien

Anon.

(Attaingnant, *Neuf basses dances,* 1530, fol. 2ᵛ)

(Tenor)

etc.

Example 41

Complainte amoureuse pour dire au luth en chant italien

Text by Mellin de Saint-Gelais

Anon.

(Text in *Saingelais,* 1547; music from *Second livre de guiterre contenant plusieurs chansons en forme de voix de ville,* 1555, fol. 14)

He - las mon Dieu, y'a -

t-il ___ en ce mon - de dueil ou en - nuy, dont

on ait con - gnois - san - ce, Qui soit

e - gal a mon do - leur pro - fon - de.

Example 42

Si j'ame ou non, je n'en dy rien

Text by Mellin de Saint-Gelais

Anon.

(Le Roy, *Premier livre de chansons en forme de vau de ville,* 1573, fol. 3ᵛ)

Si j'ame ou non je n'en dy

rien Cha-cun en pen - se ce qu'il veut ...

Example 43

(a) Bramo morir

Costanzo Festa

(*Il terzo libro di madrigali d'Archadelt*, 1541, p. 26)

Bra - mo mo - rir   per non pa - tir   piu mor - te

(b) Contre raison

Claudin de Sermisy

(Attaingnant, *Trente et quatre chansons*, 1529, fol. 10)

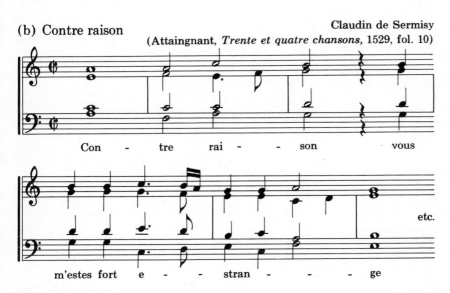

Con - tre rai - - son   vous

m'estes fort   e - - stran - - - ge

Example 44

(a) Lieti fior

Costanzo Festa

(*Madrigali*, 1530, no. 1)

Lie - ti fior   ver - di fron-de che fo - le - te

fior   frond'   herb'   ombr'   antr'   ond'   au -

re ——————   sua - - - - vi

[251]

(b) Con lacrime sospir

Philippe Verdelot
(Ibid., no. 2)

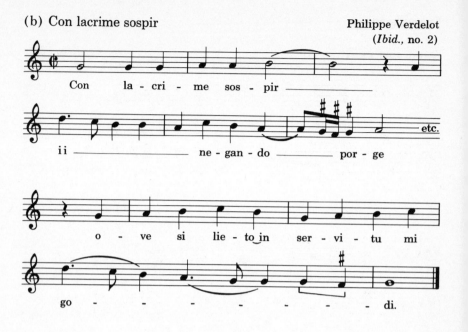

Con la - cri - me sos - pir

ii — ne - gan - do — por - ge

o - ve si lie - to_in ser - vi - tu mi

go - - - - - - - - di.

Example 45

Tous mes amis

Claudin de Sermisy
(Attaingnant, *Trente et deux chansons,* 1529, fol. 3)

Tous mes a - mis ve - nez moi

se - - - cou - - - - rir

de mon a - mi de mon a -

mi dois je pour - tant — mou - - rir.

Example 46

Se del mio amor temete

Philippe Verdelot
(*Madrigali,* 1530, no. 11)

Se   del mio a-mor te - me - - -

- - - - - - - te

Dun - que gran tort a - ve - te   Se

del mio a - mor te - me - - -

Example 47

Madonna qual certezza

Philippe Verdelot
(Verdelot, *Il primo libro de madrigali,* 1533, no. 4)

Lines of text:	Sections	Length	Cadences
1			
2	A	28 ◊	g
3			
4			
5	B	25 ◊	D
6			
7			
8			
9	C	24 ◊	g (with link
10			leading to the
11			reprise)
[1]			
2	A	28 ◊	g
[3]			

Example 48

O bon, egli è bon

Marchetto Cara

(Bossinensis, *Tenori e contrabassi intabulati . . . Libro II,* 1511, fol. 23)

[Fine]

[Da Capo dal segno*]

INDEX

INDEX

INDEX

"Che farala che dirala," Pesenti, 65n, 66, 115

Chesney, Kathleen, 2n

"Chon tutta gentileça" (Ex. 18), Busnois, 52–53, 177

"Christus vincet, Christus regnat," Mouton, 105

citaredi, 75

Claudin, *see* Sermisy

Clement VII, pope, 101, 106

"Comment peut avoir joye," Josquin, 19n

Commynes, Philippe de, 91

Compère, Loyset, 3, 24, 62, 63, 71, 86, 114, 122

"Complainte amoureuse pour dire au luth en chant italien" (Ex. 41), Saint-Gelais, 119, 250

"Con lacrime sospir" (Ex. 44b), Verdelot, 122, 123, 251

"Con suave parlar," Verdelot, 70

Conseil, Jean (Consilium), 93, 102, 106, 107, 127

"Consumo la vita mia," Prioris, 36n

"Contre raison" (Ex. 43b), Claudin, 121, 128, 251

Coppinus, Alexander, 59, 61, 62, 75, 79

Corbinelli, Jacopo, 98

Cornago, Johannes, 38

Correggio, Niccolò da, 56, 73

Corte, Andrea della, 65n

Cortegiano, Il (*The Courtier*), Castiglione, 54, 89, 92

Crétin, Guillaume, 2, 3, 14; "Déploration . . . sur le trespas de feu Okergan . . . ," 2n; "Plainte sur le trespas de feu . . . Lourdault, chantre," 2n

Cristoforo da Piacenza, 94

"Cueur langoureulx," Josquin, 14n, 16n

"Cueurs desolez / Plorans ploravit," Josquin, 13n

D'Accone, Frank, 58n, 60n, 78n, 79n, 80, 84

"Dal lecto me levava," Pesenti, 64, 86

Daniel, Jean, 110

D'Asola, Francesco, 98

"De che te pasci, Amore" (Ex. 21), Ghiselin, 58, 184

"De la da l'acqua," F(rancesco) P(atavino), 66

"De profundis," Josquin, 12

"De resjouyr," 30n

"De tous biens playne," 138n; Hayne van Ghizeghem, 13; Josquin, 12

"De tous regretz," Mouton, 27, 29, 42, 107

De Villiers, Pierre, 97

Decrue de Stoutz, Francis, 2n

Deslouges, Philippe (= Verdelot), 102

Diane de Poitiers, 5, 99

"Dieu gard de mal," Mouton, 27n

"Dieu te gart," Brumel, 45, 63

discant-tenor technique, 8, 15, 18, 19, 24

"Dit le burguygnon," 39, 40

"Dite di non amor, quanto vi piace" (Ex. 36), 96, 110, 245

"Don, don al foco al foco," A. Stringari, 68

"Dona i ardenti rai," Dufay, 52

Doni, Antonfrancesco, 97, 98n; *I Marmi*, 102

"Donna benche di rado," 68

"Donna di dentro," Isaac, 63

"Donna gentile, bella come l'oro," Dufay, 52, 132

"Donne, venete al ballo," Patavino, 67

"Dont vient cela," 33n

Dorico, Valerio, 95, 97, 103; *Madrigali de diversi musici libro primo* (1530), 103, 122, 123

"Douleur me bat," Josquin, 14n, 16, 17

Droz, Eugénie, 7n, 8, 40, 134n

Du Bellay, Joachim, 118

"Du bon du cueur," Mouton, 27n

Du Colombier, Pierre, 91

Du Fau, Lancelot, bishop of Luçon, 137

"Du mien amant," Josquin, 16n

Dufay, Guillaume, 13n, 38, 49, 52, 83, 132

"D'un bel matin d'amore" (Ex. 27), Zesso, 66, 76, 209

"E dont venez vous Madame Lucette," Verdelot, 103; as "Almande VIII" in Attaingnant, *Troisième livre de danceries* (1530), 103n

"E d'un bel matin d'amore," Capriolus, 66, 76

écurie, 94

Einstein, Alfred, 59n, 65n, 68n, 74, 79, 80, 86n, 87n, 97, 103, 105, 106, 111n, 115, 119, 123

Eitner, Robert, 44n, 70n

Eléonore, queen of France, 94

"En amours n'a sinon que bien" (Ex. 6), Févin, 22, 23, 154

"En l'ombre d'un buissonet," Josquin, 12n, 19n, 34n

"En l'ombre dung aubepin," Ninot, 63

"En non saichant," Josquin, 16n

"En regardant son gratieux maintien," 33n

"En venant de Lyon," Mouton, 27n

Engel, Hans, 60, 62n, 121

"Entre je suis," Josquin, 12n, 19n

Erasmus, Desiderius, 92

Este, Ippolito d', Cardinal, 100, 102

"Este merci," Claudin, 109

INDEX

INDEX

INDEX

INDEX

INDEX

INDEX